RHYTHMIC ALTERATION IN SEVENTEENTH- AND EIGHTEENTH-CENTURY MUSIC

RHYTHMIC ALTERATION IN SEVENTEENTH- AND EIGHTEENTH-CENTURY MUSIC

Notes Inégales and Overdotting

Stephen E. Hefling

Schirmer Books
An Imprint of Macmillan Publishing Company
NEW YORK

Maxwell Macmillan Canada
TORONTO

Maxwell Macmillan International
NEW YORK   OXFORD   SINGAPORE   SYDNEY

SCHIRMER BOOKS
An Imprint of Macmillan Publishing Company
866 Third Avenue
New York, NY 10022

MAXWELL MACMILLAN CANADA, INC.
1200 Eglinton Avenue East, Suite 200
Don Mills, Ontario M3C 3N1

Macmillan Publishing Company is part of the Maxwell
Communication Group of Companies

LIBRARY OF CONGRESS CATALOG CARD NUMBER: 92-11958

Printed in the United States of America

printing number
1   2   3   4   5   6   7   8   9   10

LIBRARY OF CONGRESS CATALOGING-IN-PUBLICATION DATA

Hefling, Stephen E.
    Rhythmic alteration in seventeenth- and eighteenth-century music :
notes inégales and overdotting / Stephen E. Hefling.
      p.   cm.
    Includes bibliographical references and index.
    ISBN 0-02-871035-5 (alk. paper)
    1. Notes inégales. 2. Musical meter and rhythm. 3. Performance
practice (Music)—17th century.   4. Performance practice
(Music)—18th century.   I. Title.   II. Title: Rhythmic alteration
in 17th- and 18th-century music.
ML437.H43   1993
781.2′2′09032—dc20
                                                                92-11958
                                                                CIP
                                                                MN

The paper used in this publication meets the minimum
requirements of American National Standard for Information Sciences—Permanence of Paper for Printed Library
Materials. ANSI Z39.48-1984. ⊗™

For Deborah

CONTENTS

Preface   ix
Acknowledgments   xv

PART I. Notes Inégales

CHAPTER 1.   Conventional Aspects of French Inequality   3

CHAPTER 2.   The Negation of Inequality, Discrepancies among the Sources, and Related Matters   21

CHAPTER 3.   Notes Inégales Outside France   37

PART II. Overdotting

CHAPTER 4.   The Value(s) of the Dot   65

CHAPTER 5.   The Earlier German Sources on Overdotting   83

CHAPTER 6.   Later Sources on Overdotting   112

CHAPTER 7.   Summary Observations   141

Notes   161
Bibliography   201
Index   225

PREFACE

Aujourd'hui le **point,** pris comme valeur de Note, vaut toujours la moitié de celle que le precede. . . . Mais cette manière de fixer la valeur du **point** n'est sûrement pas la meilleure qu'on ait pû imaginer, & cause souvent bien des embarras inutiles.

Today the **dot,** as a rhythmic value, is always worth one half that which precedes it. . . . But this manner of fixing the value of the **dot** is surely not the best one could imagine, and often causes a good deal of useless embarrassment.

—Jean-Jacques Rousseau, 1768[1]

As social theorist, Rousseau was something of a prophet; but Rousseau the music lexicographer probably never anticipated that these remarks about the dot would prove so true for the twentieth century. Today the secondary literature on rhythmic alteration in the performance of baroque music is longer than Rousseau's entire *Dictionnaire de musique.* And it has become so confusingly polemical—laced with such terms as "jerky style," "counter-reformation," and "paradigm of inconsistency" —that hitherto anyone wishing to make well-informed decisions on the matter had to master all the sources set forth in the Bibliography below.

There is a significant relationship between *notes inégales* and overdotting (and it will be examined in chapter 4 below). Nevertheless, it is essential to distinguish between the two procedures. *Notes inégales* is a historical name for the relatively consistent French custom of performing diminution-like passages as uneven pairs of notes, despite their notation in equal values; the practice applied most commonly to eighth notes in the meters **2** and **3,** and it is discussed by more than forty French writers from the latter half of the seventeenth century until the Revolution. There were other contemporary terms for this: *poincts alternatifs,*[2] *pointer,*[3] *inégaliser,*[4] *passer les croches,*[5] or *croches inégales,*[6] plus a few special designations to be discussed presently; but in modern usage *notes inégales* has become standard. "Overdotting," however, is a term evidently coined by Erwin Bodky in the 1950s;[7] there is no historical equivalent, and substantially less contemporary information about this practice than there is concerning *notes inégales.* In modern musical literature,

overdotting has been chiefly, though not exclusively, linked with the
so-called French overture style, and it is used to mean performing dotted
rhythms longer than their notation indicates, in degrees that range from
very slight to intense "ultra-dotting."[8] Failure to observe the basic differences between *notes inégales* and overdotting results in considerable
confusion.[9]

The history of the conflict concerning rhythmic alteration has been
sketched by others, and need be reviewed only briefly here.[10] The major
impetus toward twentieth-century revival of these customs came from
three British writers—Arnold Dolmetsch, Thurston Dart, and Robert
Donington—beginning with Dolmetsch's pioneering handbook, *The Interpretation of the Music of the Seventeenth and Eighteenth Centuries*
(London, 1915). On the basis of somewhat limited documentation and
occasionally mistaken exegesis, Dolmetsch recommended both inequality and overdotting for a rather wide range of repertoire. *Notes inégales*,
he felt, would be welcome not only in French music, but also in many
pieces by Bach and Handel; of overdotting he suggested that "we can but
feel justified in treating all the old music alike in this respect."[11] Dart's
discussion (1954) of inequality is extremely brief and apparently pertains
only to French music.[12] But his sweeping advocacy of overdotting was
among the most extreme and influential endorsements of the practice:

> Rhythms that are already written as dotted notes, whether they are
> iambic or trochaic, need to have the disparity between the lengths of the
> notes emphasized; otherwise they will sound lazy. . . . In an overture in
> the French style . . . for instance, all the parts should move together,
> jerkily, even when their written note-values do not suggest that this is
> how they should be played. *All* dotted rhythms should be adjusted so that
> they fit the shortest one in the piece. . . .

> This conventional lengthening of the dotted note and shortening of
> the complementary note was in very widespread use over a very great
> length of time, and ignorance of this fact is one of the gravest defects of
> present-day performances of old music. It is a fashion that lasted from the
> early years of the seventeenth century down to the last years of the
> nineteenth. . . . It is required in Monteverdi and Purcell . . . ; in the over-
> tures to Handel's oratorios and operas; in the overtures to Bach's orches-
> tral suites and to such works as the harpsichord Partita in C minor. It
> applies to marches and to sicilianos, to jigs and to Andantes. Quantz and
> C. P. E. Bach are unanimous in saying that it applies to the music of their
> own time. It is found in some of Gluck's operas, as well as in those of
> Sarti. Leopold Mozart (1756) prescribes it for Adagios or in any piece
> that would otherwise sound lazy. It is implied in Haydn, Mozart, and
> Beethoven. . . .[13]

Relying on the researches of Dolmetsch and a few others, Dart provided virtually no historical evidence for these assertions. But in 1963 the first edition of Donington's *Interpretation of Early Music* mustered more documentary material from treatises and scores than had either of its predecessors. From these data Donington concluded, as Dolmetsch had earlier, that *notes inégales* was an international custom, and suggested that it extended to the generation of Beethoven. Although more circumspect than Dart on the issue of overdotting, Donington nevertheless broadly advocated it "when the dotted notes (i) are persistent enough to dominate the rhythm; or (ii) form a distinct rhythmic figure or formula; or more generally (iii), would sound sluggish if taken literally. . . ."[14]

Every tenet of this emerging orthodoxy was vigorously reexamined by Frederick Neumann in two articles published in 1965.[15] On the basis of extensive research, Neumann argued that *notes inégales* was customary only among French musicians, who employed the practice only in specific rhythmic and melodic contexts. Allowing for very few exceptions, he claimed that rhythmic inequality was not prevalent in Germany, and should not be applied to the music of J. S. Bach. Neumann also insisted that overdotting be limited to German *galant* music from approximately 1750–90, and concluded that "for the period from Lully to Rameau, the so-called French style is essentially a legend, and its first formulation by Dolmetsch is an invention which has been wrongly taken for a discovery."[16] From that point until the present, the issues of rhythmic alteration have been debated, often heatedly, in a long chain of writings by Donington, Neumann, Michael Collins, David Fuller, Graham Pont, and others. All too often bits of old treatises were fired like bullets from an assault rifle, and by the late 1970s David Fuller would, with some justification, divide the partisan camps into "right" (Neumann) and "left" (nearly everyone else).[17] The hapless observer of these musicological volleys was likely either to be swayed by the intensity of the most recent offensive, or to be left baffled by the confusion of it all.

I must acknowledge from the outset that pat answers to the problems of rhythmic alteration cannot be given here and are not likely to be revealed in future. Each interpreter will have to exercise taste and judgment in deciding about particular situations; so too, presumably, did performers during the period under consideration. The goal of present-day historical performance practice is, I take it, to bridge the gap of time through historical imagination (as Collingwood discusses it); the process is a dialogue of question-and-answer whereby we can inform and develop our own taste and judgment on the basis of what is intelligible in data that survive from the past.[18] Accordingly, the primary purpose of this book is to provide an accurate and dispassionate account of what is known about *notes inégales* and overdotting. Given the controversy that has surrounded these issues, this involves reviewing yet again a good deal of material that has already been at least partially presented by other authors. And although I cannot avoid noting apparent misunderstandings in previous writings, I do not press the viewpoints of the 'right' or 'left'; insofar as possible, explicit engagement with those arguments has been restricted to the endnotes.

Much (though not all) of the evidence examined here comes from treatises, prefaces, dictionaries, and the like, rather than from music scores, for two reasons: (1) On the whole, music notation of the seventeenth and eighteenth centuries provides very few clues that would lead the uninitiated interpreter to alter the indicated rhythms; but for the surviving written accounts, *inégalité* and overdotting would probably never have become concerns of twentieth-century musicians. The first order of business, then, is to assess the verbal documentation as carefully as possible. (2) As suggested above, what scores of the period do present is a multitude of situations—literally thousands—requiring interpretation based upon judicious weighing of the available data—and upon taste. Moreover, as every performer knows, a wide range of contextually interdependent variables must be considered simultaneously in making interpretive decisions: affect, tempo, texture, contour, articulation, ornamentation, and so on. To isolate rhythmic alteration as though it were an independent matter is, to be sure, artificial; yet for the moment it is also necessary. In the concluding chapter I offer brief commentary on certain aspects of interpreting and applying the documentary information presented in parts I and II—but this is by way of summary and review: no reasonably sized selection of pieces could possibly constitute a representative sampling of the manifold situations performers will face.

One important issue of rhythmic interpretation in seventeenth- and eighteenth-century music is not discussed here: binary versus ternary conflicts and synchronizations. The reason for this omission is that my researches turned up nothing that substantially augments what is already known on this subject. Neumann's article "Conflicting Binary and Ternary Rhythms: From the Theory of Mensural Notation to the Music of J. S. Bach" provides a good review of the matter, and concludes with a set of general guidelines for performers with which I would largely concur.[19]

This volume is designed to serve a wide range of readers. Those needing a quick assessment of its coverage can glean that from the closing chapter, "Summary Observations," plus the tables in chapters 1, 5, and 6. Performers who wish to become more thoroughly versed in the source materials surveyed here should find that the text can be grasped with little or no reference to the documentation and amplification provided in the endnotes. Specialists, of course, will want to examine the whole.

To facilitate further reference and research, the bibliography is divided into three parts: (I) *Notes inégales;* (II) Overdotting, and Variable Value of the Dot; and (III) Related Issues. Primary sources are listed chronologically, and bracketed dates are from *RISM* Bvi unless a more accurate date could be established. (In the body of the book, for convenience, I have attempted always to cite both author and date of primary sources.) Secondary sources in all sections of the bibliography are arranged alphabetically, and the Overdotting and Related Issues portions of the source list contain shortened references to works already cited in a previous section. For readers' convenience I have made note of facsimile and reprint editions of which I am aware, but these come and go quickly, and my listing should not be considered exhaustive. Library sigla used in this volume are those established in *RISM* and also adopted in *The New Grove Dictionary of Music and Musicians.* Unless otherwise noted, basic information about the musicians and musical centers discussed here is taken from *The New Grove;* regrettably, the large number of articles consulted precludes my acknowledging each of them individually. Translations are my own, except for the citations from J. J. Quantz's *Versuch einer Anweisung die Flöte traversiere zu spielen* (Berlin, 1752), which rely heavily on Edward R. Reilly's fine English version, *On Playing the Flute,* 2d ed. (New York: Schirmer Books, 1985). Original orthography has been preserved in treatise quotations. Whenever possible, Neumann's numerous articles on rhythmic alteration are cited as reprinted in his *Essays in Performance Practice* (Ann Arbor: UMI Research Press, 1982).

My hope is that the present pages, despite their limitations, will provide a firm and useful foundation from which to proceed in addressing issues of rhythmic alteration as they crop up in context. It will be convenient to begin with a review of *notes inégales,* and then take up the more problematic matter of overdotting.

ACKNOWLEDGMENTS

During the dozen years of the book's gestation many people gave me valuable advice and assistance, and I should like to acknowledge as many as possible, with apology in advance to anyone I have overlooked. Raymond F. Erickson, professor of music at the Aaron Copland School of Music and director of the Aston Magna Academy, first invited me to speak on problems of rhythmic alteration at the Aston Magna Academy in Great Barrington, Massachusetts, during the summer of 1979; subsequent versions of that preliminary lecture were presented at Yale University in 1980, and at chapter meetings of the American Musicological Society in New England (1981) and northern California (1982). Professors Edward Reilly of Vassar College and Lenora McCroskey of the University of Texas, Denton, read earlier versions of my work and offered much useful information and advice. Two of the most prolific writers on the issues at hand, Professors Frederick Neumann (emeritus, University of Richmond) and David Fuller (SUNY Buffalo), have graciously responded to all my requests for data from their files. Professors Charles E. Brewer (University of Alabama), Bruce L. Gustafson (Franklin and Marshall College), Craig A. Monson (Washington University), John G. Suess (Case Western Reserve University), Walter Winzenburger (Baldwin-Wallace College), Jaap Schröder (Schola Cantorum, Basel, and Yale University), Richard Rephann (Yale University), Marian Smith (University of Oregon), Thomas Christensen (University of Pennsylvania), David Tartakoff (University of Illinois, Chicago) and Dr. Patricia Ranum (Baltimore) all provided various sorts of assistance for which I am grateful. To Professor Charles C. Hefling, Jr. (Boston College), who was convinced the thing would never see the light of day, I am especially indebted. Troy Sartain and Gary Wright of the Center for Music and Technology at Case Western Reserve, and my research assistant, Julie Andrijeski, provided expert help with technical matters in the preparation of the tables.

Many libraries have provided access to the information on which this book is based, and I wish particularly to thank: the Département de Musique of the Bibliothèque Nationale, Paris; Bibliothèque de l'Arsenal, Paris; the Musiksammlung of the Österreichische Nationalbibliothek, Vienna; the Archiv of the Gesellschaft der Musikfreunde, Vienna (Dr.

Otto Biba, director); the Staats- und Universitätsbibliothek, Hamburg; the Music Division of The Library of Congress, Washington, D.C. (especially Wayne Shirley); The Newberry Library, Chicago; the New York Public Library; the John Herrick Jackson Music Library at Yale University (particularly Deborah R. Miller, now Deborah Hefling); the Eda Kuhn Loeb Music Library at Harvard University; the Music Library of Stanford University; the Music Library of the University of California, Berkeley; the Kulas Music Library of Case Western Reserve University (Stephen Toombs, librarian); and the Cleveland Public Library.

For permission to reproduce rare and copyrighted materials I am grateful to: the American Musicological Society; A-R Editions, Madison, Wisconsin; Baerenreiter Music Corporation, Englewood, New Jersey; Boethius Press, Aberystwyth, Wales; the British Library, London; the Bibliothèque Nationale, Paris; C. F. Peters, New York; Early Music (Oxford University Press); the Fitzwilliam Museum, Cambridge; the Institut für Mittelalterliche Musikwissenschaft (L. A. Dittmer, Vorsteher); Jerona Music Corporation, Hackensack, New Jersey; The Library of Congress, Washington, D.C.; Music Associates of America, Englewood, New Jersey; the Österreichische Nationalbibliothek, Vienna; the Sibley Music Library, Eastman School of Music (especially Louise Goldberg); the Staats- und Universitätsbibliothek, Hamburg; Theodore Presser Co., Bryn Mawr, Pennsylvania; and the University of California, Berkeley, Music Library.

RHYTHMIC ALTERATION IN SEVENTEENTH- AND EIGHTEENTH-CENTURY MUSIC

PART I

NOTES INÉGALES

Conventional Aspects of
French Inequality

EARLIEST SOURCES

The earliest account of French-style rhythmic inequality is probably that of Loys Bourgeois, published in Geneva in 1550:

> La maniere de biē chāter les demiminimes en ces signes diminués $\text{O}\mathbb{C}$ O_1^2 C_1^2 O2 C2 est de les chāter come de deux en deux, demourant quelque peu de tēps d auantage sur lapremiere, que sur la seconde: cōme si la premiere auoit vn poinct, & que la second fust vne fuse. A cause que la premiere est vn accord, & que la seconde est le plussouvent vn discord. . . . A cause aussi qu'elles ōt meilleure grace à les chāter ainsi que ie dy, que toutes egales, comme il sensuit.

Il faudra faire le semblable des Fuses, en ces signes entiers O C O2 C2 ainsi:[1]

The manner of singing well the semiminims [♩s] under these diminished signs $\text{O}\mathbb{C}$ O_1^2 C_1^2 O2 C2 is to sing them two by two, dwelling some little bit of time longer on the first, than on the second—as though the first had a dot and the second were a fusa [♪]. The reason is that the first is a consonance, and the second most often a dissonance. . . . It is also because they have more grace when sung in this way, as I have indicated, than if they were all equal, as it would appear [see first example above].

It is necessary to do the same for the fusae under these undiminished
signs O C O2 C2, as follows: [see second example above]

The passage is curious because it is so insular: written by a Calvinist
church musician in Geneva, it antedates by more than a hundred years all
the Parisian accounts of inequality. That notwithstanding, Bourgeois has
introduced five principles that will recur repeatedly in much later discussions of *notes inégales:* (1) There is a definite relationship between
meter and the note values rendered unequal: in duple time (as in the cases
Bourgeois cites), it is the fourth part of the beat that is affected. (2) The
characteristic way of unequalizing is long–short, "two by two," as he
puts it. (3) The degree of inequality is some indefinite little bit, which is
then likened to dotted notation. (4) "More grace" is a reason for inequality; Bourgeois also mentions the metric placement of consonance and
dissonance, but this is not a factor in later accounts of inequality. And (5)
his musical examples indicate that the rhythmic alteration applies to
diminutions in stepwise motion, a condition subsequently made explicit
by a number of writers, as we shall see.

*Late sixteenth- and seventeenth-century Italianate rhyth-
mic alterations.* As noted, for more than a century we find no further
discussion of inequality written in French; but several treatises from
Spain and Italy refer somewhat sporadically to rhythmic liberties that
may be taken in performing diminutions. Tomás de Santa Maria (1565)
indicates that to play "in good taste" one should execute semiminims (♩s)
long–short, and may play *las Corcheas* (♪s) in one of three ways, listed in
order of increasing elegance: (1) long–short, in contrapuntal pieces and
both lengthy and brief diminutions; (2) short–long, in brief diminutions;
or (3) in groups of four, by hurrying through the first three notes and
dwelling on the fourth; this,he says, is good for either short or extended
passages.[2] Like Bourgeois, Tomás illustrates his intended executions with
dotted notation, but he stresses that the alteration should not be too
much—rather, "just enough to be perceptible."[3] In Italy both Bovicelli
(1594) and Caccini (1602) suggest that certain conjunct ornamental passages be rendered unequally to increase their gracefulness; Caccini also
illustrates a type of tempo rubato whereby selected long notes are held
and the succeeding shorter values are hurried.[4] Cerone (1613) writes of
long–short treatment of semiminims, while Frescobaldi (1615) observes
that in passages of his toccatas where the harpsichordist encounters
eighths and sixteenths in both hands, the sixteenths may be somewhat

dotted, short–long.[5] And Puliaschi (1618) briefly mentions that dotting the first note and shortening the second is among the singer's expressive resources in the execution of diminutions.[6]

The rhythmic liberties these writers advocate are linked to two developments in Italianate musical style from roughly 1560 to 1640: (1) rising virtuosity, manifest in florid written-out *passaggi* as well as in diminution treatises published to promote the skill of extemporaneous ornamentation; and (2) the free declamatory style of vocal monody, which also affected instrumental writing. Like the complex articulation patterns prescribed by the diminution tutors, rhythmic alteration is part of the soloist's expressive vocabulary; but it would also appear to have been both more radical and more arbitrary than the ordinary agogic accentuation of passage-work through articulation.[7]

France, ca. 1660–90. After the second decade of the seventeenth century, we find next to nothing about rhythmic alteration in Italian sources before 1800. During the latter half of the century in France, however, a number of writers present brief and slightly haphazard accounts of *notes inégales*, rather as though they were attempting to record an oral tradition, as Saint-Arroman observes.[8] In 1665 Nivers notes that

> il y a encore un autre [mouvement] particulier et fort guay, qui est de faire comme des demipoints apres la 1.ere 3.me 5. et 7. croche de chaque mesure, (supposé qu'il y en ait huit) c'est a dire d'augmenter tant soit peu les dites croches, et diminuer tant soit peu et a proportion les suivantes . . . ce qui se pratique a discretion, et plusiers autres choses que la prudence et l'oreille doivent gouverner.[9]

> there is yet another special sort of *mouvement, fort guay,* which is to make as though half-dots after the 1st, 3d, 5th, and 7th eighth notes (assuming that there are eight of them); that is to say, to augment ever so slightly the aforementioned eighths, and to diminish ever so slightly in proportion those that follow . . . which is practiced according to discretion, and many other things which prudence and the ear have to govern.

He also makes sporadic use of the irregular notation ⌐⌐⌐ , apparently to suggest rhythmic rubato, and this device occurs even more frequently in his third collection of 1675.[10] A "half-dot" notation of inequality – ♪. ♪ ♪. ♪ – is found in Nivers's second book of organ music (1667).[11]

The following year Bacilly's singing treatise advocates similarly subtle and flexible execution of ornamental writing; for pedagogical purposes, he identifies two passages where the singer should interpolate dots that yield irregular, rubato-like rhythms, which, he says, are never marked on the page. Beyond this, he also discusses the practice of *poincts alternatifs* in diminutions:

> Quoy que ie die qu'il y a dans les Diminutions des Poincts alternatifs & supposez, c'est à dire que de deux Nottes il y en ait l'ordinaire vne pointée, on a jugé à propos de ne les pas marquer, de peur qu'on ne s'accoustume à executer par *sacades*, ie veux dire par *sautillemens*, à la maniere de ces Pieces de Musique que l'on nommes *Gigues*, suiuant l'ancienne Methode de Chanter qui seroit presentement fort desagreable. Il faut donc faire ces sortes de Nottes pointées si finement que cela ne paroisse pas, si ce n'est en des endroits particuliers, qui demandent ex-pressément cette sorte d'execution, & mesme il faut entierement les éuiter en certains endroits. . . .[12]

> Although I say that in diminutions there are dots, alternate and assumed, which is to say that of two notes, one is ordinarily dotted, it has been deemed appropriate not to mark them, for fear that one might accustom himself to execute them by *jerks*, I mean by *leaps*, in the manner of those pieces of music called *gigues*, according to the ancient method of singing, which would currently be very disagreeable. Hence it is necessary to execute these sorts of pointed notes so delicately that it is not apparent, if it is not in the specific places that expressly demand this sort of exe-cution, and similarly it is necessary to avoid them entirely in certain places. . . .

Bacilly's use of language is not especially clear, nor are the examples he cites particularly instructive.[13] Nevertheless, it does seem certain that he favors a very subtle sort of rhythmic liberty, in contrast to some previous style of singing which he considers unpleasant.[14]

Perrine's lute book (ca. 1680) tells us only that "to find the true *mouvement* of all sorts of pieces for the lute, the first parts, or first parts of parts of the beats of the measure should be played longer than the others."[15] And the organist Gigault is similarly casual about inequality: "One could also animate one's playing more or less by adding dots where one wishes,"[16] although he has already added them to the text in the vast majority of possible places. Jullien, on the other hand, added such dots to only one of his pieces, a *Trio pour une élévation*, as an example of how one could treat the others "more or less lightly, according to the *mouve-ment*"; the meter is 𝄵, and the dotted rhythms (long–short) occur at the rhythmic level of the eighth note.[17] The anonymous "Maniere de toucher lorgue . . ." (ca. 1685) indicates that the purpose of rhythmic alteration (*bien pointer, pointement*) is to lend "grace, *mouvement*, beauty, and charm . . . without which the pieces are dull, without taste," a description that echoes Bourgeois's much earlier commentary. So too does the im-precise analogy between performance mannerism and written notation (which several later writers make as well): the first of paired eighths is lengthened "as though there were a dot," and the second is shortened accordingly.[18] The degree of inequality varies according to the type of piece: the trio is to be pointed "with great fire and great boldness . . . one cannot point it too much," and one must "point extremely" in the duo; solos for the *cornet* registration, however, are to be "very fast and lively without pointing."[19]

FRANCE, CA. 1690–1790

Beginning with the treatise of Jean Rousseau (1687), French writers are increasingly explicit and concordant about the relation between meter and inequality, which had already been foreshadowed by Bourgeois in 1550. According to Rousseau, in duple meter (**2**) "it is necessary to mark a little the first, third, etc., of each measure; but it is necessary to take care not to mark them too roughly." In **C**, sixteenths rather than eighths are thus treated. In triple meter (**C3**), however, one marks only the first eighth of the measure and renders the others equally; and quarters in $\frac{3}{2}$ are to be played in the same manner.[20] This last statement is curious because virtually all later writers indicate that the eighths in **3** and the quarters in $\frac{3}{2}$ are unequal; otherwise, however, they essentially agree with Rousseau about the note values to be rendered unequally in **C** and **2**, and they extend the practice of *notes inégales* to most other meters as well. The basic principle is a refinement of notions expressed by the earlier writers: at the rhythmic level of diminutions, "the first parts, or first parts of parts of the beats," as Perrine put it, are unequal. In triple meters, this is ordinarily the half-beat (eighth notes in **3** being the most common case); in duple meters, the quarter-beat is usually affected (eighths in **2**, sixteenths in **C** or $\frac{2}{4}$.)

This broad consensus concerning meter and inequality was documented by Neumann in a table representing the views of thirty treatise writers,[21] which is reproduced below, with minor corrections, as table 1-1. More than a dozen other French writers have subsequently been uncovered, all of whom essentially concur with the patterns Neumann established; these sources are included in the column "Meter-Inequality Relationship" in table 1-2 below.[22] Minor discrepancies are found among the treatises, and these will be discussed in chapter 2. Nevertheless, it is indisputable that by the end of the seventeenth century (and perhaps somewhat earlier) the French custom of rhythmic alteration, which apparently developed haphazardly, was being systematically organized with regard to meter, and in other respects to be reviewed presently. Such

Table 1-1.   Meter-Inequality Relationships as Formulated by 30 Contemporary Authors.

	$\frac{3}{2}$	2	¢ IN TWO	¢ IN FOUR	C	$\frac{2}{4}$	$\frac{3}{4}$	3	$\frac{6,9,12}{4}$	$\frac{3,4,6,9,12}{8}$
Rousseau (Jean) 1687 a]	♩	♪	♪		♪			♪		
Loulié 1696 b] c]	♩	♪	♪	♪	♪			♪		
L'Affilard 1697, 1705		♪	♪		♪	♪				♪
Muffat 1698 f]	♩ d]	♪	♪	♪	♪	♪ d]		♪ e]	♪ d]	♪ d]
Saint-Lambert 1702	♩	♪	♪		♪			♪		
Montéclair 1709, 1736 g]		♪	♪		♪	♪ h]		♪	♪	♪ i]
Dupont 1718 c]	♩	♪	♪	♪	♪			♪		♪
Saurin Borin* 1722 i]* r]*	♩	♪	♪	♪	♪			♪	♪	♪
Démotz 1728 i] k]	♩	♪	♪	♪	♪	♪ h]	♪ h]	♪	♪	♪
Vague 1733 b]	♩	♪	♪	♪	♪			♪	♪	
David 1737 b]	♩	♪	♪	♪	♪	♪	♪	♪	♪	♪ i]
Dupuit 1741 l]	♩ m]	♪			♪			♪*	♪	♪
Corrette 1741, 1770 l] n]	♩ m]	♪	♪	♪	♪	♪	♪	♪	♪	♪
Duval —1741—* i]	1775: ♪*	♪*	♪*		♩ OR ♩*	♪ h]	♪ h]	♪	♪	♪
Vion 1742 i]	♩	♪	♪ [?]*		♪			♪	♪	♪
Denis 1747					♪	(♪ IMPLIED)*	♪ p]*		♪	♪

Rollet 17–	g)										♩ h]	
QUANTZ 1752	l)										♩ i]	
St. Philbert 17–		♪ m]									♩ h]	
Bordet 1755	l)										♩ h]	
Villeneuve 1756			IMPLIED* (♪)									
Bordier 1760	l)	♪ m]		✗ *				♪ p]*				
Choquel 1762						♪ o]	♪ h]					
Brijon 1763												
Duval (abbé) 1764	i)						♪ p]*	♪ p]*				
Lacassagne 1766	l)							♪ p]*				
Dard 1769	i)											
Métoyen 17–				♪*	♪ h] [?]*	♪ h]	♪ p]	♪ p]			♪ h]	
Cajon 1772	l)	♪ q]		♪*			♪ p]					
Raparlier 1772												

a) Rousseau uses the term *marquer* which might imply a combination of dynamic and agogic accent. b) First category in duple meters, second category in triple meters. c) Equates equality with detached articulation. d) Derived from Muffat's examples. e) If "fairly fast" (un peu gai). f) St. Lambert's listings implied by: 8th unequal except in 4 where 16ths unequal; quarter-notes unequal in "slow triple meter." g) Any four-fold subdivision of the beat is unequal. h) Implied by: 8th equal. i) Specified for 3/8. j) Inequality is *cumulative*: when shorter notes occur than those eligible for inequality, both the shorter *and* the longer notes are unequal. k) Démotz spells out cumulative inequality in every single instance. m) Sometimes equal' implying unequal 8ths. n) 'Sometimes equal'* in Sonatas or Concertos. o) With the unusual comment that only quarter and 8th notes occur in 2/2 meter, meaning probably: *if* only quarter and 8th notes occur. p) Equal if 16ths occur. q) If no 8ths occur, quarter notes are unequal. r)* Borin also indicates that half notes are unequal in 3/1 meter. *Source*: Compiled by Frederick Neumann (with minor revisions denoted by asterisks by the present author). Reproduced by kind permission of the American Musicological Society.

TABLE 1–2.   Comparative Table of Source Material on Inequality (ca. 1680–1785).

COUNTRY	METER/INEQUALITY RELATIONSHIP	STEPWISE MOTION	LONG-SHORT	SHORT-LONG	MILD**	VARIABLE	STRONG	CANCELLED BY:	EXPECTED = E / POSSIBLE = P
France	a) Rousseau 1687 b) L'Affilard 1694 c) Loulié 1696 d) Saint-Lambert 1702 e) Hotteterre 1707, 1719 f) Montéclair 1709, ca. 1735, 1736 g) Dupont 1718 h) Borin 1722 i) Démotz 1728 j) Cappus 1730 k) Vague 1733 l) Corrette 1738, 1741, ca. 1742, 1748, ca. 1780 m) de-LaChapelle 1736 n) David 1737 o) Duputi 1741 p) Vion 1742 q) St. Philbert 1743 r) Denis 1747 s) Métoyen 17?? t) Buterne 1752 u) Dumas 1753 v) Bordet 1755 w) Villeneuve 1756 x) Anon., ca. 1760 y) Bordier 1760 z) Morel deLescer, ca. 1760 aa) Rollet 1760 bb) Bouin 1761 cc) Choquel 1762 dd) Brijon 1763	b) c)+ e) 1719+ f) 1709+ Couperin 1717+ i)+ k)+ n) v) w) x) y) aa) (et. all) [+ = explicit]	Nivers 1667 Anon., ca. 1685 c) d) e) f) g) j) l) m) q) t) u) v) w) Anon., ca. 1760 aa) bb) cc) Rousseau 1768 ff) gg) hh) jj) kk) mm) oo) pp) qq) rr) tt) Cleret 1786	c) Couperin 1713	Nivers 1667 Bacilly 1668 a) c) Freillon-Poncein 1700 f) m) w) aa) cc) Rousseau 1768 hh) mm) qq) rr) ss)	Anon., ca 1685 d) ff) kk) mm) uu)	n) o) ee) Cleret 1786	"detaché" "notes égales" strokes or dots above notes (⋅⁚) "martelé" ('goût')	E: a) through uu), plus others

France (*continued*)	ee) Duval 1764 ff) Lacassagne 1766 gg) Dard 1769 hh) Bailleux 1770 ii) Caion 1772 jj) Raparlier 1772 kk) Tarade 1774 ll) Anon. 1775 mm) Duval 1775 nn) Engramelle 1775, 1778 oo) Pollet 1775 pp) Roussel 1775 qq) Torlez, ca. 1775 rr) Azaïs 1776 ss) Mercadier 1777 tt) Mussard 1779 uu) Marcou 1782			
Germany*	a) Muffat* 1698 b) Quantz 1752	a)	a) b)	b)
				b): , ' '		E: b)
Netherlands	a) Frischmuth 1758 [implied]	a)		b)
				E: Courante, Allemande
England	a) Burwell lute MS, ca. 1668–71 (one example b) Roger North's diaries (MS) (one example?)	a) b) c)		P: a), b)
	c) Prelleur 1731			E: c)

*Muffat writes specifically to introduce French music and its performance style.

**Probably not more than 2–1.

***German sources often unjustifiably cited as evidence for *notes inégales* include C.P.E. Bach (1753–62) and Leopold Mozart (1756).

regularization almost certainly reflects Lully's domination of French musical taste; his student Georg Muffat, who sought to introduce the French manner in Germany, explicitly identifies *notes inégales* as Lullian.[23] In any case, the practice became so common in France that in 1717 François Couperin could dispose of it in a brief but revealing paragraph:

> Il y a selon moy dans notre facon d'ecrire la musique, des deffauts qui se raportent à la manière d'écrire notre langue. C'est que nous écrivons différemment de ce que nous éxécutons: ce qui fait que les étrangers joüent notre musique moins bien que nous ne fesons la leur. au contraire les Italiens écrivent leur musique dans les vrayes valeurs qu'ils L'ont pensée. Par exemple, nous pointons plusieurs croches de suites par degrés-conjoints; Et cependant nous les marquons égales; notre usage nous a asservis; Et nous continüons.[24]

> In my view there are defects in our way of writing music, which correspond to the manner of writing our language. It is that we write differently than we play: which causes foreigners to play our music less well than we play theirs. By contrast the Italians write their music in the true values in which they conceived it. For example, we point several eighths that proceed by conjunct degrees; however, we mark them equal; our custom has enslaved us; and we continue.

Fortunately other writers were more specific: the information they provide is summarized in table 1-2 and will be reviewed below under the headings shown in the table. The letter symbols in the second through ninth columns of table 1-2 are identified by author in its first column.[3]

Stepwise motion. The treatises listed in the second column of table 1-2 indicate, as Vague puts it, that "notes in disjunct intervals are ordinarily equal."[25] The six sources marked + state this specifically, and the others imply it by the musical examples they cite in explaining inequality. Several apparent exceptions to this rule suggest, however, that it was not an extremely rigid one. Monteclair provides a short illustration (example 1-1) that includes, in addition to typical conjunct eighths, two leaps of a fourth specifically marked unequal: the first note of the pair is to be *appuyé,* a term further discussed below. In his earlier *Nouvelle methode,* however, Monteclair states that "when the melody proceeds in

EXAMPLE 1-1. Monteclair, *Principes de musique . . .* (Paris, 1736), 21.

disjunct intervals, the eighths are ordinarily equal" (at least in $\frac{3}{4}$ meter).[26] And Corrette provides an example of sixteenth notes in broken thirds (meter: **C**) which are to be unequal.[27] Disjunct motion (especially extended arpeggiations) is generally more characteristic of Italian music than French, which may be a factor in the theorists' excluding it from inequality. (If so, however, Corrette is self-contradictory; see below.) In any case, the stricture against inequality in leaps apparently applied to passages in which disjunct motion predominates, and performers could adjust their rhythmic execution accordingly within a piece.[28]

Long–short vs. short–long. As the third and fourth columns in table 1-2 show, the French custom of rhythmic inequality was to pair notes by lengthening the first beyond its written value and shortening the second, "long–short": more than thirty writers attest to this. As Neumann has shown, two problematic sources, Loulié and Couperin, led certain twentieth-century scholars to assume that French *notes inégales* could also be short–long patterns, at the discretion of the performer.[29] Loulié raises this possibility as an afterthought: in the second part of his treatise he had described ordinary long–short inequality in some detail, including its relation to meter, and the relative degree of alteration (see below). Then in the third part he returns to the topic, as follows:

> On avoit oublié de dire dans la 2. Partie en parlant des Signes de Mesures de trois Temps, que les premiers demi-Temps s'executent encore d'une quatriéme maniere, sçavoir en faisant le 1. plus court que le 2. Ainsi.[30]

> One has forgotten to say in the Second Part, in speaking of the metrical signs of triple time, that the first halves of beats are executed in yet a fourth way, namely, in making the first shorter than the second. Thus: [see example above]

And in the manuscript additions to his treatise Loulié illustrates a "mixed" manner of inequality, in which the seemingly irrational rhythmic notation suggests gentle short–long inequality in a ratio of approximately 2:3 (example 1-2).[31]

EXAMPLE 1-2.   Loulié, MS addition to *Elements ou principes de musique.*

Mixed (Meslé)

Abgedruckt mit Erlaubnis des Institutes für Mittelalterliche Musikwissenschaft.

EXAMPLE 1-3.   François Couperin, *Premier livre* (1713), ornament table.

Loulié's rather sporadic application of his short–long pattern suggests that it might be akin to the arbitrary rhythmic liberties vaguely advocated by Santa Maria, Frescobaldi, Nivers, and Bacilly many years earlier. But with respect to all subsequent discussions of *notes inégales*, it is clearly a maverick. Moreover, in French music the Lombardic rhythm (♪♩.) frequently occurs in contexts where ordinary long–short performance of the written eighths was surely expected; apparently, then, the short–long pattern was a special effect requiring explicit notation.

Couperin's ornament table in his first book of harpsichord pieces enigmatically introduces an unusual notational device described as "Slurs, wherein the dots indicate that the second note of each beat must be more stressed [*plus appuyée*]" (example 1-3).[32] This was copied almost verbatim by Fouquet, without further explanation, and Marpurg uses the marking once in his very French *Pieces de clavecin*.[33] Later in the century, however, Engramelle identifies the notation ⌒ as a short–long pattern that he calls *secondes coulées* (example 1-4).[34]

The principal ambiguity concerning Couperin's slur-plus-dot is the term *appuyer*, which ordinarily means to support, sustain, lean upon, help or favor, or stress.[35] Bacilly, Marais, Dupont, Anon., Dard, and Roussier, for example, all use the term in conjunction with agogic or dynamic emphasis.[36] But as we have seen, Montéclair uses *appuyer* to mean the rhythmic lengthening of long–short inequality (example 1-1);[37] so, too, does Quantz in the French translation of his famous flute treatise.[38] Given the harpsichord's narrow dynamic range, all of this suggests that Couperin's unusual notation (copied by Fouquet and Marpurg) means

EXAMPLE 1-4. Engramelle (1778), "Secondes coulées."

short–long inequality.[39] And the main point to be grasped is that a special notation was required to achieve this: it was not a customary procedure, whereas long–short inequality clearly was.[40] The slur-and-dot marking is, in any case, very rare.[41]

Indeed, so customary was the trochaic performance of diminutions that it was applied even in the revisionist form of liturgical chant known as *plain-chant musical* or *figuré*. The oft-reprinted method book by François de La Feillée states:

> Les grandes breves sont inégales, c'est-à-dire, que l'on soutient légérement la premiere, & l'on passe vîte la seconde. . . .
>
> . . . Enfin s'il y avoit quatre breves, après avoir soutenu la quarrée, on appuieroit sur la premiere & sur la troisieme très-légérement, & l'on passeroit fort vîte sur la seconde & sur la quatrieme, pour aller soutenir la quarrée qui seroit après: *voyez le cinquieme exemple.*[42]

> The large breves [equal to two small-typeface breves] are unequal, which is to say that one lightly sustains the first, and passes the second quickly. . . .
>
> . . . Finally, if there were four breves, after having sustained the square note, one would stress the first and third breves very lightly and would pass quite quickly over the second and fourth, to arrive and dwell upon the square note that would follow: *see the fifth example* [above].

The degree of inequality. How strongly the written rhythms of French music were altered is among the most crucial issues concerning *notes inégales.* The evidence is summarized in table 1-2 under the headings "Mild," "Variable," and "Strong." In general, it would seem that *inégalité* was mild—less than the 3:1 ratio occasioned by a dotted note, and in no case known to exceed 3:1. According to Nivers (1665), it is as though one placed "half dots" after odd-numbered eighths to augment them "ever so slightly" (see p. 5 above). Bacilly's commentary suggests that ordinarily *notes inégales* should be executed "so delicately that it is not apparent" (see above, p. 6), and Jean Rousseau cautions that one "must take care not to mark them too roughly" (see p. 7). Loulié uses the term *lourer* for mild inequality, whereby one makes the first notes of pairs "a little bit longer" (*un peu plus longs*);[43] and in the manuscript additions to his treatise he illustrates a ratio of approximately 3:2, as shown in example 1-5.[44]

Strong inequality is termed *piquer* or *pointer* by Loulié, but he observes that here "the first half-beat ought to have a dot," and he illustrates it that way in his later handwritten annotations.[45] At least twelve treatise writers use the expression *un peu* in describing the rhythmic alteration of *notes inégales.*[46] Moreover, Vague observes that "it is necessary to distinguish this inequality of which we are speaking from that which requires the dot, which is greater."[47] And while de-La Chapelle introduces inequality with a pedagogical example of dotted notation, he indicates that this is only an approximation; when the music actually includes written dots, one dwells longer on the first (dotted) note than when executing *notes inégales:*

> a la mesure du quatre tems les doubles et triples croches se gouvernent a peu près de cette Facon. ♩♪♪♪♪♪♪ on reste sur la premiere et l'on passe vite la segonde, mais l'orsquelle sont pointées on y reste un peu plus, voila pourquoy je dis a peu pres, et la raison de les pointez pour faire connoitre ceux ou l'on doit le plus rester. . . .[48]

> In the four-beat measure the sixteenths and thirty-second notes regulate themselves approximately in this fashion: [see rhythmic notation]. One dwells on the first and passes the second quickly; but when they are dotted one dwells a bit more—there you see why I say approximately, and the reason for dotting them, in order to indicate those where one must dwell the most. . . .

Rollet, in discussing the meter $\frac{3}{4}$ (or **3**), observes that "it is necessary to shorten a bit the second of two eighths, without however singing them by jerks."[49]

But the treatise writers are not unanimous on this issue.[50] We have already noted the commentary advocating strong inequality for certain

EXAMPLE 1-5.   Loulié, MS addition to *Elements ou principes de musique.*

Abgedruckt mit Erlaubnis des Institutes für Mittelalterliche Musikwissenschaft.

sorts of pieces in the anonymous "Maniere de toucher lorgue" (see above, p. 7). Saint-Lambert observes that

> quand on doit inégaliser les Croches ou les Noires; c'est au goût à décider si elles doivent être peu ou beaucoup inégales. Il y a des Piéces où il sied bien de les faire fort inégales, & d'autres où elles veulent l'être moins. Le goût juge de cela comme du mouvement.[51]

> when one must inequalize the notes, it is up to taste to decide whether they should be a little or strongly unequal. There are pieces where it is good to make them strongly unequal, and others where they should be less. Taste judges this, as in the case of tempo.

Lacassagne writes of unequal eighths where "the first is much longer than the second, in proportion to the tempo that one executes."[52] François David clearly seems to advocate 3:1 inequality when he notes that

> il faut demeurer, & rester sur la premiére des deux, continuant de deux en deux, de même que si la premiére avoit après elle un point qui l'augmentât de la moitié de sa valeur; de sorte qu'ayant dérobé la moitié de la valeur de la seconde Note par ce point supposé, il faudra que la seconde se passe au quart de la valeur de la premiére. . . .[53]

> it is necessary to dwell and remain on the first of the two, continuing two by two, the same as if the first had a dot after it, which would augment its value by one-half, in such a manner that, being robbed of half of its value by this supposed dot, the second note would have to go by at a fourth of the value of the first. . . .

Dupuit's diagrams for cranking the vielle show only precise 3:1 inequality.[54] L'Abbé Duval writes that first notes in pairs of eighths must be substantially longer ("bien plus longues").[55] Tarade specifies that a *marche pointée* is to be pointed as though the first eighth had a dot and the second were a sixteenth—in other words, 3:1 inequality.[56] And Cleret *fils* describes inequality in eighth-note motion as giving half again as much value to the first and passing quickly over the second.[57]

While the passages just cited from David, Tarade, and Cleret seem unambiguous, they also draw our attention to the potentially confusing illustrations and terminology used in a number of treatises, as Neumann has pointed out.[58] Musical examples that employ dotted notes to explain *notes inégales* do not necessarily mandate 3:1 inequality.[59] We have already seen this in Bourgeois's early account, which provides an example in dotted notation, yet describes the degree of inequality as "some little bit" (see above, p. 3). Monteclair writes that the first note in an unequal pair "should be almost as long as though it were dotted,"[60] and gives the illustration that ♪ 𝄐𝄐𝄐𝄐 is like 𝄐𝄐𝄐𝄐 (and similarly for other meters). He closes this discussion, however, by stating that the first note is always "a little longer" (*un peu plus longue*) than the second, and his latest treatise presents a very similar account.[61] Denis uses the analogy of the dot in discussing inequality in **C** meter, where "the sixteenths must be unequal as though they were dotted, that is, the first of each beat long, the second short."[62] And J.-J. Rousseau, after explaining inequality in terms of dotted notes, concludes that in French music one always points the eighths "un peu" (unless the meter is **C** or the piece marked *croches égales*).[63]

Related to this problem is the frequent use of the verb *pointer* to mean "play unequally": *le point* is the traditional term for the dot of addition, and *pointer* can also mean "to dot," i.e., to add dots to the notation. It is already clear from the commentary by Nivers, Bacilly, Loulié, and Vague cited above that in discussions of *notes inégales*, these words need not imply a 3:1 rhythmic ratio. Thus, for example, in his allemande "La laborieuse" (example 1-6) Couperin writes "les double croches un tant-soit-peu pointées," meaning very mild inequality for the sixteenth notes,[64] and Dornel marks the *rondeau* "La badine sérieuse" "un peu

EXAMPLE 1-6.   François Couperin, allemande "La laborieuse" (1713), opening.

pointéz et liées."[65] Late in the century Pierre Duval objects to such seemingly contradictory language by writing that *"pointer* is improperly used
to mean making eighths unequal."[66] This problem does not arise in the
work of the numerous authors who use other terms — *inégaliser, reposer/
passer plus viste, notes* (croches, etc.) *inégales, inégalité, tenir/passer,* etc.
Apparently, however, the distinction between notated dots of addition
and the unnotated custom of *notes inégales* was never fully established:
as late as 1782 Pierre Marcou (ordinaire de la Musique du Roi) writes that

> parmi les gens de l'art, il en est qui prétendent que ce principe ne doit
> avoir lieu que lorsque ces notes sont précédées chacunes d'un point; il en
> est d'autres qui reconnoissent une différence sensible entre la maniere de
> donner une valeur égale à ces notes, de les pointer légérement de deux on
> deux, ou de les pointer d'une maniere plus marquée, lorsqu'elle est in-
> diquée par les points qui précedent les notes breves. Comme on n'est pas
> parfaitement d'accord sur ce principe, on choisira dans les trois manieres
> celle qui sera la plus propre au genre de musique qu'on exécutera.[67]

> among people of the art, there are those who claim that this principle [of
> inequality] does not have to be applied except when each of these notes
> is preceded by a dot; there are others who recognize a palpable difference
> between the manner of giving equal value to these notes, or pointing
> them lightly two by two, or pointing them in a more marked manner
> when it is indicated by dots that precede the short notes. Since there is
> not perfect agreement on this matter, one chooses among the three man-
> ners that which will be most appropriate to the genre of music one plays.

The most precise indications concerning the degree of *inégalité* are
found in Père Engramelle's writings on the pinning of mechanical organs — in Bedos de Celles's *L'art de facteur d'orgues* (1778),[68] and more
especially in his own volume *La tonotechnie.*[69] Here Engramelle stresses
that the extent of the inequality is most important for the proper expression of a piece, and notes that it often varies within the same piece "if one
wishes to express certain passages in a more interesting manner," according to taste.[70] He establishes a range of unequal ratios from 7:5 up to 3:1.
Marches receive the strongest inequality — 3:2 and 2:1 in the pieces notated in the plates, and 3:1 prescribed for the "Marche du roi de Prusse,"
for which no music is provided.[71] Minuets are generally smoother: "The
least marked differentiation, as in many minuets, is 3 to 2, 7 to 5, etc.,"[72]
and the examples in the plates show ratios of 1:1, 7:5, and apparently 5:3
("Minuet de roy de Prusse"). But in certain minuets, such as the "petit
menuet Trompette," the inequality is to be 2:1.[73] For all other pieces he
mentions or notates, Engramelle advocates ratios smaller than 2:1. It is
both fascinating and instructive to hear these pieces as realized according
to his detailed instructions by Houle; but it is difficult to generalize about

them beyond Engramelle's own summary remarks in *L'art de facteur d'orgues:*

> Cette *inégalité* doit varier suivant le genre d'expression de l'air; dans les airs gais, elle doit être plus marquée que dans les airs gracieux & d'une expression tendre, dans les marches que dans les menuets; cependant il se trouve bien des menuets de caractere dans lesquels l'*inégalité* est aussi marquée que dans les marches. Le goût, ou plutôt l'usage du notage, fera sentir cette différence.[74]

> This *inequality* ought to vary according to the nature of the piece; in gay airs it should be more marked than in those that are gracious and of tender expression, more in marches than in minuets; however, there are a number of minuets of character in which the *inequality* is as marked as in marches. Taste, or rather the use of *notage*, will make this difference sensible.

The sum of the evidence on this issue is shown in table 1-2. Of those writers who discuss the degree of *inégalité*, sixteen suggest that it is mild ("un peu," etc.); four mention only strong rhythmic alteration; and six indicate that the ratio of inequality is variable.

These, then, are the main points of consensus about *notes inégales* among French writers from about 1690 until the Revolution: the relationship between meter and inequality; the general rule of stepwise motion; the essentially trochaic nature of rhythmic alteration (long–short); and the degree of inequality—on the whole mild, but certainly variable. In the next chapter we shall take up matters on which the sources are notably less concordant.

The Negation of Inequality, Discrepancies among the Sources, and Related Matters

THE NEGATION OF INEQUALITY

Not later than the turn of the eighteenth century, *notes inégales* had become so common in French performance style that a composer needed to provide special instructions if the custom were not to apply; Pierre Duval declared that "the only exception to this rule [of inequality] is when one is forewarned either by dots or little perpendicular lines."[1] To be sure, *notes* or *croches égales* is the most common countermand, mentioned by a number of theorists and found in many scores by Couperin, Clérambault, Bernier, la Ferté, Caix d'Hervelois, Dandrieu, Dornel, and others. But as Duval observes, dots or strokes placed above the notes also negate inequality.[2] So too does the word *détaché*.[3] And according to two writers, *notes martelées* indicates equality as well.[4] This suggests that staccato articulation is generally inimical to *inégalité*, which "slurs the song and renders it more flowing," as Choquel puts it.[5] Indeed, phrases that typically appear in the treatise discussions of inequality—"*liées de deux en deux, se passent longues et breves de deux en deux, pointer de la première à la seconde*," etc.—suggest that, although not actually slurred, the notes were closely bound together through their unequal apportionment of a beat. And short slurs, especially of two notes, are not uncommon in passages that are to be played unequally.[6] Thus, the indication of *détaché* or dots was apparently adopted to suggest separating the bond between paired unequal notes; these markings may, but do not necessarily, mean staccato articulation as well.

Modern writers often assume that the terms *marqué, piqué,* and *mesuré* also cancel inequality. But these words are problematic and can be understood only in the context where they appear. Brossard associates *marqué* with performing in strict time, as opposed to the free style of *récitatif*.[7] As Saint-Arroman has documented, such was fairly common usage;[8] but this has no specific bearing on the performance of *notes in-égales*. As we have seen (p. 164–65, n. 20), *marquer* is actually Jean Rousseau's term for *inégalité*; on the other hand, Loulié links *marquer* with playing evenly, as written, in the manuscript additions to his treatise.[9] The verb indicates emphasis and inequality in Demotz de la Salle's definition of *lourer* (see p. 170, n. 6), while other writers use *marquer* simply to suggest accentuation.[10] Morel de Lescer's vocal treatise includes a *leçon* marked "mouvement decidé" (in **C**) with the added comment that the eighths are equal "because the *mouvement* is marked."[11] (The suggestion that eighths in **C** might otherwise be rendered unequally in 1760 is unusual in itself: see below). But later in the same volume (p. 14) a piece in $\frac{6}{4}$ is marked "Mouve. marqué Les croches et les doubles croches sont inégales," which seems at variance with the author's previous association of *marqué* and rhythmic equality. Boüin writes that in overtures or marches the eighths are always "inégales & marquées."[12] On the other hand, Couperin's fourth book for harpsichord contains an "Air dans le goût polonois" (in $\frac{3}{4}$ marked "Vivement: Les notes égales; et Marquées," with *détaché* dots over many of the eighths as well.[13] Thus the term has no consistent meaning with respect to inequality and must be interpreted in context.

Piquer (or *picquer*) also presents difficulties. For Loulié it means sharp 3:1 inequality that should be indicated by notated dotted rhythms (see above, p. 16). But only one other writer seems clearly in accord with this meaning: Lacassagne, who mentions only relatively strong *notes inégales* (see above, p. 17), uses *se piquer* to describe them.[14] The lexicographer Sebastian Brossard, who was on close terms with Loulié, might appear to adopt Loulié's understanding of *picquer* when he defines *lourer* as mildly lengthening the first of two paired notes "sans cependant *la pointer* ou *la picquer*."[15] But Brossard's entry for *picquer* refers us to the Italian term *staccato*: dry, separate bow strokes, well detached or separated, "almost what we call in French *Picqué* or *Pointé*."[16] And this seems to be the most common meaning of *piquer*, reflected in J.-J. Rousseau's definition as well: for him, the *note piquée* is to be dry and strongly marked.[17] In both of these dictionaries, as well as that by Meude-Monpas,[18] the issue is slightly confused because *pointer*, which usually indicates rhythmic inequality (with or without notated dots), is used for the addition of a *staccato* dot (or stroke). (Although not common in the treatises, this possible meaning of *pointer* should be considered when the word appears in scores of the period; see also below.)

Campra marks several movements *piqué* in his first book of cantatas; in "L'heureux jaloux," two of them (in **3** and **₵**) contain no eighths eligible for inequality, which suggests that *piqué* means staccato.[19] Hotteterre, in explaining the various sorts of measure, uses the term to characterize duple meters: **2** is ordinarily "vive et piquée," and appropriate for the beginning of overtures, entrées, marches, bourées, gavottes, etc. Predictably, "the eighths are unequal" (*les croches y sont pointées*): given this additional directive plus the wide variety of pieces Hotteterre associates with the meter **2**, *piquée* would seem to mean crisp articulation, rather than strong inequality in Loulié's sense.[20] Hotteterre's "1.ᵉʳ Trait" for flute in the same volume (p. 20), which is labeled "Rondem.ᵗ et croches égales," includes a brief passage where the eighths are marked both "piqué" and with staccato (or *détaché*) dots: apparently, then, the word means staccato in his works. For Boüin, the meter **2** (or ₵) is associated with pieces "grave & picqué" in character, such as marches or overtures; he goes on to explain that the eighths are always to be unequal and *marqué*, which again suggests that *picqué* describes articulation.[21] Bordet explains that notes with strokes above them are to be "piquées et coupées," and he distinguishes these from ordinary *notes detachées*, which bear no marking and merely receive separate bow or tongue strokes;[22] evidently for him the term means a sharp staccato. Dard also links *piquer* with staccato dots and strokes.[23] And according to Pierre Duval, *notes piqués* must be "equal and well marked."[24]

The anonymous *Nouvelle methode pour apprendre a jouer du violon* [ca. 1760] provides a uniquely detailed explanation of *piquer*. In his discussions on meter and inequality the author establishes a difference between *notes detachées*, which are to be equal in duration but alternately strong and weak (*fort et foibles*), and *notes articulées*, which are to be rendered *inégales* according to the usual meter-inequality relationship; the shorter of the *notes inégales* are to be connected to the longer (presumably without articulation space between them).[25] The treatise's "First Lesson on the Four-beat Meter" (*1.ᵉʳᵉ leçon sur la mesure à quatre temps*) is thoroughly marked with articulations and inequality; the author discusses the seventh measure, shown in example 2-1, as follows (p. 30):

> Les points qu'on voit entre les noms des notes articulées [= sixteenths] indiquent les longues et les breves. La ligne perpendiculaire qu'on voit sous chaque note pointée dans le troisieme et le quatrieme temps de la septieme mesure [see below], marque qu'on doit détacher l'archet à chaque note articulée, quand elle est suivie d'un point; celle qui est marquée triple croche doit être jointe avec la note suivante comme les breves dans les notes articulées, mais d'une maniere beaucoup plus sensible; cette maniere d'éxécuter les notes s'appelle piquer.

> The dots one sees between the names of the articulated notes [= sixteenths] indicate the longs and shorts. The perpendicular line that one

EXAMPLE 2-1.   Anon., *Nouvelle methode pour apprendre à jouer du violon* [ca. 1760], 30.

sees beneath each dotted note in the third and fourth beats of the seventh measure indicate that one must detach the bow at each articulated note when it is followed by a dot; the note marked as a thirty-second must be joined with the following note, like the shorter notes of the articulated ones, but in a much more noticeable manner; this manner of executing the notes is called *piquer.*

Here *piquer* clearly means detached articulation; it is also associated with dotted rhythms, as in Loulié's definition, but the dots are notated (as Loulié suggested they properly should be). Detaching the bow between the dotted note and the thirty-second and linking the thirty-second to the next dotted note yields crisp articulation between them: this is one of very few clues found in French treatises about the difference between *notes inégales* and dotted notation at the level of inequality (see also below, pp. 32–34).

Several additional instances of the term in musical works seem to confirm that *piqué* ordinarily means staccato. An "Air piqué" by la Ferté (example 2-2) is apparently to be detached (the "slurs" in the bass indicate prolongation of harmony rather than legato). Dandrieu's "La lyre d'Orphée" from his second book of *pièces* is marked "grave et piqué" (example 2-3); the leaping eighths would not customarily be eligible for inequality, whereas shortening their duration evokes the pluck of the lyre.[26] Mondonville's *Titon et l'Aurore* contains passage-work for violins, "Vite et piqué," that hardly lends itself to strong inequality; staccato is apparently intended (example 2-4).[27] In Mondonville's *Isbé* we find the passage shown in example 2-5, wherein the strong 3:1 rhythmic ratio is fully notated; "piqué" must mean crisp articulation.[28]

The sum of this evidence, then, suggests that *notes piquées* were usually to be shortened, even clipped, and probably well marked or accented; according to some authors, they could occur in the context of *notes inégales,* while for other writers crisp articulation, like the signs of dot and stroke, was linked with rhythmic equality. Individual musical works in which the term occurs must be evaluated in context—but it would appear that Loulié's definition of *piquer* as strong inequality was not common usage.[29]

EXAMPLE 2-2.   La Ferté, *Premier livre de sonates* (1707), 28.

EXAMPLE 2-3.   Dandrieu, "La lyre d'Orphée," *Second livre* (1728), 5.

EXAMPLE 2-4.   Mondonville, *Titon et l'Aurore* (1753).

None of the sources examined here uses *mesuré* to cancel inequality.[30] According to J.-J. Rousseau, *mesuré* is the equivalent of the Italian *a tempo*, meaning to sing in strict time (as opposed to the free style of *récitatif*).[31] François Couperin had used it with similar meaning in *L'art de toucher le clavecin*: preludes, he writes, are to be played "in an easy manner without adhering too greatly to precision of tempo, unless I have expressly indicated this by the word **Mesuré**,"[32] and he maintains this usage in subsequent collections.[33] Later in the century Duval writes that *mesuré* "indicates greater precision in each beat of the measure."[34]

It is sometimes claimed that allemandes should be excluded from the custom of *notes inégales*,[35] but there is only one ancient source that hints at this: in the preface to his second collection (1701) Marais refers to the allemande as a case in which taste does not require rhythmic inequality, and he therefore assumes it unnecessary to mark dots to negate the custom; Marais does not, however, advert to specific note values involved.

EXAMPLE 2-5.   Mondonville, *Isbé* (Paris, n.d.), 141.

But the following year Saint-Lambert stipulates that for pieces in quadruple meter, such as allemandes, inequality descends to the level of sixteenth notes (if there are any), owing to the slowness of the tempo in this meter.[36] As noted previously, in 𝄴 or $\frac{4}{4}$, the sixteenth is customarily the altered rhythmic value (see tables 1-1 and 1-2); since the allemandes in Marais's second book contain relatively few sixteenths (rather, they crop up in the succeeding *doubles*), his comment may have been based on the characteristic relation between meter and inequality rather than on the nature of the allemande as a piece. In any case, as noted above (p. 18), Couperin expressly indicates mild inequality for the sixteenths of an allemande in his *Premier livre.* Later in the century Corrette advocates unequal sixteenths for allemandes in three of his several treatises; and both Hotteterre and Vion include the allemande in their discussions of inequality as well.[37]

One writer—L'Abbé Lacassagne—suggests that eighths become equal when mixed with syncopations ("mêlées . . . de Notes syncopées").[38] No other source concurs.

DISCREPANCIES AMONG FRENCH
SOURCES

As discussed above, French writers of the eighteenth century are generally in accord about the relationship between meter and inequality. But
on this issue and several others, discrepancies occur, which will now be
reviewed. One of the most prominent differences of opinion concerns the
treatment of rhythmic values smaller than those ordinarily rendered unequal. As Neumann has observed, treatise writers who address this matter fall into two groups: those for whom inequality *descends*, and those
who postulate that it is *cumulative*.[39] The notion of cumulative inequality is neatly summed up by Borin: ". . . in whatever measure, when one
species of note is unequal, it follows that the smaller species are also."[40]
This would surely produce unusual rhythmic clashes in keyboard or ensemble music, but none of the sources mentions such a problem. On the
other hand, several authors assert that inequality must descend to the
smallest rhythms present, whereby the (larger) note values usually altered
become equal. As Azaïs puts it:

> La loi de l'égalité ou de l'inégalité des croches n'a rien de commun avec
> la maniere correcte ou vicieuse de désigner une mesure. Cette loi se tire
> du principe simple, mais général, que c'est toujours les notes de moindre
> valeur, employees dans une mesure qui se passent inégalles.[41]

> The law of equality or inequality has nothing in common with the cor-
> rect or faulty manner of indicating a meter. This law is derived from the
> simple but general principle that it is always the notes of least value
> employed in a measure that are rendered unequal.

None of the writers provides convincing rationale for either of these
opposed positions; presumably performers resolved the issue according to
taste and the nature of the piece at hand.

Inequality in $\frac{3}{4}$ time is another matter on which sources disagree. As
table 1-1 shows, some writers regard $\frac{3}{4}$ as equivalent to **3** (*triple simple*),
whereby eighths are unequal; for others, inequality descends to the level
of sixteenths in $\frac{3}{4}$. Corrette, Denis, and Rollet declare that $\frac{3}{4}$ is merely the
Italian equivalent of **3**; yet while Rollet advocates unequal eighths in
either meter, Corrette and Denis remain vague about $\frac{3}{4}$.[42] As we shall see
below, it would appear that Italian music was largely exempt from the
custom of *notes inégales*; therefore modern writers sometimes suggest
that precisely the association of $\frac{3}{4}$ with Italian composition engendered
the confusion about this meter.[43] But the treatises themselves do not
establish convincing reasons for the discrepancy,[44] and rather late in the

eighteenth century Azaïs declared that the purportedly different treatment of *notes inégales* in **3** and $\frac{3}{4}$ was an absurdity.[45]

A few additional disagreements about meter and inequality crop up
sporadically in the French treatises. Monteclair observes that

> il est tres difficile de donner des principes generaux sur l'égalité ou sur
> l'inegalité des nottes, car c'est le gout des Pieces que l'on chante qui en
> decide, cependant il faut observer qu'en quelque mesure que se soit, les
> nottes dont il en faut quatre pour remplir un tems, sont toujours inegalles
> la premiere un peu plus longue que la seconde.[46]

> it is very difficult to give general principles concerning the equality or
> inequality of notes, because it is the taste of the pieces one sings that
> decides this; however, it is necessary to observe that in whatever mea-
> sure it be, the notes of which it takes four to make up a beat are always
> unequal, the first a little longer than the second.

Demotz de la Salle, who presents the basic rules of *notes inégales* in the
various meters with exemplary clarity (see table 1-1), also introduces the
following exceptions:

> Dans l'éxpression des Airs déclamatifs, Recitatifs ou Recits mesurez *à
> deux ou trois Tems simples*, les Notes Croches ♪ qui sont dites *inégales*,
> s'éxpriment très-souvent égales aux autres Croches par rapport à l'ex-
> pression de la Parole, & selon le goût du Chant.

> Et dans les Recitatifs, Recits de Basse ou autres, Mesurez *à quatre
> tems simples*, les Croches qui sont naturellement égales dans leur mar-
> che, se chantent au contraire souvent inégales, aussi selon le goût du
> chant, & suivant que les sortes d'Airs sont plus ou moins régulierement
> écrits, & qu'ils éxpriment plus ou moins bien la parole.[47]

> In the rendering of declamatory airs, recitatives, or solos *in ordinary
> duple or triple time* [**2** or **3**], the eighths ♪ which are called *unequal* are
> often rendered equal to the other eighths, in keeping with the expression
> of the text, and according to the taste of the melody.

> And in recitatives, or solos for bass or others, which are *in ordinary
> quadruple meter* [**C**], the eighths that are naturally equal in their course
> are on the contrary often sung unequally, also in accordance with the
> taste of the melody, and according to whether the types of airs are more
> or less regularly written, and whether they express the text more or less
> effectively.

Antoine Dumas, contrary to most writers (cf. table 1-1), indicates that
eighths are unequal in **C** unless sixteenths are present, in which case the
inequality descends to the sixteenths. And he includes an exercise in **C**,
composed largely of conjunct eighths (but no sixteenths), labeled

"Croches inégales" (example 2-6).[48] Thus apparently, like Azaïs, Dumas considers the level of diminution in the music more significant than the traditional rule relating inequality to meter; this approach recalls much earlier examples of unequal eighths in C found in Nivers (1667), Gigault (1685) and Jullien (1690), as well as Perrine's comment about "the first part, or first parts of parts of the beats."[49] Morel de Lescer's treatise also suggests that eighths in C might occasionally be altered, as noted above (p. 22); his comment on this meter is that "eighths are *sometimes* equal, while sixteenths are ordinarily always unequal, even though they are not so marked" (emphasis added).[50] On the same page he presents a *leçon* beginning in C marked "lentement *Croches inegales*," without further comment (example 2-7).

This little exercise raises a number of issues: given the presence of sixteenth notes, it is apparently not a case of 'ascending' inequality (as was the Dumas exercise in example 2-6); presumably, the ratio of inequality for Morel's eighths in C would be milder than the 3:1 ratio of the dotted notes; and presumably this mild inequality would carry over into the 3 section, with little or no change in the basic tempo of the quarter note. But the text does not address these problems.

These differing opinions about inequality in C may stem from ambiguity inherent in the nature of the meter itself. The vast majority of French writers state that it is beaten in four; but while some emphasize that the tempo is slow (*à quatre tems graves*), others indicate that C can also be a measure of four quick beats (*à quatre tems legers*). The situation is similar for ₵: it could be taken either in two slow beats or four quick ones. And as table 1-1 shows, a number of treatises reflect this distinction in their treatment of *notes inégales:* when ₵ is taken in two, the eighths are unequal; in four, sixteenths are altered.[51] Furthermore, a few writers note the similarity in practice between duple and quadruple meters; Bouin, for example, observes that "sometimes there are pieces marked by a simple C that ought to be played like pieces marked by a 2, in which one does not find sixteenth notes, particularly when these pieces . . . are of gay or quick tempo, and when one does not find any sixteenths in them."[52] According to Bordet, "there are some who beat in two in the measures of C and $\frac{12}{8}$, but this is a poor practice which is contrary to principle."[53] And Tarade also suggests that C could be beaten in quarters or halves.[54] Thus, although contrary to the usual rules, eighths in C were probably taken unequally on occasion. In Lully's overture to the second part of the *Ballet royal d'Alcidiane* (1658), for example, two out of seven sources show the meter as ₵, while the others have C;[55] it is difficult to imagine that this discrepancy reflects an intentional difference in the performance of the eighth notes. Similarly, the opening sections of Dieupart's overtures for

EXAMPLE 2-6. Dumas, *L'art de la musique* [1753], 201.

EXAMPLE 2-7. Morel de Lescer, *Sçience de la musique vocale* [ca. 1760], 11.

keyboard move primarily in eighth notes; in the printed version the meter
is **C**, whereas in the Babell manuscript four of them are notated in **¢** (see
example 2-8). Again it seems unlikely that a difference in execution was
intended.[56]

RHYTHMIC ALTERATION OF TRIPLETS

Ordinarily, triplets and the ternary groups of compound meters (such as
eighths in $\frac{6}{8}$) are not subject to any rhythmic alteration. Several writers
address this; among the most specific is Tarade, who explains $\frac{12}{8}$ thus:
"These three eighths are always equal among themselves unless the author makes exception to the rule by double-flagging the middle one and
placing a dot between the first and second, in order to give half again as
much value to the first."[57] But three authors take exception to the rule,

Example 2-8.   Dieupart, Overture for keyboard, 24-Babell #25 (1702).

British Library, reproduced by permission.

without double-flagging the second eighth. Cappus, in a substantial dis-cussion of triplets, offers several possibilities for their execution:

> . . . ces notes se passent le plus souvent egalement, il arrive cependant quelque fois que l'on passe ces notes comme si les deux dernieres des trois croches etoient doubles, ou comme si les deux premiers etoient doubles, ou en fin comme si la premiere avoit un point et que la seconde fut double, le Gout et le mouvement determinent ces differentes manieres. . . .[58]

> . . . these notes are most often performed equally; it sometimes happens, however, that one performs these notes as though the last two of the three eighths were sixteenths, or as though the first two were sixteenths, or finally, as though the first had a dot and the second were a sixteenth; taste and *mouvement* determine these different styles. . . .

According to Raparlier, in $\frac{3}{8}$ "the style of the song very often demands that the eighths be unequal, the first long, the second short, and the third long"[59] — in other words, approximately ♩♫ . Pollet suggests the same for $\frac{12}{8}$.[60] And Mercadier de Belesta presents the following options:

> S'il en faut six, elles sont inégales, comme les précédentes, excepté lorsque ces notes sont mises pour quatre de la même espèce: auquel cas elles doivent être égales, ou bien la première & la quatrième doivent être un peu plus longues aux dépens de la seconde & de la cinquième. S'il n'en faut que trois, ou que, dans une mesure quelconque, on mette trois notes pour deux de la même espèce; on doit les passer également, ou soutenir la première un peu plus, & la seconde un peu moins que la troisième.[61]

> When there are to be six notes [to a beat], they are unequal, like the preceding, except when these notes are substituted for four of the same species: in which case they must be equal, or else the first and fourth must be a little longer, at the expense of the second and fifth. If there are only to be three [notes per beat], or else, in whatever measure, one sub-stitutes three notes for two of the same species; one must play them equally, or else sustain the first a little more, and the second a little less, than the third.

Such alterations of ternary groupings, like the rhythmic liberties advo-cated by Demotz de la Salle, stand apart from ordinary French practice as it is documented in the treatises; they are not, in any case, directly related to the custom of *notes inégales*. But they again remind us that, despite the relatively systematic approach of so many French writers, taste remained the ultimate touchstone in matters of rhythmic alteration; *le bon goût* provided "the freedom that musicians give themselves to transgress their own rules," as Saint-Lambert put it.[62]

THE QUESTION OF INEQUALITY
NOTATED BY DOTTED RHYTHMS

As late as 1782, dozens of treatises notwithstanding, Marcou reports that there was not "perfect agreement" concerning the distinction between notated rhythm and *notes inégales* (see above, p. 19), and this issue remains controversial to the present day.[63] During the early years of the custom's formation (ca. 1660–1700), some French composers may well have used dotted rhythms to indicate rhythmic alteration, as Gigault apparently did. When this seems to be the case, one must weigh whether the dotting represents the subtle lilt described by Nivers, Bacilly, and Jean Rousseau, or whether a vigorous 3:1 ratio might be intended. Muffat, for example, explains *notes inégales* in the preface to the first of his *Florilegia*; in both collections, however, he occasionally uses dotted notation at the rhythmic level of inequality for the highest part (violino), but only inconsistently or not at all for the lower voices. It seems unlikely that a difference in execution was intended, particularly when the parts move in parallel motion, as in example 2-9.[64] The plentiful later discussions of inequality, which are often very detailed, make it difficult to suppose that many eighteenth-century French musicians attempted to write out what performance tradition would provide as a matter of course; despite some inconsistencies among the sources, the essential features of the practice must have been general knowledge, and the numerous composers who used terms and symbols such as *pointé*, dots or strokes, *notes égales*, etc., assumed as much. Thus, for example, when Couperin consistently writes dotted 16th/32d patterns in "La Mézangére" (meter: 𝄴), it seems clear that he is specifying 3:1 ratios rather than *notes inégales* in quadruple time;[65] when he mixes straight sixteenths with dotted 16th/64th groupings in "La Raphaéle" (meter also 𝄴), it seems equally clear that he is differentiating sharp ratios from milder *notes inégales* (see example 2-10).[66] The latter situation—dotting at the customary level of inequality mixed with straight notes—is legion in French music. And in such cases, one must consider whether the dotting is to be distinguished from a milder degree of unwritten inequality, as Vague and de-La Chapelle indicate it should be

EXAMPLE 2-9.   Muffat, *Florilegium Secundum* (1698), fasc. I, Ouverture (*DTÖ* II/2, 58).

EXAMPLE 2-10.   Couperin, "La Raphaéle," *Second livre* (1717), 22.

(see above, p. 16). As we have seen (p. 23–24), one anonymous source, the *Methode pour apprendre a jouer du violon* [ca. 1760], suggests that dotted notation within the context of *notes inégales* means both a sharper rhythmic ratio and crisp articulation.

Still, anomalies do crop up: when we encounter passages like those shown in example 2-11 in the music of Monteclair, who explains conventional inequality clearly in three treatises, the inconsistency is vexing;[67] but the solution is simply that the instrumentalists and singer must come to agreement about the rhythms of the diminutions. Similar situations occur in the works of Rameau and other composers as well.

EXAMPLE 2-11. Monteclair, "Ariane et Bacchus," *Air gay* (1728) (ed. Anthony and Akmajian).

Whether persistent dotting might be a notation of French-style inequality in the music of other countries is an issue to be considered presently.

NOTES INÉGALES IN RELATION TO "GOOD AND BAD NOTES"

As Neumann has shown, French inequality intersects with, but is not identical to, the international notion of *quantitas intrinseca* or "good and bad notes"; because there is no longer substantial disagreement on this issue, it need not be minutely examined here.[68] In brief, the notion that rhythmic groupings consist of intrinsically long (or strong) and short (or weak) pulses is very old, considerably antedating any known references to *notes inégales*; by the time of Zarlino's *Istitutioni* (1558) such syllabification of musical rhythm was directly intertwined with contrapuntal practice. Diruta may have been the first to speak of *nota buona* and *nota cattiva* in describing metrical order, and thereafter a variety of sources in German, French, and English discuss the topic.[69] But whereas the distinction between good and bad notes applies to all levels of rhythmic subdivision, from the whole bar to the smallest notes present, the French applied their custom of *notes inégales* to a much more restricted range of rhythmic values and circumscribed the practice in other ways, as we have seen. Moreover, the vast majority of French writers do not confuse the two issues. Many treatises that present the typical meter-inequality relationship make no mention of good and bad notes whatever; on the other hand, Roussier discusses strong and weak metric divisions at some length, but never really focuses on *notes inégales*.[70] Writers who treat both topics generally place them in separate sections of the volume.[71] As it happens, the long–short pairs of French inequality may coincide with good and bad notes, but the two concepts are neither identical nor interdependent.[72]

In chapter 1 we reviewed those aspects of French inequality about which contemporary writers were generally in agreement. But the discrepancies and problems of terminology examined here suggest that the "systematic" presentations of *notes inégales* were a somewhat artificial product of the Age of Reason, written at least in part to simplify the teaching of a performance custom that is not inherently rational. To be sure, many (although by no means all) of the French tutors are directed to beginners and amateurs. Among professionals, and especially soloists, treatment of inequality may have been rather more subtle and varied than most treatises would indicate. And virtually all the "rules" concerning

notes inégales have been bent or broken by some seventeenth- or eighteenth-century source. Still, the evidence suggests that to ignore the custom would have been highly irregular; its application must be determined
by taste, as Saint-Lambert, Monteclair, Demotz de la Salle, Engramelle,
and others remind us. How far the taste for inequality extended beyond
French borders is among the most controversial issues concerning rhythmic alteration, and the one to which we now turn.

∽

CHAPTER THREE

Notes Inégales Outside France

Although one's taste might occasionally reject the convention of *notes inégales*, the bulk of the evidence—nearly sixty tutors, plus a variety of other sources—indicates that inequality was virtually de rigueur in France from the time of Lully until the Revolution. By comparison, documentary evidence of the custom outside France appears meager: this is summarized in table 1-2 (p. 11 above). As we have already noted, in the first decades of the seventeenth century scattered Italian (and Spanish) sources advocate rhythmic liberties for diminutions, in terms that do not differ greatly from the casual discussions of early French authors such as Nivers and Bacilly. But during the period of the numerous and detailed French treatises reviewed above (ca. 1690–1790), only three authors writing beyond French borders—Muffat, Quantz, and Prelleur—unmistakably describe the relatively systematic French custom of inequality; they are clearly exceptional and will be discussed presently.

Several French sources indicate that foreign music—meaning chiefly Italian—is exempt from *notes inégales*. The earliest of these is the second edition of Loulié's treatise (1698), published in Amsterdam. As in the Paris print, we read that eighths are equal in disjunct motion (p. 39); but then follows an italicized line not included in the earlier edition: "*& dans toute sorte de Musique etrangere ou l'on ne pointe, jamais qu'il ne soit marque*" ("*and in all types of foreign music, where one never inequalizes unless it is marked*"). In defining the Italian term *andante*, Loulié's friend Brossard observes that "especially for the basso continuo, it is necessary to make all the notes equal"; and according to Borrel, one of Brossard's motets is marked "The term andante indicates that it is Italianate music, and not pointed."[1] A dozen years later François Couperin observes that the Italians write music "in the true values in which they conceived it," whereas the French play evenly notated rhythms unequally.[2] Hotteterre's *L'art de préluder* contains several references to Italian style, indicating that he, too, was well aware of national differences in music; in the section on "Mesure du Triple Simple" (**3** or $\frac{3}{4}$) Hotteterre advises us that "the eighths are almost always unequal in French music."[3] Monteclair's third treatise contains two Italianate pieces — "Gavotte à l'Italienne" and Courente [*sic*] à l'Italienne" — both of which are specifically marked "Croches egales" in meters that would otherwise mandate inequality.[4] David writes that in triple meter the half-beats are unequal "according to the practice of the French."[5] Jean-Jacques Rousseau, an ardent Italian partisan during the Querelle des Buffons, is quite explicit on the issue:

> Dans la Musique Italienne toutes les Croches sont toujours égales, à moins qu'elles ne soient marquées *pointées*. Mais dans la Musique Françoise on ne se fait les Croches exactement égales que dans la Mesure à quatre Tems; dans toutes les autres on les pointe toujours un peu, à moins qu'il ne soit écrit *Croches égales*.[6]

> In Italian music all the eighths are always equal, unless they are marked *pointées*. But in French music one makes the eighths exactly equal only in the four-beat meter [**C**]; in all the others one always makes them a little unequal, unless they are marked *Croches égales*.

And Mondonville's preface to his *Pieces de clavecin avec voix ou violon* (1748) directs that it is necessary "above all to distinguish the phrases in French style from those that call for Italian taste";[7] inequality was presumably among the chief means of doing so.

But other sources suggest the situation may not have been so straightforward. Despite Couperin's claim that Italians write in "true values," he himself wrote a "Courante a L'italiéne" in running eighths that is to be played "pointé-coulé" (pointed and slurred; example 3-1). The Italian violinist Giovanni Antonio Piani, who had been active in Paris since 1704, published a set of sonatas there in 1712: Piani's *Avertissement* explains that dots placed above the notes mean rhythmic equality — a customary cancellation of *notes inégales* (example 3-2).[8] And such dots appear in a movement that could otherwise be a textbook example of French *notes inégales* (example 3-3). Clearly this Italian was familiar with the convention: Did he then apply it in the usual contexts throughout these pieces? Did he maintain the custom of *notes inégales* during later years in Vienna (1721–57)? Or did he merely adopt the mannerism while in Paris, to curry favor with the French? We simply do not know.

The prolific treatise writer Michel Corrette presents inconsistent views on the issue of national style and inequality. In his violoncello method (1741) Corrette states flatly that "in every meter the eighths are played equally in Italian music: as in the courante of the seventh sonata from Corelli's op. 5," and his treatise for pardessus de viole [1748] says much the same thing.[9] But in *L'ecole d'Orphée* for violin, Corrette explains unequal sixteenths in **C** with reference to one of his "Studies for

EXAMPLE 3-1.   François Couperin, "Courante a L'italiéne," *Troisiéme livre* (1722), Suplement, *Concerts royeaux,* 24.

EXAMPLE 3-2.   Piani, *Sonate* (Paris, 1712), preface.

EXAMPLE 3-3.   Piani, Sonata no. 10 (1712) (ed. Jackson).

Reproduced by permission of A-R Editions, Madison, Wis.

EXAMPLE 3-4.   Corelli, Sonata, Op. 5, No. 10, Gavotta (ed. Joachim and Chrysander).

violin to learn to play in Italian style" (*Leçons de Violon pour apprendre a joüer dans le goût Italien*), found at the end of the volume. Moreover, in this treatise he observes that the meter $\frac{3}{8}$ occurs frequently in "the Italian operas of Messrs. Handel, Bono[n]cini, Pepus[c]h, Scarlatti, Porpora, and all the sonatas composed by our illustrious French. . . . It is necessary to play the eighths equally and pass the second sixteenth more quickly" (i.e., sixteenths are unequal, as usual).[10] Corrette's flute tutor advises us that while sixteenths are ordinarily unequal in **C**, "sometimes one also plays them equally in allegros or prestos of sonatas and concertos"—presumably because these are Italianate movements. But in the paragraph explaining $\frac{6}{4}$, he recommends inequality for English vaudevilles and contradances such as "Bartholomew Fair," "Hunt the Sanerel," and "Hooptpettycoat."[11] The same author's *L'art de se perfectionner dans le violon* gives the usual explanation that dots above the notes mean equality.[12] The book is full of Italian pieces by Corelli, Vivaldi, Tartini, and a host of others; but there are virtually no dots to indicate that inequality does not apply in them.

In Vion's treatise the section on *measures* and *notes inégales* includes four examples from "Opera 5$^{\text{ta.}}$" by Signor Roberto Valentine, the English flautist and composer who lived in Rome and published a good deal of music both there and in Amsterdam.[13] Later in the century Azaïs, criticizing the purported distinction between **3** and $\frac{3}{4}$, observes that "all the foreigners unanimously utilize the signature $\frac{3}{4}$, yet nevertheless make the eighths unequal in ordinary triple time."[14] And, contrary to Corrette, Mussard cites the famous F-major gavotte from Corelli's Opus 5 as an example of unequal sixteenths in **C**! (see example 3-4).[15] Thus, just as the French assimilated features of Italian style into their own compositions, so too some of them extended the native performance convention of *notes inégales* to foreign music.

Germany

Only rarely outside France do we find a fully developed explanation of *notes inégales* such as those commonplace in French tutors of the eighteenth century. Yet although treatise information is slim, there are traces of the practice making its way abroad. Printz's *Musica Modulatoria Vocalis* (1678) rather vaguely suggests that

ehe wir dieses Capitel beschliessen/erinnere ich erstlich/daß alle laufende *Figur*en gehemmet werden können/durch Hinzuthun eines Puncts zu denen Notis quantitate intrinseca longis, (so mit ungerader Zahl gezehlet werden/) und *Minui*rung der darauf folgenden. *E. gr.* [16]

before we close this chapter I would recall first of all that all running figures can be held back by placing a dot by the notes of intrinsically long quantity (which are called odd-numbered) [i.e., the "good" notes], and diminishing the notes that follow. For example: [see above]

The first line of Printz's example is obviously an ornamental dotting of diminutions, although it bears no explicit relation to meter. But the freer configurations in the second line are utterly foreign to French discussions of *notes inégales* (although they would not seem out of place in an Italian *passaggi* tutor); thus it is not certain that Printz's short remark reflects French practice.[17]

But two decades later Georg Muffat, who as a youth had gone to Paris for six years' study with Lully and others (1663–69), clearly advocates the Lullist manner of performance for his *Florilegia* (1695–98), two large collections in the style of French ballet music.[18] His brief discussions of inequality link it to the customary note values in **2**, ¢, **3**, and **C**; and he suggests that to play such diminutions equally would be "boring, crude, and insipid." Prior to the publishing of the *Florilegia* in Augsburg and Passau, Muffat had worked in Vienna, Prague, and Salzburg, and had also studied in Rome; very likely he shared his firsthand knowledge of French style in all of these cities. Although he would later claim he was the first to introduce French style to German-speaking lands,[19] Muffat was preceded in this by several other composers. Froberger had been to Paris in 1652, where he almost certainly met Louis Couperin and Chambonnières; his keyboard suites reveal clear French influence, and he may have carried French performance style back to Vienna, where he spent the years 1653–58. Johann Sigismund Kusser was another student of Lully's who had spent six years in Paris and was engaged in 1682 to teach violinists in Ansbach the French style of orchestral playing; Kusser's *Composition de musique suivant la methode françoise* appeared in Stuttgart in 1682, and it is scarcely imaginable that he did not perform these very French pieces with *notes inégales*.[20] Kusser continued to compose instrumental music in French style, and also became well versed in Italian opera. From 1690–94 he was Kapellmeister in Wolfenbüttel, a city where three of Lully's works had been produced in the 1680s. Kusser subsequently worked in Hamburg and Stuttgart, making frequent guest appearances in other Germany cities until his departure to London in 1705. (He spent the remainder of his twenty-two years there and in Dublin.) Similarly, Johann Fischer (1646–1716) worked five years as a copyist for Lully before holding numerous short-term positions in Stuttgart, Augsburg, Ansbach, Lüneburg, and Schwerin. Rupert Ignaz Mayr (1646–1712) was sent by the Munich court to study with Lully, whence he returned in 1685. Agostino Steffani visited Paris between 1678 and 1679; the operas he subsequently wrote for Munich and Hannover were considerably influenced by Lullian style, from their overtures to their ballets and dance-style arias; he, too, would certainly have known of French rhythmic alteration.

French musicians had arrived in the Hannover Hofkapelle in the middle of the seventeenth century; it was there and in nearby Wolfenbüttel that Telemann became thoroughly acquainted with French style between 1698 and 1701. He then moved to Leipzig (1701–5), where he founded the Collegium Musicum (which Bach would later direct). In 1705 Telemann became Kapellmeister in Sorau, where he wrote numerous French overtures upon request for Count Erdmann II of Promnitz, who had recently returned from Paris. While employed in Eisenach (1708–12) Telemann was influenced by the virtuoso violinist and dulcimer player Pantlon Hebenstreit, who possessed "unusual adroitness in French music and composition," and who, as leader of the orchestra, demanded characteristically French precision.[21] At the court of Celle the wife of Duke Georg Wilhelm was French, and the French Hofkapelle flourished there under the direction of Philipp LaVigne from 1666 to 1705. During this period seven to ten (or more) musicians from France were among its members, and court records show that during the 1680s two of them also served as ballet masters.[22] Young J. S. Bach certainly heard this ensemble, and may have played in it, when he was a student at the Lüneburg Michaelisschule (1700–2); nearby at the Ritterakademie, the French dancing master was Thomas de la Selle, also a violinist in the Celle Hofkapelle, who may have been responsible for Bach's access to the court. According to C. P. E. Bach, his father "acquired a thorough grounding in the French taste" during his Lüneburg years.[23] And as numerous treatises show, inequality was as basic to French musical practice as counting rhythms and reading pitches. Beyond these centers of French influence, a number of German composers wrote in Lullian style—e.g., Johann Caspar Horn (ca. 1630–85), Philipp Heinrich Erlebach (1657–1714), Johann Abraham Schmierer (1661–1719), Johann Georg Conradi (d. 1699) and Johann Caspar Ferdinand Fischer (ca. 1670–1746)—and it is quite possible they were sufficiently versed in French performance practice to expect *notes inégales* in their works. In 1732 J. G. Walther's *Musicalisches Lexicon* reproduced Brossard's definition of *lourer;* yet Walther provides neither a German equivalent for the term nor any additional information about inequality.[24]

Quantz's discussion of inequality. The most detailed German writer on inequality, and today certainly the best known, is J. J. Quantz. Quantz studied the flute in Dresden with the French virtuoso Pierre Gabriel Buffardin, and he was also impressed by the leadership of the Hofkapelle's French concertmaster, J. B. Volumier. But his most influential mentor was the assistant concertmaster, J. G. Pisendel, whose style Quantz describes as "a mixture of the Italian and the French, for he had already travelled through both countries as a man of ripe powers of discernment." Quantz also deepened his knowledge of national styles through travels to Italy, Paris, and England.[25] Both Quantz's widely disseminated *Versuch einer Anweisung die Flöte traversiere zu spielen*[26] and his *Solfeggi* for flute (ca. 1770) suggest that he applied inequality ("unegal," "ungleich") to a wide variety of music.[27] Neither of these pedagogical sources provides a thorough exposition of *notes inégales* in the manner of the best French tutors, nor does Quantz specifically identify the practice as French; yet there can be no question whence he absorbed the custom. In the *Versuch* he first mentions inequality in the chapter on tonguing (VI/i/9), observing that

> bey geschwinden Passagien thut die einfache Zunge keine gute Wirkung, weil die Noten dadurch alle einander gleich werden; welche doch, dem guten Geschmacke gemäß, etwas ungleich seyn müssen. s. XI. Hauptstück 11. §

> in quick passage-work the single tongue does not have a good effect, since it makes all the notes alike, and to conform with good taste they must be a little unequal. See chapter XI, §11 [*recte:* §12].

In XI/12 (cited in full below, p. 44ff.), Quantz speaks of long–short alterations in the traditional meter-inequality relationships, but points out that "this lengthening must not be as much as if the notes were dotted"; he also advocates inequality descending to the smallest values present,

EXAMPLE 3-5.   Quantz, *Solfeggi* (ed. Michel and Teske, 1978), 40 and 55.

1. 2 Sehr ungleich und ri stark gestoßen

diese Passagen brauchen zwar nicht egal, doch auch nicht zu unegal seyn

Reprinted by permission of Music Associates of America, U.S. representatives for Amadeus Verlag.

and indicates that dots above the notes cancel rhythmic alteration. In the *Solfeggi* he indicates varying degrees of inequality by such annotations as "sehr ungleich [very unequal]," "zwar nicht egal, doch auch nicht zu unegal [certainly not equal, but also not too unequal]," and the like (see example 3-5).[28] All of this smacks of French practice. Nevertheless, Quantz introduces a few idiosyncrasies of his own. In the treatise inequality is said to be a consequence of "good" and "bad" notes (a confusion not characteristic of French writers); a number of passages in the *Solfeggi* that are to be played unequally contain numerous leaps; and there is at least one example of unequal eighths in **C**.[29] Moreover, the *Versuch* also introduces some new exceptions to the custom: Since quick passage-work in very fast tempo does not allow for ordinary inequality, "one therefore need only apply length and strength to the first of every four tones"; also exempt are roulades for the voice (unless they are to be slurred), several successive notes of the same pitch, and slurred groupings of more than two notes.[30] None of these exceptions is found in French sources. The complete text of Quantz's principal commentary on inequality is as follows:

> Ich muß hierby eine nothwendige Anmerkung machen, welche die Zeit, wie lange jede Note gehalten werden muß, betrifft. Man muß unter den **Hauptnoten**, welche man auch: **anschlagende**, oder, nach Art der Italiäner, **gute** Noten zu nenne pfleget, und unter den **durchgehenden**, welche bey einigen Ausländern **schlimme** heißen, einen Unterschied im Vortrage zu machen wissen. Die Hauptnoten müssen allezeit, wo es sich thun läßt, mehr erhoben werden, als die durchgehenden. Dieser Regel zu Folge müssen die geschwindesten Noten, in einem jeden Stücke von

mäßigem Tempo, oder auch im **Adagio,** ungeachtet sie dem Gesichte nach einerley Geltung haben, dennoch ein wenig ungleich gespielet werden; so daß man die anschlagenden Noten einer jeden Figur, nämlich die erste, dritte, fünfte, und siebente, etwas länger anhält, als die durchgehenden, nämlich, die zweyte, vierte, sechste, und achte: doch muß dieses Anhalten nicht so viel ausmachen, als wenn Puncte dabey stünden. Unter diesen geschwindesten Noten verstehe ich: die Viertheile im Dreyzweytheiltacte; die Achttheile im Dreyviertheil- und die Sechzehntheile im Dreyachttheiltacte; die Achttheile im Allabreve; die Sechzehntheile oder Zwey und dreyßigtheile im Zweyviertheil- oder im gemeinen geraden Tacte: doch nur so lange, als keine Figuren von noch geschwindern oder noch einmal so kurzen Noten, in jeder Tactart mit untermischet sind; denn alsdenn müßten diese leztern auf die oben beschriebene Art vorgetragen werden. Z. E. Wollte man Tab.IX Fig. 1. die acht Sechzehntheile unter den Buchstaben (k) (m) (n) langsam in einerley Geltung spielen [see excerpt below]; so würden sie nicht so gefällig klingen, als wenn man von vieren die erste und dritte etwas länger, und stärker im Tone, als die zweyte und vierte, hören läßt. Von dieser Regel aber werden ausgenommen: erstlich die geschwinden Passagien in einem sehr geschwinden Zeitmaße, bey denen die Zeit nicht erlaubet sie ungleich vorzutragen, und wo man also die Länge und Stärke nur bey der ersten von vieren anbringen muß. Ferner werden ausgenommen: alle geschwinden Passagien welche die Singstimme zu machen hat, wenn sie anders nicht geschleifet werden sollen: denn weil jede Note von dieser Art der Singpassagien, durch einen gelinden Stoß der Luft aus der Brust, deutlich gemachet und markiret werden muß; so findet die Ungleichheit dabey keine Statt. Weiter werden ausgenommen: die Noten über welchen Striche oder Puncte stehen, oder von welchen etliche nach einander auf einem Tone vorkommen; ferner wenn über mehr, als zwo Noten, nämlich, über vieren, sechsen, oder achten ein Bogen steht; und endlich die Achttheile in Giguen. Alle diese Noten müssen egal, das ist, eine so lang, als die andere, vorgetragen werden.[31]

Here I must make a necessary observation concerning the length of time each note must be held. One must know how to make a distinction in performance between the **principal notes,** also called accented or, as the Italians are wont to name them, **good** notes, and those that are **passing,** which some foreigners call **bad** notes. Where it is possible, the principal notes must always stand out more than the passing ones. In consequence of this rule, the quickest notes in every piece of **moderate tempo,** or even in the **Adagio,** although they appear to have the same value, must nevertheless be played a little unequally, so that the stressed notes of each figure, namely the first, third, fifth, and seventh, are held somewhat longer than the passing, namely the second, fourth, sixth, and eighth, although this lengthening must not be as much as if the notes were dotted. Among these quickest notes I mean the quarters in three-two time, the eighths in three-quarter and the sixteenths in three-eight time; the eighths in alle breve, the sixteenths or thirty-seconds in two-four or in common time [**C**]: but only so long as no figures of still more rapid notes, or doubly quick ones, are mixed in, whatever the meter—for in that case these latter would have to be executed in the manner de-

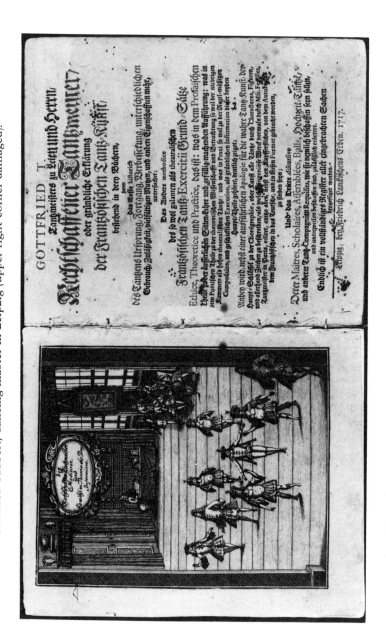

FIGURE 3-1. Frontispiece and title page of *Rechtschaffener Tanzmeister* . . . [*The Honest Dancing Master, or a Fundamental Explanation of the French Art of Dancing* . . .] [Leipzig, 1717), by Gottfried Taubert, dancing master in Leipzig (upper right corner damaged).

scribed above. For example, in table IX, fig. 1 [see below], if one were to play the eight sixteenths at letters (k), (m), and (n) slowly with the same value, they would not sound so pleasing as if one let the first and third of four be heard somewhat longer, and stronger in tone, than the second and fourth. Excepted from this rule, however, are, first of all, the fast passages in a very fast tempo, where time does not allow them to be executed unequally, and in which one therefore need only apply length and strength to the first of four notes. Further excepted are all quick passages for the human voice, if they ought otherwise not to be slurred, because each note in this sort of vocal passage-work must be made distinct and be marked by a gentle thrust of air from the chest; therefore inequality finds no place here. Also excepted are notes above which dots or strokes are found, or several successive notes on the same pitch. Further exceptions are: when a slur occurs over more than two notes (namely over four, six, or eight); and finally, the eighth notes in gigues. All of these notes must be executed equally, that is, one as long as the other.

TABLE IX, FIG. I

As Reilly has pointed out, Quantz's flute treatise reflects to a considerable extent the style of performance prevalent in Dresden from about 1720–40.[32] And it is scarcely surprising that French inequality should be among the practices of the Dresden Hofkapelle: French violinists had been active there since 1675, and wind players since 1696; between 1709 and 1732 seven or eight Frenchmen were regularly among the twenty-six to forty-four members of the ensemble. The cellist du Tilloy, who played in it from 1699 until 1733, also served as copyist of French music; and the repertoire included dozens of French suites. A French ballet corps was established in 1709 and continued until the closing of the theatrical establishments in 1769. J. B. Volumier, who had been trained at the French court and had served as both dancing master and concertmaster in Berlin from 1692 to 1708, was engaged as concertmaster in Dresden until his death in 1728. (It was he who reportedly organized Bach's aborted contest with Louis Marchand in 1717.) And a number of leading Dresden musicians—Volumier, Schmidt, Pisendel, Richter, and Pezold—absorbed French style firsthand during a visit to Paris with the Kurprinz in 1714–15.[33] Italian music, particularly opera, was certainly cultivated in Dresden as well, and eventually Italianate performers would outnumber the French; nevertheless, it would appear that the Hofkapelle maintained certain links with French performance style through Pisendel, Volumier's successor as concertmaster, until his death in 1755.

When Frederick the Great became king of Prussia in 1740, he was at last able to build the musical ensemble he had so long desired. His goal was both to emulate and surpass the Dresden Hofkapelle; he had already secured the services of the composer C. H. Graun, the violinist and composer J. G. Graun (a pupil of Pisendel's), and violinist Franz Benda, all of whom had studied or worked in Dresden. In 1741 he finally lured Quantz to Berlin. Marpurg, who had lived in Paris, remarked rhetorically of this stellar cast, "Do not Quantz, Benda, and Graun play very French?"[34] The opening of the Berlin Opera in late 1741 launched C. H. Graun's long series of operas in the style of Hasse, whose work Frederick had first heard in Dresden thirteen years earlier. And the king established a French dance corps as well.[35] Thus, the Dresden "mixed" manner of composition and performance became the official style in Berlin, and remained so throughout Frederick's reign: This is the essential background for Quantz's treatise, which appeared in French as well as German in 1752. Reception of the book was generally positive, and Telemann, Agricola, Marpurg, Adlung, J. E. Bach, Tromlitz, Gerber, Forkel, and Sulzer were among the eminent readers who recommended the whole or portions of it; three complete German editions were required during the eighteenth century, and various excerpts and translations also appeared. Only one objection to Quantz's treatment of rhythm, written by Marpurg, has come to light (see below, p. 106).[36]

Other German musicians must have been familiar with French performance style as well.[37] As Mattheson observed, "France is and remains the proper dance school,"[38] and in 1711 Bonin reported that masters of French dancing were active in Eisenach, Leipzig, Naumburg, Altorff, Nuremberg, Berlin, Saxony, Gotha, and Hannover; several of these were either native Frenchmen or had been trained by the French. It was a long-standing tradition that during instruction dancing masters played the tunes on the pochette — undoubtedly with French rhythmic alteration. In addition, more than half a dozen treatises on French court dance were published in Germany between 1700 and 1760 (see figure 3-1, p. 46).[39] Telemann, who was well acquainted with French style, left Eisenach in 1712 to become director of music in Frankfurt am Main, and held the same position in Hamburg from 1721 until his death in 1767. In 1737–38 Telemann spent eight months in Paris, where six of his "Paris" quartets were published, and also performed by excellent Parisian players. Much of his music (particularly the *Musique de table*) shows strong French influence, a fact both he and his contemporaries acknowledged in print.[40] Telemann had been a friend of J. S. Bach's since about 1709, and was godfather to Emanuel Bach. As noted above, J. S. Bach heard French performance at Celle in his youth, and probably had occasion to hear both French dance music and the "mixed" style during several later visits to Dresden and Berlin; in Cöthen his bassoonist was one J. C. Torlée; and several French dancing masters taught and published in Leipzig around the time of his tenure there.[41] He knew keyboard works by De Grigny, Le Roux, Dandrieu, and Marchand; and according to Marpurg, Bach had particularly high regard for the music of François Couperin.[42] Bach's cousin, the lexicographer J. G. Walther, cites writings of Bourgeois, Brossard, Saint-Lambert, and Hotteterre,[43] and Bach was the Leipzig distributor for the volume. Thus it seems virtually certain that he was acquainted with the custom of notes inégales.

The prolific writer on music Johann Mattheson was familiar with writings by Brossard, Jean Rousseau, and Rameau; Jakob Adlung's Anleitung zu der musikalischen Gelahrtheit reveals that author's acquaintance with the work of Demotz de la Salle, L'Affilard, Monteclair, and Rousseau, all of whom discuss notes inégales.[44] It is reasonable to suppose that other educated Germans also read French books on music, and that conscientious German performers who encountered such directives as croches égales or pointé in French music would have sought an explanation.

Nonetheless, except for Muffat, Quantz, and perhaps Printz, German music tutors are silent on the matter of French inequality.[45] But so, too, are a substantial number of French treatises:[46] the crucial difference lies in the sheer volume of French sources that do prescribe the custom, many of which introduce it from the earliest stages of musical instruction. French children and adult musical amateurs were taught notes inégales and basic meters simultaneously; in Germany such was not the case. Nor is this surprising: well before the influx of French style in the latter half of the seventeenth century, German composition and performance had been heavily influenced by Italian practice, dating from the time of Schütz, Schein, and Scheidt. As early as 1718 Telemann, for example, comments upon "how essential and useful it is to be able to distinguish these species [of French and Italian style] in their intrinsic sorts of pieces," and he also speaks of the "gemischten Goût" that unites them. According to Marpurg, "old Bach in Leipzig" declared that "in all sorts of music and in the music of all nations, there is bad stuff, and yet also something beautiful." And Quantz, who held that the mixed style was the best, also pointed out the necessity of distinguishing between French and Italian styles in performance.[47] Considered as a whole, the evidence suggests that Germans who were acquainted with inégalité learned it from musicians familiar with the French custom, and that they associated it with native French music, plus other works clearly written in imitation of that style (Kusser, Muffat, Johann Fischer, Mayr, and others); this situation apparently obtained in other nations as well, as we shall see. In Dresden and Berlin, inequality may well have been introduced into a wider variety of repertoire — certainly in performances by Quantz and his royal pupil. Yet it is notable that several members of Frederick's court did not follow suit in their own writings: Quantz's student Agricola favored Italian style over French, and makes no mention of *notes inégales* in his expanded translation of Tosi's singing treatise; Marpurg, who had visited France, and whose earliest keyboard works (ca. 1741–48) are very French, is also silent on the issue, as are C. P. E. Bach and J. F. Reichardt.[48]

THE NETHERLANDS

Within three years of initial publication, Loulié's *Elements* and Hotteterre's *Principes de la flute* were reprinted in Amsterdam by Roger (1698, [1710]), who also brought out editions of Brossard (ca. 1708), L'Affilard (1710), Saint-Lambert (ca. 1710), and Jean Rousseau (ca. 1710); in 1728 Le Cene issued a Dutch translation of the Hotteterre *Principes.*[49] Quantz's treatise was also published in Dutch, just two years after it appeared in German and French; although the Dutch edition is slightly abridged, the text of the section on French-style inequality is a virtually literal translation.[50] In 1758 Leonard Frischmuth's clavier treatise states that

> zyn 'er in de Allemande geen tittultjes agter het eerste en derde sestiende, en in de Courante agter de agtstens, moeten ze dog zo gespeelt werden, als of die daar stonden.[51]

> if in the allemande there are no dots after the first and third sixteenth, and in the Courante after the eighths [i.e., first and third], they must nevertheless be played as though they were there.

Frischmuth's association of meter and inequality in French dances, together with the analogy of dotted notation in this passage, certainly suggests French influence. Yet in his comments on the sarabande, minuet, bourée, and gigue, Frischmuth says nothing about rhythmic alteration, and his remarks as they stand do not approach a comprehensive account of *notes inégales*. Rousseau's *Dictionnaire* appeared in Amsterdam (in French) the same year it was published in Paris (1768); the passage on *notes inégales* (s. v. "Pointer") is identical with the original edition, save for minor changes in orthography.

The Netherlands appears to have been a musical crossroads during the seventeenth and eighteenth centuries: the influence of English style in keyboard and lute music is apparent from the days of Sweelinck, Thy-sius, and others; French and Italian performers appeared there frequently; and publishers in Amsterdam brought out a wide variety of music and writings on music. During the 1680s Lully operas and *opéra-ballets* were presented in both Amsterdam and The Hague. It is certain that French performance style was known in the Netherlands, but as in the case of Germany, the extent of its influence is difficult to gauge.

ENGLAND

London was yet more cosmopolitan. The Restoration brought Charles II back from exile in France, whereupon he established both the Twenty-four Violins of the King and the Private Musick in imitation of Louis XIV's Grande Bande and Petits Violons. Roger North goes so far as to suggest that "in the time of King Charles 2 there was no musick enter-teined but the French theater; consisting in branles and tunes. What other musick subsisted in those days appeared only in corners, and private assemblies . . ."; moreover, "all the compositions of the towne were strained to imitate Baptist's vein," which became "vernacular."[52] Nicho-las Lanier (ii), who had visited France, was Master of the King's Musick, and the leading violinist, John Banister (i), was sent to Paris in 1661, almost certainly to become better acquainted with performance at the court of Louis XIV. The French composer Louis Grabu (fl. 1665–94) be-came the Master of the Music and director of the Twenty-four Violins upon the death of Lanier in 1666, and Banister subsequently established public concerts in London in 1672. Pelham Humfrey (Purcell's teacher) was also sent to France (as well as to Italy) in the mid-1660s. In 1673 the successful French organist and composer Robert Cambert came to Lon-don, in collaboration with his former pupil Grabu. And around the years 1668–71 the Burwell lute tutor was compiled, a manuscript that probably records the teachings of John Rogers, successor to the French lutenist Jacques Gaultier in Charles II's Royal Music. In this manuscript (chap. 12) we find a discussion of "the humouring of a Lesson":

> Besides this [i.e., choice of tempo and rubato] wee have that which we call the Soule of the lute the humour and fyne ayre of alesson which cannot be taught but is stollen better by the Ears in hearing those that play well yet we will give some Rules for it with a Demonstration you may gett that art by breaking the Stroakes that is devideing of them by stealing halfe a note from one note and bestoweing of it upon the next note that will make the playing of the Lute more aerye and skipping.

The heareing of Violins and singing is agreat helpe to learne this livelines and Sweetnes which wee have tearmed the Soule of the Lute. . . .

The Demonstration for the humouring of a Lesson

You see heere six single Quivers if you will humour them make the D of the Sixth which is the first Quiver a Quiver and halfe then make of the A of the Fifth a Semyquiver and soe of the twoe other Couples in this manner following. . . .[53]

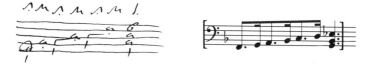

As Roger North observes, it was "the French from whom wee had the lute,"[54] and these brief instructions are similar to the sketchy French discussions of *notes inégales* from the third quarter of the seventeenth century (see above, pp. 5–7). North's own manuscripts also contain brief comments on rhythmic alteration; of the "point" (= dot of addition) he observes:[55]

. . .in short notes it gives a life and spirit to the stroke, and a good hand will often for that end use it, tho' not express't. . . . And next it gives a spirit to swift playing which they call devision, thus:

where the air is smarter, than if the notes were played plaine. . . . That wee call pick't notes in common time, which is thus:

differs not much from:

And then in a tripla way it comes to the same account, for then it is thus:

Once again, the discussion is casual and limited; nor does North here mention French style, which he clearly knew. Nevertheless, his comments contain hints of the practice so common among French performers.

French harpsichord music of the seventeenth century is present in a number of English manuscript sources, most notably 23-Tenbury and 24-Babell (both compiled by Charles Babell).[56] The performance style of these works may have been transmitted across the channel as well.

As noted above, Kusser, a student of Lully's, arrived in England in 1705; James Paisible (d. ca. 1721) and Charles Dieupart (ca. 1667–ca. 1740) were among the native French musicians active in England around the turn of the eighteenth century. In 1706 J. E. Galliard (ca. 1687–1749) moved to London from Celle, where he had studied flute and oboe with a Frenchman, and had served for eight years as a member of the French Hofkapelle. Hotteterre's *Principes de la flute* came out in English in 1729, and two years later Prelleur published an unacknowledged abridgement of it.[57] Waring's translation of the Rousseau dictionary appeared ca. 1775 and 1779, and Marcou's *Elémens* (1782) was published (in French) in both Paris and London.

But Italian style was also influential in England and gradually gained the upper hand; by the end of the seventeenth century Italian singers were active in London, and Handel's arrival in 1710 firmly established Italian opera in the capital. Terence Best reports that an organ clock by Charles Clay (d. 1710), which plays arrangements of pieces by Handel, does not add a trace of *notes inégales*; nor does the Holland barrel organ (ca. 1790, Colt Collection, Kent) in its performances of Handel concertos.[58] In 1771 Anselm Bayly, Subdean of the Chapel Royal, actually denounces the practice of inequality:

> The scholar would do well to practise the marked divisions carefully free of any motion with the chin, first slow, then by degrees quick, avoiding to mark them unequally, unless so directed with a peck by the composer.... Marking divisions unequally, without leave of the composer, often produces an ill effect alone, but especially in parts, while one sings the division equally, and another unequally.[59]

Bayly then lists specific spots from anthems of Croft and Purcell where "to mark the division unequally . . . is beside the author's intention, and takes away the state and dignity of the word."[60] All of these divisions are sixteenths in $\frac{4}{4}$ or ₵, which would very likely be unequal according to French custom; an interesting example is the verse cited from Purcell's "O Give Thanks" (example 3-6a), because earlier in this anthem we find dotted diminutions at the eighth-note level in $\frac{3}{4}$ (i.e., the traditional value subject to alteration by the French in this meter—see example 3-6b).[61] The sum of this evidence indicates that although Bayly did not approve of improvised inequality, some performers clearly indulged in it, and that the performance practice of "marking divisions unequally" (which, of course, was the root of French *inégalité*) was to some extent associated with written-out dotted rhythms ("so directed with a peck by the composer"). This may mean that Croft, Purcell, and some later Englishmen dotted their divisions when they wished them rendered unequally, and otherwise expected a generally even performance of diminutions.

ITALY

It is not surprising that virtually no direct evidence of French-style inequality in Italy has come to light: as noted previously (pp. 37ff.), Loulié, Brossard, Couperin, Corrette (on some occasions), Rousseau, and others state that *notes inégales* was not a feature of Italian performance. Nevertheless, two Italian authors—Tosi (1723) and Lorenzoni (1779)—have been misinterpreted as advocates of *inégalité*. Tosi's unusual comments about "dragging" in singing suggest a powerfully expressive sort of rubato:

> Ma è ormai tempo, che si parli della bellezza dello strascino, che se 'l patetico tornasse al Mondo un Cantore sappia conoscerlo....
>
> Quando sul movimento eguale d'un Basso, che lento cammini di croma in croma un Vocalista mette la prima voce sugli acuti strascinandola dolcemente al grave col forte, e col piano quasi sempre di grado con disuguaglianza di moto, cioè fermandosi più su qualche corda di mezzo, che su quelle che principiano, o finiscono lo strascino, ogni buon Musico crede per indubitato, che nell' arte migliore del Canto non vi sia invenzione, nè studio più atto a toccar il cuore di questo....[62]
>
> §27. But it is now time that we speak of the *Dragging*, that, if the *Pathetick* should once return again into the World, a Singer might be able to understand it....
>
> §28. When on an even and regular Movement of a Bass, which proceeds slowly [from quaver to quaver], a Singer begins with a high Note, dragging it gently down to a low one, with the *Forte* and *Piano*, almost

Example 3-6. Purcell, "O Give Thanks" (1693), (a) mm. 89–92, and (b) mm. 6–10 (ed. Lewis and Fortune).

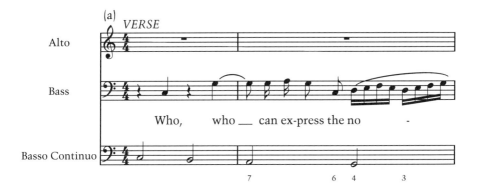

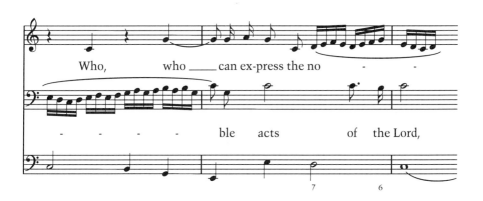

gradually, with Inequality of Motion, that is to say, stopping a little more on some Notes in the Middle, than on those that begin or end the *Strascino* or *Dragg.* Every good Musician takes it for granted that in the Art of Singing there is no Invention superior, or Execution more apt to touch the Heart than this. . . .

Agricola, who was acquainted with Italian singing, and probably with *notes inégales* as well, found this passage incomprehensible.[63] But Tosi had given concerts in London in 1692–94, and also spent the years from about 1725 to 1727 in England; among his friends was J. E. Galliard, translator of his treatise, who provides the illustrations of the "Dragg" shown in example 3-7. North also heard Tosi, and apparently he, too, attempted to notate an approximation of "smooth and sliding graces, [whereby] the great secret is to break and yet keep the time," as in example 3-8.[64]

Anselm Bayly provides another discussion of Tosian rubato. He explains "gliding" as the perfectly smooth slurring of two equally rendered notes, without added ornamentation. And:

Dragging is much the same motion as that of gliding, only with inequality, hanging as it were upon some notes descending, and hastening the others so as to preserve the time in the whole bar, with the forte and piano artfully mixed to render them more lulling and exquisite. "The stealing of time in the *pathetick,* says *Tosi,* is an honourable theft. . . ."[65]

Among Bayly's examples for practicing the drag is the phrase from Maurice Greene's anthem "Lord, How Are They Increased" (example 3-9).[66] In such a context, *notes inégales* are simply not an issue. Later in the treatise Bayly discusses gliding and dragging as two of several means whereby one may vary repeated passages in another solo anthem by Greene.[67] Thus, whatever Tosi and his interpreters had in mind, it seems clear that *lo strascino* is by no means identical to the custom of rhythmic alteration discussed by dozens of French writers.[68]

Antonio Lorenzoni's flute treatise (1779) contains the following short paragraph:

Regola per le note buone, e cattive. Le note buone, quando sono di qualche prestezza, debbono essere rilevate preferibilmente alle cattive; cioè, si dee dare più tempo alle note buone, che alle cattive, non per altro quanto se avessero de' punti (ww).[69]

Rule for good notes and bad. The good notes, when they are of some rapidity, should be brought out in preference to the bad; that is, more time is given to the good notes than to the bad, not, on the other hand, as much as if they had dots (ww).

EXAMPLE 3-7. Galliard, examples of the "Dragg," from his translation of Tosi (1743, plate VI).

EXAMPLE 3-8. Roger North, "smooth and sliding graces."

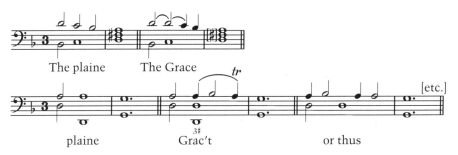

For notes falling away in oixts the upper laggs a little behind:

EXAMPLE 3-9.   Greene, "Lord, How Are They Increased" [1747].

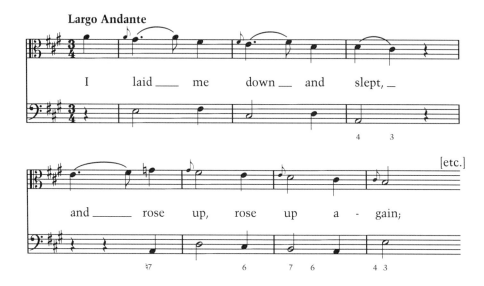

As Reilly points out, Lorenzoni's tutor is in part an unacknowledged plagiarism of Quantz and other writers. His comments on good and bad notes are lifted from Quantz's discussion of inequality (chap. XI, §12), but without the refinement and detail that reveal Quantz's unmistakable connections with French practice.[70] Elsewhere in the treatise (and in other contexts) Lorenzoni cites Loulié's *Elements* and Rousseau's *Dictionnaire* — writings that provide a reasonably clear picture of *notes inégales*. But he mentions nothing about the customary French meter-inequality relationships, the cancellation of inequality, and so forth: thus, if Lorenzoni really understood the French custom (which is by no means certain), he chose not to present it fully and clearly. Instead, he seizes upon the concept of "good" and "bad" notes, long familiar to Italians, and applies Quantz's suggestion that good notes be slightly lengthened, without accepting any other features of French *inégalité*. This hardly constitutes advocacy of *notes inégales*.[71]

The manuscript of a complete Italian translation of Quantz, formerly the property of Padre Martini, is preserved in Bologna. Although neither the translator nor the date of the manuscript has been established, it seems clear that this Italian version was made from the published French edition.[72] While the translation plus Quantz's correspondence with Martini suggests that Quantz and his treatise were better known in Italy than one might otherwise suppose, it is impossible to gauge how widely he was read there, or whether the commentary on rhythmic alteration had any impact on Italian performers.

Another unusual source is the *Methode ... pour le forte-piano ou clavecin* [1786] by F. P. Ricci, coauthored (according to the title page) by J. C. Bach. Although published in Paris, the tutor was written "for the Naples Conservatory." Among the Italian terms defined at the beginning is *pontato*, which "indicates that one must strongly mark the *Pointé*, that is, make clearly apparent the inequality of proportions, alternatively long and short, between the notes. *Pointé* [= the French equivalent]."[73] Today scholars consider J. C. Bach's coauthorship doubtful.[74] Ricci was *maestro di cappella* at Como, and is known to have visited Paris prior to the appearance of the treatise; yet it seems odd that he should publish in Paris a tutor intended for students in Naples. The book's definition of *pontato* clearly indicates familiarity with the terminology of *notes inégales*, yet neither *pontato* nor *pointé* appears in any of the exercises or examples. Taken at face value, the instructions suggest that one would not play unequally unless the directive *pontato* or *pointé* appeared: this would make sense in the context of Italian performance practice but would seem quite unusual to French readers, who took *inégalité* for granted unless directed *not* to play unequally. Perhaps the definition was included merely because the volume was published in Paris. In any case, Ricci, like many Germans, English, and perhaps other Italians, may have known of the French custom — but he is certainly not advocating it as a general procedure.

French dance style was well established in northern Italy by the 1660s, particularly in Modena, by such composers as Uccellini, Colombi, G. M. Bononcini (i), and G. B. Vitali; some of their pieces are even marked *in stil francese*.[75] The marriage of Alfonso IV d'Este in 1655 to Laura Martinozzi, niece of Cardinal Mazarin, precipitated a lively period of cultural exchange between the Modenese and French courts: French musicians visited Modena, and hundreds of utterly French dances by Colombi are still preserved in manuscript. In 1687 the performance of Lully's *Psyché* in Modena was among the earliest productions of French *opéra-ballet* in Italy. Thus, *inégalité* was almost certainly known and applied to French music in Modena; how far geographically the custom may have spread remains a matter of conjecture. Muffat, who was well versed in French style, visited Rome in the early 1680s, where came to know Corelli and Pasquini; in 1690 Lully's *Armide* was produced in the *urbs aeterna*. But this was also the period of emerging currents in Italian opera and instrumental music that struck Frenchmen like Raguenet and Le Cerf as distinctly foreign;[76] and evidently such music was not subject to inequality.

Some modern writers, especially Donington, have claimed that manuscript variants in Italian music (as well as German or English) prove that inequality was internationally commonplace: when even notes in one source correspond to dotted passages in another, the latter are purportedly an effort to record the customary performance practice. Similarly, if parallel passages within a single source are notated here with dotting but elsewhere evenly, the dotted version is assumed to indicate the composer's true intention.[77] But this sort of argument is problematic in several respects. Careful establishment and evaluation of source transmission is essential to the validity of such investigations; yet for the Italian works Donington cites—variant readings in pieces by Vulpio, Alessandro Scarlatti, and Steffani—precise information about the relationship of the sources either to the composer or to each other is lacking: variants could crop up for any number of reasons, from revision by the author to caprice of the copyist. We have already seen that the relation between dotted notation and the performance practice of *notes inégales* is by no means clear in French music: as in France, composers from other lands may have intended crisp 3:1 rhythmic ratios in passages of dotted diminutions, rather than the "little bit" of inequality that appears to have been the most common degree of French rhythmic alteration. Moreover, the discrepancies in Donington's manuscript citations (and many others) include differences of pitch and basic rhythmic configuration as well as the supposed notation of *inégalité*—which is itself inconsistent. As regards varying rhythms between parallel passages within a single source, we cannot be sure they are not intentional. Given all of this, plus contemporary French testimony denying that *notes inégales* was an Italian practice, it is currently difficult to accept the notion that manuscript variants prove inequality was common in Italy (or elsewhere).

Passages of consistently notated dotting in situations where the usual conditions of *notes inégales* have theoretically been fulfilled will continue to pose puzzles that can probably be solved only provisionally, on the basis of musical style and taste. Neumann denies that such dotting could ever represent the French performance custom, while Fuller continues to argue the possibility that it might. But as Fuller has also shown, the written-out "dotted style" in European music of the seventeenth and eighteenth centuries occurs in an enormous variety of formal, textural, and affective contexts;[78] only some of these might reasonably be associated with typical French applications of inequality. Further stylistic investigations of the sort Fuller has initiated are likely to provide the most useful starting point for intelligent interpretation in the future.

To summarize briefly: The available evidence suggests that French *inégalité* was certainly known to musicians in several areas of Germany, as well as in the Netherlands and England, and also in Modena (at least during the latter half of the seventeenth century). The custom was transmitted by Frenchmen who went abroad, as well as by visitors to Paris who subsequently imitated French style, and also by French musical writings (both in the original language and in translation). Very likely inequality was applied to music of French origin and to works that obviously emulated French style; to what degree *notes inégales* may have been extended to pieces less closely related to French models remains uncertain. But the Germans, Dutch, and English were also well acquainted with Italian music and performers, and if, as Couperin, Rousseau, and others claim, the Italians did not play unequally, it is only reasonable to suppose that musicians of other nations followed suit when performing Italianate repertoire; Telemann and Quantz in particular suggest the desirability of distinguishing between French and Italian styles. And a plethora of eighteenth-century writings—from the simple French tutors to the lengthy essays of Mattheson and Marpurg to the polemical volleys of the Querelle des Buffons—testify to widespread awareness of national distinctions in musical style. In any case, there seems to be no evidence that anyone outside France assumed inequality as a matter of course, with the exception of Quantz and possibly some of his colleagues in Dresden and Berlin.

PART II

OVERDOTTING

CHAPTER FOUR

The Value(s) of the Dot

With the foregoing review of *notes inégales* well in mind, let us now approach the more controversial problem of overdotting. The earliest writer to discuss what we now understand as overdotting per se is Quantz (1752): presently we shall treat of his and his contemporaries' commentaries on the matter, but first a review of background is in order.

The Meaning of the Dot

It is perfectly clear that throughout Europe during the seventeenth and eighteenth centuries, the dot of addition had the same standard meaning it does today: one-half the value of the preceding note or rest. More than fifty French sources define it thus; many give subdivided musical examples (♩ . = ♪♪ , etc.); and occasionally, as in Dupont's catechetical treatise intended for the instruction of eight-year-old Louis XV, the explanation is even more specific:

D[emande] Que vaut un point.
R[éponse] Il vaut la moitié de la notte, qui le precede.
D Comment connaître un point.
R Lorsque vous trouverez une petite piqure de plume, faite ainsy • cela s'appele un point.
D A quoy sert ce point.
R A prolonger la note, apres la quelle il est posé, de la moitié de sa valeur.
D Qu'entendez vous, par ce mot, à prolonger de moitie. Exemple.
R C'est a dire, si je dois estre une demi heure, à chanter une ronde quand elle est seule, je dois estre trois quarts d'heure, lors qu'elle est suivie d'un point, et une blanche a proportion.[1]

Q[uestion] What is the value of a dot?
A[nswer] It is worth half of the note which precedes it.
Q How do you recognize a dot?
A When you encounter a little prick of the pen, made thus •, that is called a dot.
Q What is the purpose of the dot?

EXAMPLE 4-1.   Titelouze, *Hymnes de l'eglise* (1623).

A To prolong the note after which it is placed by one-half of its value.
Q What do you mean by this expression, to prolong by one-half? An example?
A It is to say that if I need half an hour to sing a whole note when it is by itself, I need three quarters of an hour when it is followed by a dot, and so on in proportion for a half note.

Non-French sources, although less numerous, also confirm the standard meaning of the dot.

Variable duration of the dot. But of course there are exceptions. In the preface to his *Hymnes de l'eglise* for organ (1623) Titelouze notes that "there are some notes elongated by a dot which I have used to indicate only a quarter of their value; it is done to save the note-plus-tie that would be necessary to indicate the value,"[2] as in the case shown in example 4-1. Thus he shortens, rather than lengthens, the value of the dot. Loulié, in the manuscript additions to his treatise, states that

> ordinarily, a dot after a note augments its value by half. Sometimes, [however,] it augments the note by ⅛, or ¼, or ⅜, or ½, or ⅝, or ¾, or ⅞. That is to say, that the dot of a quarter-note sometimes has the value of a thirty-second note, or a sixteenth-note, or three thirty-second notes, or an eighth-note. . . . [etc.; cf. example]

In any [given] place, the time-value of the dot is regulated by the notes which follow.[3]

Metoyen (n.d., 17) says much the same thing:

> Il arrive souvent que le point n'a pas une valeur determinée, c'est
> lorsqu'il se trouve un trait de doubles ou triples croches après lui; il sert
> a soutenir le son à proportion de la quantité de Nottes qu'il y a apres;
> pour lors, si dans le trait il y a nombre pair, la 1e. notte est longue; si il
> y a nombre impair, la 1e. notte est breve. Exemple.[4]

> It often happens that the dot does not have a fixed value, as when there
> is a brace of sixteenths or thirty-seconds after it; it serves to sustain the
> sound in proportion to the quantity of notes that follow; then, if there is
> an even number [of notes] in the brace, the first note is long; if there is
> an odd number, the first note is short. Example: [see above]

These commentaries by Loulié and Metoyen may help explain some
of the curious extra beaming found, for example, in works by Gigault and
Couperin (although Gigault writes that "it is unnecessary for the eighths
that are beamed several times to frighten them [i.e., organists], since one
must regard them as though they were only sixteenths"[5]). But this unusual notation occurs as well in situations where it is unrelated to dotted
rhythm.[6]

That the dot could stand for a tie (e.g., ♩. ♫ = ♩♪♫) is also im-
plicit in Titelouze, Loulié, and Metoyen. This notation, found occasionally in French music, Bach autographs (and even Mahler's sketches), is
explicitly discussed by the German theorists Sperling and Schmelz. According to Sperling,

> in bißweilen doch selten findet man absonderlich vor kurzen zusammen
> gestrich- oder gezogenen Noten einen Punct welcher *absolute* nicht
> mehr gilt als die folgende Note. . . . Zum Exempel[7]

occasionally, although seldom, one finds, particularly before short notes
that are drawn or spun-out together, a dot that is *absolutely* not worth
more than the following note. . . . For example [see above]

EXAMPLE 4-2.   (a) L'Affilard, *Principes* (1705), notation and execution of the
double cadence coupée (pp. 16–17); (b) J.-J. Rousseau, *Dictionnaire* (1768), notation and execution of the *cadence pleine*
(plate B, fig. 13).

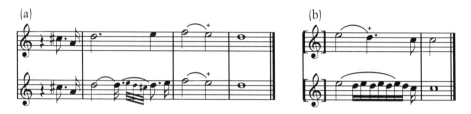

Sperling goes on to say that this is probably done to save time in copying.
Schmelz's discussion of the dot includes the observation that

> folgen aber nach ihme [i.e., the dot] 3. Noten, gilt es so viel, als eine dieser
> 3. Noten.[8]

[Solmization syllables omitted from example.]

> if, however, three notes come after it [the dot], it is worth as much as one
> of these three notes. [see example above]

The dot may also stand for a triplet — 𝄽 in place of 𝄽 ; the latter
notation is very rare during the period in question.[9] Gigault states that
"when there is a sixteenth above an eighth, it is necessary to play them
together"; in dotted contexts (e.g., ♩· ♪ ♪), this effectively yields double
dotting for the sake of rhythmic synchronization.[10] And it should be
noted that dotted notes bearing ornaments were sometimes (but not always) held beyond their literal value to allow fuller execution of the
embellishments;[11] two such cases are shown in example 4-2 above.

OVERDOTTING CONCOMITANT WITH
NOTES INÉGALES

Of much greater import is the lengthening of the dot occasioned by *notes
inégales*. Common sense would suggest that in a situation such as this:
♩· ♪ ♪ the eighth after the dotted quarter should coincide with the
shorter of the *croches inégales* in the lower part. Four French theorists

confirm this, and provide additional insight into the situation. Hotteterre observes in his musette treatise that

> dans les mouvemens où les *Croches* sont inégales, le point qui est après la *Noire*, fait un équivalent à la *Croche* pointée; de sorte que la *Croche* qui suit une *Noire* pointée, est toûjours brève.[12]

> in *mouvemens* where the eighths are unequal, the dot which is after the quarter note is the equivalent of a pointed eighth, such that the eighth which follows a dotted quarter is always short.

Morel de Lescer, writing for singers, comments as follows:

> NB. Je demontre que le point apres une noire (lorsque les croches sont inegales) vaut plus d'une croche par la raison qu'il tient lieu d'une premiere croche qui est longue par sa nature; il s'en suit de la, que la derniere du tems qui est apres le point etant breve et affoiblie par la longueur de la premiere croche, ne vaut plus qu'une double croche. consequemment d'un point placé apres la croche qui doit avoir le meme raport. j'ai eté bien aise de demontrer cet article clairement ayant Eprouvé moi meme la peine qu'ont les Maitres de faire pointer exactement aux Ecoliers avec beaucoup de vitesse les Nottes qui se trouvent apres le point de quelque nature qu'elles soient, pour toutes les mesures en general. Ce que je demontre du point doit aussi servir pour les silences, car si un demi soupir qui vaut une croche est placé a l'endroit d'une I.re croche laquelle par sa nature doit être longue, la croche qui vient apres ce demi soupir ne doit valoir qu'une double croche. consequemment des quards de Soupir, etc.[13]

> NB. I point out that the dot after a quarter note (when the eighths are unequal) is worth more than an eighth for the reason that it takes the place of a "first" eighth, which is long according to its nature; it follows from this that the latter part of the beat which comes after the dot, being short and weakened by the length of the "first" eighth, is worth no more than a sixteenth. And so too for a dot placed after an eighth, which has to have the same relationship. I have been very happy to demonstrate this point clearly, having witnessed myself the great difficulty masters have in making plain to students exactly and quickly the notes following the dot, of whatever type they may be, for all meters in general. What I am demonstrating for the dot ought also to apply to rests, because if a rest equal to an eighth note is put in place of a "first" eighth, which must by its nature be long, the eighth which comes after this rest must be worth no more than a sixteenth. And so on for sixteenth rests, etc.

Metoyen, after giving the standard definition of the dot, adds that "when the eighths are unequal, the dot which is after the quarter note must always be the value of a long eighth, and that which comes after the dot is always short."[14] And Engramelle's instructions for pinning the serinette, or monophonic barrel organ, also make the distinction between "first" and "second" eighths in *notes inégales*. In explaining his detailed diagrams, Engramelle points out that the dotted quarter "must be prolonged by the value of a 'first' eighth . . . and in consequence the eighth that follows the dot, being a 'second,' " is to be reduced proportionately.[15] The same procedure applies to single pickups that begin a piece, which are generally "seconds," and therefore short in proportion to the degree of inequality being executed.[16]

Here, without question, we have overdotting, in direct proportion to the degree of rhythmic alteration occasioned by *notes inégales*. If one's taste demanded strong inequality (3:1)—which, as we have seen, is certainly possible (pp. 16–20 above)—then dotted quarters would effectively become double-dotted quarters, as Morel de Lescer suggests; where inequality is milder, the overdotting would be proportionately less. It will also be observed that the treatise writers introduce this sort of overdotting independently from the issue of assimilating conflicting rhythms in keyboard or ensemble music; in particular, Engramelle is writing about a mechanical instrument that plays melodies only. If even musette players, serinette pinners, and singing students practicing alone were expected to prolong dotted notes in proportion to inequality, such overdotting must have been commonplace in French music, despite the relatively small number of writers who discuss it.[17] And it must have been essential for the precise ensemble playing demanded by Lully. Geographically, the practice would have been as widespread as *notes inégales* themselves; as Fuller aptly observes, "wherever inequality goes there also goes overdotting."[18] What remains at issue is its relative strength, and how it became an independent mannerism.

DOUBLE-DOTTING

We have seen that in performance the dot could be lengthened in proportion to the notes following it, or in proportion to the prevailing degree of *inégalité*. But it must be recalled that musicians of all nations could and did notate sharp 7:1 rhythmic ratios through appropriate combinations of dotting, ties, and rests (e.g., ♩. ♪, ♩♫); and Graham Pont has drawn up a list of 147 composers from Byrd to Jommelli who do so.[19] While notation of the double dot was not commonplace until about the middle of the eighteenth century, it was nevertheless fairly well known to French *clavecinistes* and organists between approximately 1650 and 1700. The most frequent users are Chambonnières, Louis Couperin (probably autograph notation in 32-Oldham), and André Raison; yet double dots also occur sporadically in works by d'Anglebert (autograph, 33-Rés-89ter), the La Barre of the Bauyn manuscript, Dumont, Richard, Vincent, and anonymous composers and arrangers. Clérambault, Hotteterre, and Muffat knew this notation as well.[20]

Prima facie, it is only reasonable to assume that when double dotting (or other 7:1 rhythms) are mixed with ordinary 3:1 ratios, the two patterns ought to be distinguished: for one example out of many, let us consider Chambonnières's allemande "Le moutier" and Louis Couperin's *double* for it, which are found in the manuscript 35-Bauyn (figures 4-1 and 4-2). The meter is ¢, but the nature of the diminutions (especially in the *double*) strongly suggests that the piece would be taken in four, meaning that inequality (if any) would descend to the sixteenths (cf. table 1-1);[21] that being the case, dotted quarters would not be affected by inequality at the eighth-note level. In the allemande, the first dotted quarter appears in m. 6; the first double-dotted quarter comes in the second half of m. 7; and in m. 8 the single-dotted rhythm returns. Each of these upper-voice rhythms is carefully synchronized with the movement of the other voices. In the *double,* Couperin varies the upper line through rearticulation and dotting in m. 6; he leaves it intact in m. 7; and in m. 8, he incorporates double-dotting to synchronize the top voice with the ornamental sixteenths and dotted rhythms he has added to the other parts. In the reprise of the allemande Chambonnières uses the double-dotted pattern in the upper voice of m. 16, again aligned with inner-voice rhythm; the alto line of Couperin's *double* imitates the double-dotting in the second half of the bar, while the tenor line simultaneously imitates the sixteenth-note divisions Couperin had incorporated in the first half of the measure. In each of these cases, it is difficult to discern any reason why the distinctions between single- and double-dotted quarters should not be carefully preserved: if Chambonnières knew a custom of general overdotting in performance such as present-day musicians frequently suppose, why would he bother with such notational distinctions? If Couperin assumed generalized overdotting, or knew that Chambonnières expected it, why would he notate double-dotting as part of his variation technique in the *double*?

For one additional example of mixed single- and double-dotting, let us turn briefly to a *Christe* for organ by Raison (1688; figure 4-3, p. 75 below). In the meter **3** eighths are customarily unequal, and single-dotted quarters in the subject of imitation (mm. 1, 3, 6, etc.) might therefore be elongated in proportion to the degree of *inégalité* (albeit none of the dotted quarters are combined with moving eighths). Yet double-dotted quarters are written in mm. 10 and 24——. The piece is essentially an asymmetrical two-part form (mm. 1–14 / 14–41), with a modified repetition beginning at m. 14; the double-dotted rhythm at m. 10 launches a homophonic precadential gesture, which leads to a hemiola (mm. 12–13) and the close on D in m. 14; there the fugato-like imitation begins anew. The return of double-dotting in m. 24 again suggests motion toward

FIGURE 4-1.   Chambonnières, allemande "Le moutier," MS. 35-Bauyn [post-1676].

Reproduced through courtesy of the Bibliothèque Nationale, Paris.

FIGURE 4-2. Louis Couperin, *double* to "Le moutier," MS. 35-Bauyn [post 1676].

Reproduced through courtesy of the Bibliothèque Nationale, Paris.

cadence; but this time the onset of a linear intervallic pattern (mm. 26–30) thwarts the expectation of closure, and the movement is considerably extended. Thus, the two 7:1 rhythmic gestures signal important structural moments in this *Christe*, and were apparently intended to stand out from the single-dotted quarters of the subject; this in turn suggests that the *notes inégales* should not be so strong as to result in obscuring the distinction between single and double dots.[22] Even in cases where the rationale for the distinction is not immediately apparent, the possibility that the composer intended it to be observed should be respected.

French keyboard sources. There are many concordances among manuscripts of French keyboard music, and it is a reasonable hypothesis that comparison of these might provide insight into the notation or performance of 7:1 rhythmic ratios. Accordingly, the following sources known to contain double dots were studied: 32-Oldham, 33-Rés-89ter, 35-Bauyn, 36-Parville, 24-Babell, 38-Gen-2348/53, 46-Menetou, 47-Gen-2356, and 51-Labarre-11.[23] But the results of this investigation are inconclusive. For example, in the case of the allemande "Le moutier" and its *double* (discussed above), there are three concordant sources: 36-Parville shows the double dots as in 35-Bauyn,[24] but 24-Babell (1702), probably the latest of the three manuscripts, omits them altogether, substituting single-dotted quarters and eighths. Nor can we suppose that Charles Babell relied upon a performance convention of overdotting to produce a 7:1 ratio: elsewhere he uses ties to notate values equal to the double dots found in other sources.[25] Similar situations occur elsewhere: Chambonnières, for example, supervised the prints of his harpsichord works;[26] these contain a number of double dots, yet in a few cases show single dotting, no dotting, or other variants from passages where manuscripts have double dots.[27] The long and short of the matter is that we confront here many of the same difficulties inherent in the study of manuscript variants with respect to *notes inégales:* issues of source transmission and possible revision remain unclear, and the data are by no means sufficiently consistent to suggest a general convention of overdotting in performance.

Perhaps the most striking item found among the manuscripts is a keyboard transcription in 46-Menetou (#98) of the overture to Lully's *Persée* (or *Andromède*), which shows fairly consistent double dotting not found in the original orchestral version (cf. figures 4-4 and 4-5). Yet in light of what we know about *notes inégales* and concomitant overdotting, the 7:1 rhythms notated in the transcription do not seem so surprising: strong inequality could result in double-dotted performance of quarters

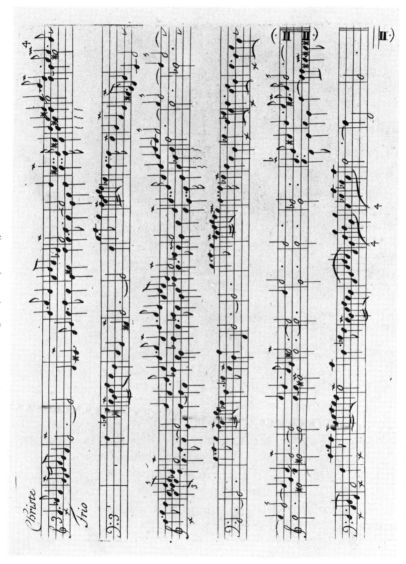

FIGURE 4-3.   André Raison, *Livre d'orgue* (Paris, 1688), *Christe.*

FIGURE 4-4.   Lully, Overture to *Persée* (*Andromède*), keyboard transcription,
MS. 46-Menetou (Berkeley Music Library MS. 777) [post-1689].

Reproduced through courtesy of the Music Library, University of California at Berkeley.

(cf. Morel de Lescer), and it seems entirely possible that the arranger of the *Persée* overture sought to make this mannerism explicit in this piece. Why he (or she) should do so here, but not in the arrangements of seven other Lully overtures found in the volume, is puzzling. Perhaps the complex motion of the bass in *Persée* would otherwise dissuade a keyboard player from lengthening the dots in the upper part(s); the bass lines are much simpler in the other Lully overtures contained in the Menetou manuscript (*Phaeton, Amadis, Roland, Armide, Isis, Bellerophon, La grotte de Versailles*). Gustafson dates the source "post 1689," and Curtis suggests that it may have been compiled by or for Françoise-Charlotte de Senneterre de Menetou; in 1689 at the age of nine she sang a number of airs for Louis XIV, supposedly of her own composition, which are included in the manuscript.[28] Almost all the remaining pieces are transcriptions from Lully operas, indicating that the compiler was quite familiar with that composer's works. Beyond this, we know nothing about the possible connections between the Menetou manuscript and Lullian performance practice, save for the obvious fact that the source is of Pa-

FIGURE 4-5. Lully, Overture to *Persée* (Paris, 1682).

risian provenance. Its double-dotted *Persée* overture must be considered in light of the many Lully overtures arranged for harpsichord in other sources that are not double dotted (even in 36-Parville, whose scribe used that notation in works by Couperin, Chambonnières, and Richard). But it is, in any case, one late seventeenth- (or early eighteenth-) century French source that spells out elongation of single-dotted rhythms, a manner of performance that was inherent in the already well-established convention of *notes inégales.*[29]

Ambiguous and misinterpreted sources. Two early French treatises have been misinterpreted as evidence of overdotting: Loulié and L'Affilard. Loulié defines the dot in the ordinary way through subdivided values, and specifically notes that "the dotted eighth is worth three sixteenths." Two pages later, but before his general discussion of inequality, he illustrates separate and slurred sixteenths and comments that "the first and the third sixteenths of each beat are long";[30] this is quite in accord with customary inequality (cf. table 1). On the same page, however, he introduces the subheading "PREMIERE CROCHE POINTÉE": essentially what he means by this is a dotted eighth that falls on a downbeat in meter **C**. He continues: "When the dot is of the same beat as the eighth that precedes it, it is necessary to hold this eighth in singing a little bit longer, and pass the following sixteenth quickly, in the same beat, without moving the hand." And he gives a short exercise. On the following page Loulié writes of the "SECONDE CROCHE POINTÉE." This, as his example makes clear, is a dotted eighth that arrives on an upbeat (♩ ♩ ♫♫), about which he says: "It is necessary to conceive and study the dot of a 'second' eighth as though it were a sixteenth."[31] The reason for these different presentations is unclear (indeed, the treatise as a whole is less systematic than many others). It may be that Loulié felt the student could manage a proper performance of the downbeat dotted eighth without mentally subdividing it ('hold it a little longer and pass the sixteenth quickly'),[32] whereas the offbeat species is trickier. Alternatively, he may have been thinking of *première* and *seconde croche* in the same sense that other writers use these terms in explaining *notes inégales;* yet nowhere else does he advert to such usage, and it does not quite make sense in the context of his comment on the "seconde croche pointée." But in light of everything Loulié says about dotted notes (including the manuscript annotations to the treatise discussed above), these remarks cannot be taken as a covert reference to some sort of generalized overdotting.

The same is true of a misinterpreted passage in L'Affilard (1694): having clearly stated that "dots are worth one-half of the note they

EXAMPLE 4-3. L'Affilard, *Principes* (Paris, 1717), 36.

EXAMPLE 4-4. L'Affilard, *Principes* (Paris, 1717), 41.

precede," L'Affilard subsequently places the following instruction on an exercise "for learning to sing dotted quarters": "To execute the dots as it is necessary, I would inform you that one suspends the dotted quarter and passes quickly the eighth that follows."[33] The treatise is written at a very elementary level, and it seems ill-advised to stretch this remark beyond its simple context.[34]

Later editions of L'Affilard include an exercise marked *pointez* as shown in example 4-3; the term had been used several pages earlier in conjunction with *notes inégales,* which are here illustrated approximately by the dotted notation. Several pages ahead (p. 38) *pointez* appears over straight eighth notes in meter **2**, obviously to indicate inequality. Still later there is an exercise marked "Pointez fort" (Point strongly) with no further explanation (example 4-4). In this context, it seems most likely that the author is telling the student either (1) to avoid sloppily curtailing the dot of the 3:1 ratio, or else (2) to make the sixteenths strongly unequal. It is by no means apparent that L'Affilard intends overdotting here.[35]

Monteclair's 1709 treatise presents a selection of "Airs de Dance, sur toutes sortes de mouvements" (pp. 34ff). The first of these is an entrée that begins as shown in example 4-5. There is no commentary about this piece, and the notation in the remainder of it is altogether ordinary. But the 7:1 ratio in the first bar is certainly unusual for an entrée, which is typically notated in single-dotted quarters and eighths—as is the reprise of Monteclair's (example 4-5b). Also unusual are the short values following the dotted quarters in the third measure: if we interpret this notation according to the guidelines set forth by Loulié and Metoyen (see p. 66–67

EXAMPLE 4-5. Monteclair, *Nouvelle methode* (1709), 34, entrée.

EXAMPLE 4-6. Monteclair, *Principes* (1736), 23.

above), the quarters are effectively double-dotted. This pattern having been established, the performer might well be inclined to maintain it, especially at the reprise. It is as though Monteclair, like the compiler of the Menetou manuscript, were trying to suggest overdotted performance; yet Monteclair's later, simpler tutor of ca. 1735 contains two entrées written in the traditional rhythmic values. In his third treatise (1736), Monteclair gives the standard definition of the dot and illustrates it with subdivided examples; he then provides three versions of a practice exercise, which are shown in example 4-6.[36] It is striking that in the sixth bar the eighths in the third line are precisely aligned with the sixteenths of the upper two lines. One might dismiss this as an engraver's caprice—yet in **2** the eighths are unequal, and the eighth after a dotted quarter will be proportionately late. In none of his treatises, however, does Monteclair clarify any of this.

Roger North's 1728 manuscripts ("The Musicall Grammarian" and "Memoires of Musick") describe performance of the entrée, which had been familiar in England since the reign of Charles II:

There are two modes of the *Grave,* which I shall just take notice of. . . . The first is striking upon a semiquaver rest, thus:

The manner was introduced by Mr. Babtist [Lully], an Italianised French-man, and all the Entrys of his *Branles,* as they were called, were of this action, but withall unexceptionable musick. And the hand nicely agrees with the foot, especially in the most stately step they call an entry. I fancy it is originally owing to the genius of the violin, of which one of the beautys is the stabb, or *stoccata,* and the other is the *arcata,* which latter hath given way and the other chiefly prevailes. I have subjoyned a *basso andante* to shew how well that sober style joynes with the desultory action of the upper part, as of one pacifying the rage of an angry person.

. . . .

And the Entrys of Babtist ever were, and will be valued as most stately and compleat harmony . . . no one could hear an *Entree* with its starts, and *saults,* but must expect a dance to follow, so lively may human actions be pictured by musick.[37]

Several points are curious here. The characteristic dotted rhythm of Lullian entrées (and overtures) is ♩. ♪; notated 7:1 patterns are rare. But equally unusual in such music is North's "walking" *basso andante:* this, according to Brossard, is an Italianism to be rendered without *notes inégales* (see above, p. 37). Even supposing North were unaware of Brossard, it seems unlikely that the "sober" and "pacifying" style he intends in his bass line would be well served by 3:1 inequality, which ratio would be needed to synchronize it with the "desultory" and "*stoccata*" upper voice. By writing the "starts" and "saults" of the entrée in 7:1 rhythmic values, North may (like the Meneton scribe and Monteclair) be freezing in notation a manner of performance that, rooted in ordinary French *notes inégales,* had emerged as an independent mannerism.[38] But given the ambiguities in his commentaries, this is by no means certain.

An apparent case of overdotting notated to reflect performance practice is found among the manuscripts for Giuseppe Torelli's *Sonate (sinfonia) a 4 trombe [and strings],* preserved at San Petronio in Bologna (D.X.16). The opening Grave of this piece clearly reflects the style of the introduction to a French overture, and originally contained many instances of the characteristic rhythm ♩. ♪. In certain of the string parts, however, this has been changed to ♩. 𝄾 ♪, presumably for a performance at San Petronio that took place sometime after the parts were first copied.[39] This is especially intriguing because virtually no evidence of Italian overdotting has come to light. Yet as noted above, French influence was strong in nearby Modena throughout the latter part of the seventeenth century; thus, the altered rhythms in these Torelli parts may represent an effort to imitate the sharpened rhythms that grew out of French *inégalité*. Arcangelo Corelli, who spent four years studying in Bologna and styled himself "il Bolognese" in his first three publications, also used brisk 7:1 rhythms in pieces that resemble French overtures; for reasons that will become apparent, however, this topic is taken up under the heading "The 'Handel Tradition' " in chapter 6.

Throughout the seventeenth and eighteenths centuries, the dot retained the basic meaning of the "dot of addition" (*punctus additionis*) in mensural notation: it augmented the preceding note value by one-half, yielding a 3:1 rhythmic relationship. But various circumstances allowed for modification of this rule in performance during the period in question. When followed by a seemingly irrational number of notes, the dot could be lengthened or shortened in proportion to what followed it; it could also stand for a tie; it could serve in makeshift notation for 2:1 rhythms in the context of triplets; it could be lengthened to allow for execution of embellishments; and it could be lengthened in conjunction with the French custom of *notes inégales*. While some musicians, especially French keyboard composers, used the double dot, this notation was apparently deployed for specific 7:1 rhythmic ratios rather than as clarification of a performance mannerism; in any case, 7:1 ratios could be and were noted through various combinations of single dots, ties, and rests. In previous chapters we have seen that the custom of *notes inégales* was virtually de rigueur in France (and quite possibly for French-style music in other countries). According to Hotteterre, Morel de Lescer, Metoyen, and Engramelle, inequality results in overdotting: the dot assumes the value of a long or "first" *note inégale*. And in France such overdotting concomitant with *inégalite* was probably the most common reason for departing from the standard meaning of the dot between about 1670 and 1790. Yet before Quantz, no known author discusses overdotting as an independent custom; after Quantz, many do, as we shall see in the following pages.

CHAPTER FIVE

The Earlier German Sources
on Overdotting

J. J. QUANTZ

When his *Versuch einer Anweisung die Flöte traversiere zu spielen* was first published, Quantz was at the peak of his career. Having studied in Dresden with the renowned French flutist Buffardin, Quantz himself had spent seven months in Paris during 1726, following a two-year study tour in Italy. During the twenty-five years from 1716 to 1741 he had absorbed and contributed to the "mixed" French-plus-Italian style in Dresden: this was the musical milieu that Frederick the Great sought to imitate, surpass, and perpetuate after he ascended to the throne in 1740. Frederick lured Quantz to Berlin in 1741; the *Versuch* was dedicated to the king in 1752; and two decades later (1772) Burney would complain that Quantz's taste was that of forty years earlier. By all accounts, musical style at Frederick's court had officially ossified; thus, Quantz's justly famous flute treatise largely represents the approach to performance current in Dresden from about 1720 to 1740.[1] And it is the first of several eighteenth-century writings, almost entirely from Germany, that treat of overdotting yet do not associate this alteration of written rhythms with *French notes inégales*. Table 5-1 summarizes the information to be gleaned from these sources. As we shall see, the custom of overdotting apparently spread from Dresden to Berlin, Leipzig, and Halle: nearly all of the German writers are linked, and in most cases their advocacy of overdotting can be traced back either to Dresden and/or Quantz, or to Berlin, where several of the principal court musicians prescribed the practice (see also table 6-1 on p. 140 below). Quantz is not only the earliest, but also the most influential, and today the most controversial source; accordingly, we must examine his commentary in some detail.

TABLE 5-1. Comparative Table of Source Material on Overdotting

AUTHOR	TYPE OF PIECE	NOTE VALUES	SHORT NOTE(S) PERFORMED	REASON	QUALIFICATIONS/COMMENTS	MEDIUM
Quantz 1752 Berlin V/21	slow or fast	c) [♫] d) [♫] e) [♫]	[♫]; c) & d) = e)	liveliness [*Lebhaftigkeit*] these notes must express	c) should be played as in f): f) [♫]	flute; (general)
" " V/23	slow or fast	a) [♫] c) [♫] b) [♫] d) [♫] e) [♫]	a) = c) b) = d) [♫] [♫]	boldness, liveliness = flattering, pleasing		" "
XII/24	Allegro	"dotted notes"	Very short [*sehr kurz*]	in Allegro, to express majesty	Dotted notes attacked sharply, executed in a lively fashion; dots are held long, and the following notes are made very short—see V/21 and 22.	flute
XVII/ii/13 " "	Adagio and Allegro "slow"	[♫] [♫] [♫] [♫] [♫]	very short very short and sharply (in slow or quick mvt.)	Dots usually express something of the majestic and sublime [*Prächtiges und Erhabenes*]	In Adagio, the first note is not played so strongly as in the Allegro. Heavy bow stroke; sustained or *nourrissant* manner; not detached, dots held to the outermost limit of their value; the following double-tailed notes are always played very short; separate bow strokes unless there are slurs.	Orchestral players " "
XVII/ii/16	Adagio and Allegro	[♫]	very rapidly			" "
XVII/ii/21	"slow"	[♫]	[♫] →		[♫] = [♫]	" "
XVII/iv/10	quick or slow	[♫]	very short and sharply			

AUTHOR	TYPE OF PIECE	NOTE VALUES	SHORT NOTE(S) PERFORMED	REASON	QUALIFICATIONS/COMMENTS	MEDIUM
XVII/vii/56	French dance music	"dotted notes"	very short and sharply		Dotted notes played heavily; heavy yet short and sharp bow stroke, more detached than slurred.	
XVII/vii/58	loure, sara- bande, cou- rante, cha- conne, entrée, etc.	in 2, 3, 4, [𝄵]	short and sharp		The dotted note is played with em- phasis, and the bow is detached dur- ing the dot. The dances listed in col. 2 are to be played "majestically" [prächtig gespielet].	
	Overtures, entrées, furies	after dot or rest	greatest possible speed		Separate bow strokes; slurring rarely used.	
Bach 1753 Berlin II/23		"dotted notes"	shorter than notated		Sometimes the disposition of parts requires exact rendering. In fast tempo, dotted notes are often not held as long as notated. Precise notation would be best; otherwise, the content of the piece helps to determine . . .	Keyboard solo
1787 ed.:		(synchronize)			= as written "when the tempo is not too slow . . . . In figures where dotted notes are fol- lowed by four or more notes, these last are, because of their number [Vielheit], short enough." Ornaments or the character of the melody may require more time for the short notes.	
Marpurg 1755 Berlin		e.g.,	as written	Notation of the double dot, or tie, is necessary for longer ex- ecution	"I don't see why one would write one way, but intend a different way of performance. . . ."	Keyboard

AUTHOR	TYPE OF PIECE	NOTE VALUES	SHORT NOTE(S) PERFORMED	REASON	QUALIFICATIONS/COMMENTS	MEDIUM
L. Mozart 1756 Augsburg I/iii/11	Adagio	[musical notation]	[musical notation]	Otherwise, "too sleepy"	"The dot should in fact be held at all times longer than its value"—Performance is thereby enlivened. Proper notation (··) recommended.	Violin (beginning students)
VII/ii/2–4		[musical notation] ·, etc.	long delayed quickly	Prevents hurrying; performance more lively; good taste promoted	Attack dot somewhat strongly; slur little note decreasingly and quietly.	
		[musical notation]	quickly			
Agricola 1757 Berlin	always, slow or fast	dotted, esp. [musical notation]	short, at the very end of their value		The note before the dot is heavy; that [those] after it is lighter.	Voice
Bach 1762 Berlin XXIX/15		"dotted"	often extremely short		*Exceptions*: disposition of voices or flattering affect may require literal performance. "If only *one* type of execution is established . . . one loses the other types. . . ."	Keyboard accompaniment
Löhlein 1773 Leipzig		[musical notation]	[musical notation]		1791 ed.: "Not a rule . . . often exceptions. . . ." Precise notation preferred.	Keyboard
Falkener London 1774		[musical notation]	as short as possible			Harpsichord

AUTHOR	TYPE OF PIECE	NOTE VALUES	SHORT NOTE(S) PERFORMED	REASON	QUALIFICATIONS/COMMENTS	MEDIUM
Kirnberger & Schulz 1775 Leipzig [in **Sulzer**]	loure overture	[♩♩|♩·♩♩] "main notes"	[♪] if several, with greatest possible speed, staccato		The main notes are usually dotted, and held longer than their value. Opening section = serious, fiery, proud character.	Orchestra " "
Reichardt 1776 Berlin & Leipzig		dotted, e.g. [♪·♪]	as short as possible	to give emphasis to the long note	The dotted note is sustained unless a rest is indicated.	Ripieno violinist
Wolf 1784 Halle		dotted			Better to hold the dot too long rather than too short; modern composers often use the double dot.	Voice
1784 & 1789 Halle		dotted	as written		Precise notation necessary, as Marpurg said.	Keyboard
Petschke 1785 Leipzig		dotted notes	proportionately shorter		Dots are generally held longer than their value would indicate. In Adagio, short notes not dispatched so briefly because of character.	Keyboard
Schlegel 1788 Graz	slow or fast	[♩·♪ etc.]	[♪ ♪]	liveliness [*Lebhaftigkeit*] these notes must express = flattering, pleasing	[Discussion drawn entirely from Quantz]	Flute

AUTHOR	TYPE OF PIECE	NOTE VALUES	SHORT NOTE(S) PERFORMED	REASON	QUALIFICATIONS/COMMENTS	MEDIUM
Türk 1789 Leipzig & Halle	Grave, sostenuto, overture	[music notation]	[music notation]		Lengthen dots worth less than one beat (½ beat in slow tempo).	Keyboard
	"singing"				Elongate the dot only a little.	
		[pickups] [music notation]		(synchronization)	—Unless synchronization makes parallel fifths, etc.	
		[music notation]	literally	(contrapuntal)		
	lively, joyous	[music notation]	[music notation]			
Rellstab 1790 Berlin		[music notation]	[music notation]		The dot usually becomes a rest; if the piece is marked *sostenuto* (as is often the case in church music and overtures), the later notes are strongly sustained, the later notes still played shorter than their value. Sometimes affect requires literal performance of dots (e.g., "flattering").	Keyboard
Tromlitz 1791 Leipzig	fast and lively	"dotted"	as though the long note were double-dotted			
	slow				Elongation milder than in quick movement. Better if composers were precise; then the foregoing vague rules would be unnecessary.	Flute
Bailleux 1798 Paris		[music notation] (1st & 3rd quarters of a bar, when dotted)	very lively, and a little later than usual		Separate, detached bow strokes [no discussion of *notes inégales*].	Violin

As table 5-1 shows, Quantz's *Versuch* contains no fewer than eight references to the practice of overdotting. The first of these appears in chapter V, an introduction to the rudiments of pitch and rhythm entitled "Of Notes, their Values, Meter, Rests, and Other Musical Signs": evidently Quantz considers the crisp performance of certain dotted patterns to be as basic as keeping the beat with one's foot. In §21 of chapter V he introduces a notion common to most later writers who treat of the issue: when dots follow notes of relatively short duration—eighth notes and smaller—one departs from the ordinary 3:1 rule and elongates the dot virtually as much as possible; according to Quantz, this is "because of the liveliness [*Lebhaftigkeit*] that these notes must express." His subdivided musical examples leave no doubt about what he means (see below),[2] and it is important to grasp his terminology from the outset: "the note after the dot in (c) and (d) must be played just as short [*eben so kurz*] as that in (e), whether the tempo is slow or fast." The entire passage runs as follows:

> Bey den Achttheilen, Sechzehntheilen, und Zwey und dreißigtheilen, mit Puncten, s. (c) (d) (e), geht man, wegen der Lebhaftigkeit, so diese Noten ausdrücken müssen, von der allgemeinen Regel ab. Es ist hierbey insonderheit zu merken: daß die Note nach dem Puncte, bey (c) und (d) eben so kurz gespielet werden muß, als die bey (e); es sei im langsamen oder geschwinden Zeitmaaße [see examples below]. Hieraus folget, daß diese Noten mit Puncten bey (c) fast die Zeit von einem ganzen Viertheile; und die bey (d) die Zeit von einem Achttheile bekommen: weil man die Zeit der kurzen Note nach dem Puncte eigentlich nicht recht genau bestimmen kann. Dieses deutlicher zu begreifen, spiele man die untersten Noten bey (f) und (g) langsam, doch ein jedes Exempel nach seinem gehörigen Zeitmaaße, nämlich das bey (d) noch einmal so geschwind, als jenes bey (c); und das bey (e) noch einmal so geschwind, als das bey (d): und stelle sich in Gedanken die obersten Noten mit Puncten vor Nachher kehre man solches um; spiele die obersten Noten; und halte eine jede Note mit dem Puncte so lange, bis die Zeit von den untersten Noten mit den Puncten verflossen ist. Die Noten mit [*sic, recte:* nach] den Puncten mache man eben so kurz, als die darunter befindliche viergeschwänzte Note es erfodert. Auf diese Art wird man sehen, daß die obersten Noten mit den Puncten bey (f), die Zeit von drey Sechzehntheilen, und einem Zwey und dreißigtheile mit einem Puncte bekommen: und daß die bey (g) die Zeit von einem Sechzehntheile und einem punctirten Zwey und dreißigtheile; die bey (h) aber, weil bey den untersten Noten zweene Puncte stehen, und die folgenden Noten noch einmal geschwänzet sind, nur die Zeit von einem Zwey und dreißigtheile, nebst anderthalbem Puncte, erhalten.

For dotted eighth, sixteenth, and thirty-second notes (see [c] [d] and [e]) one departs from the general rule because of the liveliness these notes must express. It is particularly important to observe that the note after the dot at (c) must be played just as short as that [after the dot] in (e), whether the tempo is slow or fast [see examples above]. As a result, the dotted notes in (c) receive almost the time of an entire quarter note, and those in (d) the time of an eighth, because one cannot actually determine the duration of the short note after the dot with complete precision. To grasp this more clearly, one should play the lower notes in (f) and (g) slowly, yet in accordance with their proper duration in each example — that is, those in (d) twice as fast as those in (c), and those in (e) twice as fast as those in (d) — and imagine the upper notes with dots.[3] Thereafter one should turn this around, play the upper notes, and hold each dotted note until the time of the lower dotted note has passed. One makes the note after the dot just as short [eben so kurz] as the sixty-fourth note underneath indicates.[4] In this way one will see that the upper notes in (f) receive the time of three sixteenths plus a dotted thirty-second note, those in (g) the time of a sixteenth plus a dotted thirty-second, but those in (h) only the time of a thirty-second note with a dot and a half, because double dots are found among the lower notes, and the notes that follow have an additional flag.

We may assume as well that Quantz intends these short little notes to be sharply articulated: in chapter VI, on tonguing for the flute, he stipulates that the tongue stroke *tiri* "is indispensable for dotted notes; it expresses them in a much sharper and livelier fashion [*viel schärfer und lebhafter*] than is possible with any other kind of tonguing."[5] And he always places the short, sharp syllable *ti* on the little note that follows the dot (VI/ii/3–6; see also VI/i/1 and 5–6). Having introduced overdotting in chapter V §21, Quantz also advocates it for the so-called Lombard rhythm (♬♩.) in V §23: "the shorter [*je kürzer*] you make the first notes in (a), (b), (c), and (d), the livelier and bolder is the expression."[6] In the situation marked (e) (♩♬), which is the reverse of (b), lengthening the dots makes the expression "more flattering and pleasing [*schmeichelnder und annehmlicher*]."

Quantz's *Solfeggi pour la flute* include several excerpts provided with abbreviated directives about overdotting that are largely concordant with the foregoing commentary from the *Versuch*.[7] Two such *solfeggi* are shown in example 5-1: in the first of these, the dotted eighths are to be held "to the utmost"; in the second, the same values are "held very long,

EXAMPLE 5-1.   Quantz, *Solfeggi* (ed. Michel and Teske 1978), 47, 69.

die Punkte äußerst gehalten.

die Punctirte Note sehr lang gehalten, die lezte sehr kurz, und scharf gestoßen.

Reprinted by permission of Music Associates of America, U.S. representatives for Amadeus Verlag.

the lattermost [i.e., the sixteenths] very short, and sharply articulated."

"Of Good Execution in General in Singing and Playing" is the title of chapter XI. We find here no specific information about overdotting; however, Quantz makes several significant comments concerning the applicability of his teachings. Good execution, he observes, is "indispensable" (*unentbehrlich*) both for performers of principal parts and for ripienists; indeed, the proper execution of ripieno parts prepares players, especially violinists, for solo performance (§8). Near the end of chapter XI (§20) Quantz announces that he will apply the "universal rules of good execution" (*die allgemeinen Regeln des guten Vortrages*) to the principal types of movements—the Allegro and Adagio—in the next three chapters (XII–XIV). And he also points out that much of chapter XVII, which concerns specific duties of ripienists, is related to the "universal rules of good execution" of chapter XI. In short, there is considerable overlap in what constitutes good execution for the singer, the instrumental soloist, and the ripienist; thus it is hardly surprising that overdotting, which Quantz had introduced together with the rudiments of notation (chap. V), also crops up in subsequent chapters chiefly (although not exclusively) directed to soloists (XII) and ripienists (XVII) respectively.

Quantz's twelfth chapter, then, is a general discussion of performing the Allegro (his generic term for a fast movement). In such pieces, he writes (§24),

> Das **Prächtige,** wird sowohl mit langen Noten, worunter die andern Stimmen eine geschwinde Bewegung machen, als mit punktirten Noten vorgestellet. Die punktirten Noten müssen von dem Ausführer scharf gestoßen, und mit Lebhaftigkeit vorgetragen werden. Die Punkte werden lange gehalten, und die darauf folgenden Noten sehr kurz gemachet, s. V. Hauptst. 21. und 22. §.

Majesty [*das Prächtige, le majestueux*] is represented both with long
notes during which the other parts have quick motion, and with dotted
notes. The dotted notes must be attacked sharply by the performer, and
must be executed with liveliness [*Lebhaftigkeit*]. The dots are held long,
and the following notes are made very short [*sehr kurz*], see chapter V,
§§21 and 22.

The cross-reference to chapter V (see above, pp. 89–90) makes it utterly
certain that he intends overdotting; but we note that here in chapter XII
he does not specifically limit the elongation of the dot to the level of
eighths and sixteenths.

Chapter XVII is devoted to orchestral ripienists, and section ii of it to
violinists in particular. In XVII/ii/13 Quantz again emphasizes that in an
Allegro, the Lombard rhythm must be executed such that "the first note,
be it a sixteenth or a thirty-second, is played very short [*sehr kurz*] and
with a forceful bow stroke," except that in the Adagio, the attack is less
strong; his musical examples are slurred, meaning that "very short" refers
to the rhythmic value of the little note(s). The fourth paragraph of this
section must be quoted at some length:

> In langsamen Stücken müssen die mit Puncten versehenen Achttheile
> und Sechzehntheile mit einem schweren Striche und unterhalten, oder
> nourissant gespielet werden. Den Bogen muß man nicht absetzen, als
> wenn anstatt der Puncte Pausen stünden. Die Puncte müssen bis zu dem
> äußersten Ende ihrer Geltung gehalten werden: damit es nicht scheine,
> als ob einem die Zeit darüber lang werde; und das Adagio sich nicht in
> ein Andante verwandele. Wenn Striche drüber stehen, so bedeuten sol-
> che, daß die Noten markiret werden müssen. Die nach dem Puncte kom-
> menden doppelt geschwänzten Noten müssen, so wohl im langsamen als
> geschwinden Zeitmaaße, allezeit sehr kurz und scharf gespielet werden:
> weil die punctirten Noten überhaupt etwas Prächtiges und Erhabenes
> ausdrücken; daher eine jede Note, sofern keine Bogen darüber stehen,
> ihren besondern Bogenstrich erfodert, weil sonst nicht möglich ist, die
> kurze Note nach dem Puncte durch einen Ruck des Bogens so scharf
> auszudrücken, als es durch einen neuen Hinaufstrich geschehen kann.

> In slow pieces dotted eighths and sixteenths must be played with a
> weighty stroke and in a sustained or *nourissant* manner. One must not
> lift the bow as though there were rests instead of dots. The dots must be
> held to the outermost limit of their value [*bis zu dem äußersten Ende
> ihrer Geltung gehalten werden*]: thereby it will not seem that one is
> bored, and the Adagio will not be transformed into an Andante. Strokes
> above the notes indicate that they must be stressed. The sixteenths fol-
> lowing the dots must always be played very short and sharply [*sehr kurz
> und scharf*], in both quick and slow tempos; and since dotted notes
> generally express something of the majestic and sublime [*Prächtiges und
> Erhabenes*], each note, if no slur stands above it, requires a separate bow

stroke; for it is not possible to express the short note after the dot as sharply with the same stroke, by detaching the bow, as can be done with a new upstroke.

Here Quantz again stipulates lengthening dots after eighths and smaller notes — "to the outermost limit of their value" — and states that the notes after the dots "must always be played very short and sharply in slow and quick tempos." His use of language — dots held very long, little notes very short and sharp — is altogether familiar from chapters V, VI (*tiri*) and XII, in which there was no doubt that Quantz intended overdotting (cf. table 5-1). Here in XVII/ii/13 he again links overdotting with "the majestic and sublime," and advocates a separate bow stroke for each note (assuming they are not slurred): this manner of bowing (retaking the bow after each dotted note, rather than "hooking" the short note in the same stroke) is characteristically French, as Muffat established much earlier.[8] But Quantz stresses that in the case of an Adagio, one must moderate the typically "short and articulated bow stroke wielded in the French manner" (as he describes it in XVII/ii/26); rather, the bowing of dotted notes must be weighty and *nourrissant*, and one must avoid shortening them on the retake "as though there were rests" — for the clipped stroke, as we shall presently see, is the typical manner of bowing for dance music.[9]

The next passage, XVII/ii/16, concerns rhythmic contraction after rests:

Wenn, nach einer langen Note und kurzen Pause, dreygeschwänzte Noten folgen, s. Tab. XXII. Fig. 29, so müssen die letztern allezeit sehr geschwind gespielet werden; es sey im Adagio oder Allegro. Deswegen muß man mit den geschwinden Noten, bis zum äußersten Ende des Zeitmaaßes warten, um das Gleichgewicht des Tactes nicht zu verrücken.

FIG. 29

If thirty-second notes follow a long note and a short rest (see tab. XXII, fig. 29), they must be played very rapidly both in the Adagio and in the Allegro. Hence with the quick notes one must wait until the very end of the time reserved for them, in order not to disturb the balance of the measure.

In light of all we have reviewed thus far, it seems fairly certain Quantz is advocating that such pickups be played late and fast (which he later prescribes for the slow introduction of an overture as well; see below). Also noteworthy in this section is the following important advice:

Wenn im langsamen Allabreve, oder auch im gemeinen geraden Tacte, eine Sechzehntheilpause im Niederschlage steht, worauf punctirte Noten, s. XXII. Fig. 30. 31, folgen; muß die Pause angesehen werden, als wenn entweder noch ein Punct, oder noch eine halb so viel geltende Pause, dahinter stünde, und die darauf folgende Note noch einmal mehr geschwänzet wäre.

FIG. 30   FIG. 31

If in slow alla breve, or also in common time, a sixteenth rest appears on the downbeat and dotted notes follow (as in figs. 30 and 31), the rest must be regarded as if it were either dotted or followed by another rest half as long, and the following note as if it had another flag.

The sort of situation shown in Quantz's Fig. 31 is quite common in Handel, for example, and also crops up in the music of Bach and numerous other composers. Then in XVII/ii/21 Quantz describes overdotting that results from execution of an ornamental *Schleifer*, whereby the rhythm is treated as shown in table 5-1 (p. 84 above). And in XVII/iv/10 he instructs violoncellists that sixteenths following dotted notes "must be executed very short and sharply [*ganz kurz und scharf*], whether in a quick or a slow tempo": this is an abbreviation of what he has already discussed in greater detail for orchestral violinists.

Now we come to the most crucial and controversial of Quantz's commentaries on overdotting, that concerning French dance music. In XVII/vii/56 Quantz observes:

Es ist zwar nicht zu läugnen, daß die französische Tanzmusik nicht so leicht zu spielen ist, als sich mancher einbildet, und daß der Vortrag sich von der italiänischen Art sehr unterscheiden muß, so fern er jedem Charaktere gemäß seyn soll. Die Tanzmusik muß mehrentheils ernsthaft, mit einem schweren, doch kurzen und scharfen, mehr abgesetzten, als geschleiften Bogenstriche, gespielet werden. Das Zärtliche und Cantable [*sic*] findet darinne nur selten statt. Die punctirten Noten werden schwer, die darauf folgenden aber kurz und scharf gespielet. Die geschwinden Stücke müssen lustig, hüpfend, hebend, mit einem ganz kurzen, und immer durch einen Druck markirten Bogenstriche, vorgetragen werden: damit man den Tänzer beständig hebe und zum Springen anreize. . . .

It is, indeed, undeniable that French dance music is not as easy to play as many imagine, and that its execution must be clearly distinguished from the Italian style if it is to be suitable for each type of piece. Dance music is usually played seriously, with a heavy yet short and sharp bow stroke, more detached than slurred. That which is delicate and singing is rarely found in it. Dotted notes are played heavily, but the notes following them are played very short and sharply [*sehr kurz und scharf*]. Fast pieces must be executed in a gay, hopping, and springing manner with a very short bow stroke, always marked with an interior stress.[10] In this fashion the dancers are continually inspired and encouraged to leap. . . .

We have heard one of these phrases repeatedly: as illustrated through musical notation in V/21, playing the notes after dots "short and sharply" means that the dot has been lengthened. Quantz also indicates that dance music is to be played "with a heavy yet short and sharp bow stroke, more detached than slurred": articulation, of course, is variable depending on the affective context (cf. XVII/ii/13); but he has already noted that crisp tonguing is generally "indispensable" for the sharp and lively performance of dotted notes (*tiri*, VI/ii/3). Two sections later (§58) Quantz becomes more specific about performing dance music:

Wenn die Welschen, im geraden Tacte, durch das große C, so ihn andeutet, einen Strich machen; so zeiget solcher, wie bekannt, den Allabrevetact an. Die Franzosen bedienen sich dieser Tactart zu verschiedenen Charakteren, als: Burreen [*sic*], Entreen, Rigaudons, Gavotten, Rondeaus, u s. w. Sie schreiben aber anstatt des durchstrichenen C eine große 2. welche ebenfalls bedeutet, daß die Noten noch einmal so geschwind gespielet werden müssen, als sonst. In dieser Tactart sowohl, als im Dreyviertheiltacte, bey der Loure, Sarabande, Courante, und Chaconne, müssen die Achttheile, so auf punctirte Viertheile folgen, nicht nach ihrer eigentlichen Geltung, sondern sehr kurz und scharf gespielet werden. Die Note mit dem Puncte wird mit Nachdruck markiret, und unter dem Puncte der Bogen abgesetzt. Eben so verfährt man mit allen punctirten Noten, wenn es anders die Zeit leidet: und soferne nach einem Puncte oder einer Pause drey oder mehr dreygeschwänzte Noten folgen; so werden solche, besonders in langsamen Stücken, nicht allemal nach ihrer Geltung, sondern am äußersten Ende der ihnen bestimmten Zeit, und in der größten Geschwindigkeit gespielet; wie solches in Ouvertüren, Entreen, und Furien öfters vorkömmt. Es muß aber jede von diesen geschwinden Noten ihren besondern Bogenstrich bekommen: und findet das Schleifen wenig statt.

Die **Entree**, die **Loure**, und die **Courante**, werden prächtig gespielet; und der Bogen wird bey jedem Viertheile, es sey mit oder ohne Punct, abgesetzet. . . .

Eine **Sarabande** hat eben dieselbe Bewegung; wird aber mit einem etwas annehmlichern Vortrage gespielet.

Eine **Chaconne** wird gleichfalls prächtig gespielet. . . .

Eine **Passecaille** ist der vorigen gleich; wird aber fast ein wenig geschwinder gespielet.

When in common time the Italians make a stroke through the large C, we all know that this indicates alla breve time. The French make use of this meter in various types of dances, such as bourées, entrées, rigaudons, gavottes, rondeaux, & c. Instead of the crossed C, however, they write a large 2, which likewise indicates that the notes must be played at twice their regular speed. In this meter, as well as in three-four time, the eighths that follow the dotted quarters in the loure, sarabande, courante, and chaconne must not be played with their literal value, but must be executed in a very short and sharp manner [*sehr kurz und scharf gespielet werden*]. The dotted note is played with emphasis, and the bow is detached during the dot. All dotted notes are treated in the same manner if time allows; and if three or more thirty-second notes follow a dot or a rest, they are not always played with their literal value, especially in slow pieces, but are executed at the extreme end of the time allotted to them, and with the greatest possible speed, as is frequently the case in overtures, entrées, and furies. Each of these quick notes must receive its separate bow stroke, and slurring is rarely used.

The **entrée,** the **loure,** and the **courante** are played majestically [*prächtig*], and the bow is detached at each crotchet, whether it is dotted or not. . . .

A **sarabande** has the same movement, but is played with a somewhat more agreeable execution.

A **chaconne** is in like manner played majestically. . . .

A **passecaille** is like the preceding type, but is played just a little faster.

Yet again, playing the notes after the dots "short and sharply" is Quantz's phrase for overdotting, the same language he has used half a dozen times previously. But we note too that he begins the discussion in §58 with French pieces in **2** or $\frac{3}{4}$: these are precisely the meters wherein eighths are *notes inégales* in French music—and, as Morel de Lescer, Hotteterre, Metoyen, and Engramelle make clear, the eighth after the dotted quarter must be late in proportion to the degree of inequality (see above, pp. 68ff.). Thus, Quantz's prescription of overdotting for dance music overlaps with French practice: this raises an important issue to be resumed in the next paragraph, but for the moment let us review the remainder of what he has said. He reminds us that the bow stroke is sharp and detached in French dance style (§56), and again advocates the characteristic French retaking of the bow in dotted figures (§58; cf. also XVII/ii/13); in French style, however, the dots are not sustained with the bow, but detached.[11] He specifically advocates overdotting for the loure, sarabande, courante, and chaconne. Moreover, in the last three sentences quoted, he observes that the entrée, loure, courante, sarabande, chaconne, and passacaille are to be played majestically—and he had earlier associated the affect of majesty (*das Prächtige*) with overdotting (XII/24 and

XVII/ii/13; see above, pp. 91–93). Concerning the overture – today the most disputed component of the French dance suite – he speaks only about contracting the thirty-second-note *tirades,* a practice he already touched upon in XVII/ii/16.[12] But the French overture is closely related to the entrée;[13] its slow introduction is often in **2** or ₵, meters Quantz singles out for overdotting at the quarter-note level; and later in the treatise (XVIII/42) he states that it must have "a majestic and grave opening [*einen prächtigen und gravitätischen Anfang*]." Quantz was not alone in associating the opening of the overture with majesty; Scheibe had already written of "a proud animation, a serious, manly, and majestic manner, and overall, a steadfast fire" that it must contain,[14] and later writers (Kirnberger/Schulz and Türk) would comment similarly. As regards rhythmic alteration, several subsequent accounts from Berlin and Halle confirm that the opening of the overture was overdotted in Prussia (see below). Thus it seems clear that Quantz was advocating overdotting for French dance music, and virtually certain that he intended it for the opening of the overture as well. Moreover, it appears that his contemporaries and followers also took him to mean this. We shall examine their commentary in due course; but in the present context it is noteworthy that Quantz's terminology is reflected in the writings of both Marpurg and Agricola, who were acquainted with Quantz's *Versuch* when they penned their own treatises. Marpurg, who raises objections about overdotting, begins his discussion thus: "If the dot is to be quite sharp [*recht scharf*], that is, if the following short notes are to be performed with more animation [*Lebhaftigkeit*] than their value would call for. . . ."[15] And Agricola introduces the issue as follows: "The short notes that come after a dot . . . are always performed, be it slow or quick tempo . . . very short, and at the outermost limit of their value [*sehr kurz, und ganz am äußersten Ende ihrer Goltung*] . . . ."[16] It should also be borne in mind that all of Quantz's comments on overdotting are presented as though the practice were commonplace, not new or out of the ordinary. And for Berlin musical life in 1752, as we have seen, what was commonplace was the Dresden mixed style of the 1730s, endorsed and enforced by Quantz's royal pupil Frederick, to whom the *Versuch* is dedicated: this was hardly the place to introduce radical new ideas on the treatment of rhythm and articulation, and there is no evidence to suggest that Quantz did so (see also below, p. 116).

At this juncture we must distinguish between two strains of overdotting in Quantz's advocacy of it. The first, introduced in Chapter V, evidently affects only dotted eighths and lesser values; for convenience, let us accept Neumann's designation of it as the 'galant' type.[17] For this there is no known precedent, although several later writers accept it to varying degrees; it can scarcely be derived from *notes inégales,* nor does Quantz (or anyone else) associate it with French music. The second type, which is at least partially congruent with the concomitant overdotting of French *inégalité*, is what Quantz advocates for French dance music, and almost certainly for the opening of overtures as well; let us call it 'French' over-dotting. Naturally one wonders why Quantz did not identify the origin of this type, and why his overdotting of certain dances and French overtures is (apparently) so strong—for it will be recalled that among the French writers who discuss overdotting concomitant with *inégalité*, only Morel de Lescer describes out-and-out double-dotting; the others suggest length-ening of the dot in proportion to the prevailing degree of inequality. Nor do Quantz's earlier instructions about *notes inégales* favor only strong (3:1) inequality, which would result in the sharp overdotting he prescribes in XVII/ii/58 (cf. pp. 43–47 above). Yet it may be that for certain types of French movements, vigorous *notes inégales* was the practice in Dresden and Berlin; it will be recalled that Engramelle indicates 3:1 inequality for the "March of the King of Prussia" (see p. 19 above).

And this may have been the case in France as well: we have seen other glimmerings of strong overdotting in French music—Monteclair's exer-cises (particularly the 1709 entrée), the Menetou transcription of the *Persée* Overture, and Roger North's somewhat perplexing description of the Lullian entrée, in addition to Morel de Lescer. It may indeed be that a mannerism of vigorous rhythmic alteration, rooted in 'inégalité' over-dotting but no longer directly dependent upon that custom, had emerged for the performance of majestic or march-like pieces. (Besides Engramelle, Tarade also stipulates 3:1 *inégalité* for a march; see p. 17). In any case, Quantz and his Francophile colleagues evidently cultivated such a man-ner in Dresden. He in turn taught the style to Frederick the Great, and it became established in Berlin, whence the Grauns, the Bendas, and others had gone from Dresden. To be sure, direct evidence from France of such pungent rhythmic spice is neither plentiful nor strong. But there is no particular reason why it should be: the issue hinges upon the degree of inequality adopted in overtures, entrées, chaconnes, etc., and whether this in turn gave rise to the customary expectation of overdotted rhythm in such pieces. In any case, as we shall see, the French overture is to be overdotted according to three later German sources, and one of these advocates such rhythmic alteration for the loure as well.

J. S. BACH: OUVERTURE, BWV 831/831A

But first let us review an intriguing case of written-out overdotting in the work of J. S. Bach—his revision of the French overture in Part II of the *Klavierübung*. The original date of this composition remains uncertain.

The earlier, C-minor version of it (BWV 831a) is preserved in two sources: a copy by Anna Magdelena, probably made between 1727 and 1731 but not later than mid-1733, as well as a manuscript by the Dortmund organist J. G. Preller (1727–86), which is probably of later origin (ca. 1745–53). The B-minor version was published in Part II of the *Klavierübung* at Easter 1735, indicating that Bach's *Stichvorlage* was probably complete by late 1734.[18] In revising the overture, Bach contracted pickups and lengthened dotted quarters from 3:1 to 7:1 (via ties or rests), as the incipits in example 5-2 show. He did not do so consistently, as Neumann has pointed out:[19] but in approximately 83 percent of the spots where it was musically reasonable to do so, Bach contracted the pickups and lengthened the dotting.[20] In Neumann's view, the composer simply changed his mind about the rhythm of this piece.

But why? Bach was familiar with French performance style from his student days in Lüneburg; it is undeniable that his revisions in the keyboard overture are much akin to Quantz's precepts for rhythmic alteration in French dance music (XVII/vii/58); and as noted above (p. 83), Quantz's teaching generally reflects common practice in Dresden from about 1720 to 1740. From the famous "Short but Most Necessary Draft" to the Leipzig Town Council of 1730, we know that Bach greatly admired the musical establishment in Dresden; and between 1717 and 1735 he made several visits to that city, twice to present organ recitals.[21] Recent scholarship has shown that in July 1733—after the C-minor version of the overture was written, but almost certainly before the piece was revised for the 1735 volume of the *Klavierübung*—Bach again traveled to Dresden, where his son Wilhelm Friedemann had just been appointed organist at the Sophienkirche. While there he and his family prepared the parts for the *Missa* (later incorporated into the B-minor Mass) that was presented to the new Elector Friedrich August II on 27 July (for which Bach was finally awarded the title of Hofkomponist to the Elector in 1736). Thus, his visit must have lasted several days at least,[22] and it is entirely likely that he renewed his acquaintance with the court musicians, including Quantz. Indeed, any of these trips to Dresden could have provided Bach the opportunity to hear (and discuss) the overdotted manner of performing French music that seems to have been prevalent there: in July of 1733, for example, the period of mourning for August I, during which music was banned, had just come to an end; the celebration of a new reign would naturally entail the resumption of social dancing and ballet. As Marshall has shown, various compositions from Bach's last two decades reveal judicious adaptation of the emerging *galant* style popular in Dresden (see n. 21); quite possibly Bach also found the overdotting of French overtures a splendid procedure, and took steps to notate it in the 1734–35 revision of BWV 831.

EXAMPLE 5-2.   Bach, Overture (a) BWV 831a, MS copied by Anna Magdelena
             Bach; (b) BWV 831, *Klavierübung* II, 1735 (*NBA* V/2, 43, 20).

Reprinted by permission of Baerenreiter Music Corporation.

It is not surprising that Bach would seek to make his intentions clearer through notation: as Scheibe would complain only two years later, "Every ornament, every little grace, and everything that one thinks of as belonging to the method of playing, he expresses completely in notes."[23] As is typical for Bach, the C-minor keyboard overture is more complex in texture and diminutions than most French works of the genre; enlivening its rhythm entailed decisions that only he could properly make. Moreover, as Neumann has observed, the Preller manuscript of BWV 831a proves that Bach could not have counted upon "the method of playing" of every keyboardist to bring about overdotting and upbeat contractions: in this source, many of the upbeats are graced with ornaments that cannot be executed in the quickened rhythms of Bach's later revision (cf. examples 5-2 and 5-3).[24] Clearly, then, overdotting à la Quantz was by no means universal—a fact confirmed by later German writers, including Bach's son Carl Philip Emanuel.[25]

EXAMPLE 5-3.   Bach, C-minor Overture BWV 831a, Preller MS (*NBA* V/2, *KB*, 87).

Reprinted by permission of Baerenreiter Music Corporation.

BERLIN (I): C. P. E. BACH, MARPURG, AGRICOLA

Quantz's views on overdotting prompted various responses from later treatise writers, some of whom were his colleagues in Berlin (cf. table 5-1). The first of these is C. P. E. Bach, whose commentary (cited in full below) is rather disorganized and confusing, as Neumann points out.[26] It begins thus: "The short notes that come after dots are always rendered shorter [*kürzer abgefertiget*] than their notation indicates; therefore it is superfluous to mark them with [articulation] dots or strokes." This first clause is what Emanuel Bach would later dub the "sure main rule" (see below). In it we note clear resonance with Quantz's terminology (*kurz*), as well as brusque rejection of Quantz's suggestion that in dotted contexts "strokes above the [short] notes indicate that they are to be stressed" (Quantz, XVII/ii/13). Bach then asserts (1) that the disposition of parts sometimes requires the dot to be rendered precisely; (2) dots after long notes, and after short notes in slow tempo, are "generally held [*insgemein gehalten*]," as are isolated dots; but (3) when several dotted figures follow each other in quick tempo, "they are often not held, even though the notation calls for it." Points (2) and (3) are ambiguous: if by "held" Bach is referring to the degree of articulation between the dotted note and the short note, then he is largely in agreement with Quantz—namely, in quick, lively pieces one articulates between the (elongated) dot and the very short little note, while in the Adagio, a more sustained or *nourris-sant* execution is required (cf. Quantz, XVII/ii/13 and XVII/vii/56 and 58). Otherwise, one must interpret this passage (as Neumann does) to mean that in fast movements persistent dotted patterns are not exaggerated beyond their 3:1 value, but perhaps played in a milder-than-3:1 ratio. Next Bach observes (somewhat ironically for us) that (4) "it is on account of such variation that it would be best if everything were indicated precisely; otherwise, one can gain a good bit of illumination from the content of the piece." Then he states (5) that when dotted notes (apparently of relatively short duration) are followed by substantially shorter values (e.g., ♩.♪ , ♩.♬), the dots are "held out [*ausgehalten*]"; assuming "held out" means "lengthened," this is also congruent with Quantz.

At this point in the 1787 edition of his book, Bach adds several sentences,[27] the first of which contradicts item (5) above: (6) "In figures where dots are followed by four or more short notes, these latter are short enough because they are so numerous"; this applies to figures such as ♩ ♬ and ♩. ♫ , and also to ♩ ♫ "when the tempo is not too slow." This is something of a departure from Quantz. So too are numerous expressive concerns that may countermand overdotting: Bach makes exceptions for sad or expressive ideas, pieces in slow tempo, and figures bearing ornaments. And the Lombard snap, if it is slurred, must not be taken too quickly, even in moderate tempo (1753, III/24); this, too, is at variance with Quantz.

Bach's rather convoluted original text of this passage is as follows:

§23. Die kurtzen Noten nach vorgegangenen Punckten werden allezeit kürtzer abgefertiget als ihre Schreib-Art erfordert, folglich ist es ein Ueberfluß diese kurtze Noten mit Punckten oder Strichen zu bezeichnen. Bey Fig. VII

FIG. VII

sehen wir ihren Ausdruck. Zuweilen erfordert die Eintheilung, daß man der Schreib-Art gemäß verfährt (*). Die Punckte bey langen Noten, ingleichen die bey kurtzen Noten in langsamer Zeit-Maasse und auch **eintzeln** werden insgemein gehalten. Kommen aber, zumahl in geschwindem Tempo, viele hintereinander vor, so werden sie offt nicht gehalten, ohngeacht die Schreib-Art es erfordert. Es ist also wegen dieser Veränderung am besten, daß man alles gehörig andeutet, widrigenfals kan man aus dem Inhalte eines Stückes hierinnen vieles Licht bekommen. Die Punckte bey kurtzen Noten, worauf ungleich kürtzere nachfolgen, werden ausgehalten Fig. VIII.

FIG. VIII

[Added to 1787 ed.:] Bey Figuren, wo auf die Puncte vier und noch mehrere kurze Noten folgen, werden diese letztern durch ihre Vielheit kurz genug; auch bey folgenden Figuren:

Wenn die Zeit-Maaße nicht gar langsam ist: so gilt obiges auch bey folgenden Figuren:

Bey den Figuren, wo die kurzen Noten zuerst vorkommen, und der Punct zuletzt stehet, werden die kurzen Noten ebenfalls kürzer abgefertiget, als ihre Schreib-Art erfordert. Das letzte Exempel hat, ohngeacht der längern Noten, bey nicht gar langsamer Zeit-Maaße, eben dieselbe Ausführung. Von Rechtswegen sollten in diesem Falle die Noten mehr geschwänzt seyn.

Die geschwinde Abfertigung aller dieser kurzen Noten ist **meistentheils** wahr, weil diese Regel zuweilen Ausnahmen leidet. Man muß die Gedanken, wobey sie vorkommen, genau beurtheilen. Wenn die kurzen Noten Manieren über sich haben, deren Vortrag einige Zeit erfordert, z. E. Triller oder Doppelschläge: so können sie nicht so geschwinde ausgeführet werden, als ausserdem. Diese letzte Anmerkung gilt ebenfalls von den kurzen Noten, wenn der Gedanke traurig oder Affectsvoll ist, und bey langsamer Zeit-Maaße vorkommt.

[1753 ed.:] §24. Die erste Note von den bey Fig. IX befindlichen Figuren,[28] weil sie geschleift werden, wird nicht zu kurz abgefertiget, wenn das Tempo gemäßigt oder langsam ist, weil sonst zu viel Zeit-Raum übrig bleiben würde. Diese erste Note wird durch einen gelinden Druck,

aber ja nicht durch einen kurtzen Stoß oder zu schnellen Ruck mar-
quirt.[29]

FIG. IX

§23. The short notes that come after dots are always rendered shorter
than their notation indicates; therefore it is superfluous to mark them
with dots or strokes. In fig. VII [see above] we see their expression. Sometimes the disposition [of part writing] requires that one proceed according
to the notation, as at the sign *. The dots after long notes, and likewise
those after short notes in slow tempo, plus all **isolated** dots, are generally
held. But if many [dotted figures] follow each other, especially in quick
tempo, they are often not held, even though the notation calls for it. It is
on account of such variation that it would be best if everything were
indicated precisely; otherwise, one can gain a good bit of illumination
from the content of the piece. The dots after short notes that are followed
by much shorter ones are held out, as in fig. VIII.

[Added to 1787 ed.:] In figures where the dots are followed by four or
more short notes, these latter are short enough because they are so numerous; and also in the following figures: [see first unnumbered example
above]

When the tempo is not altogether too slow, the foregoing also applies to
the following figures: [see second unnumbered example above]

In figures where the short notes come first and the dot is at the end, the
short notes are likewise dispatched shorter than their notation calls for.
The last example, notwithstanding the longer note values [= 2 sixteenths and a dotted quarter], has just this same performance if the tempo
is not too slow. By rights the notes should have more beams in this case.
[see third unnumbered example above]

The quick dispatch of all these short notes is proper **most of the time,**
because this rule occasionally suffers exceptions. One must precisely
assess the ideas wherein they [the short notes] appear. When the short
notes have ornaments, whose performance requires some time, e.g., trills
or turns, then they cannot be played as quickly as otherwise. This last
remark applies likewise to short notes when the idea is sad or expressive,
and occurs in a slow tempo.

[1753 ed.:] §24. In the figures found in fig. IX, the first note, because it
is slurred, is not dispatched too shortly if the tempo is moderate or slow,
since altogether too much temporal space would remain left over. This
first note is marked by a gentle pressure, but not by a short shove or too
quick a jolt.

The second part of C. P. E. Bach's keyboard essay, which treats of
accompaniment, contains a section on general aspects of performance

(1762, XXIX): this begins with the observation that it is wrong to suppose the rules of good performance apply only to solo playing. Several paragraphs later (§15), Bach offers a brief synopsis of his views on the rendition of dotted notes:

> In der Schreibart der punctirten Noten überhaupt fehlet es noch sehr oft an der gehörigen Genauigkeit. Man hat daher wegen des Vortrags dieser Art von Noten eine gewisse Hauptregel festsetzen wollen, welche aber viele Ausnahme leidet. Die nach dem Punct folgenden Noten sollen nach dieser Regel auf das kürzeste abgefertiget werden, und mehrentheils ist diese Vorschrift wahr: allein bald machet die Eintheilung gewisser Noten in verschiedenen Stimmen, vermöge welcher sie in einem Augenblicke zusammen eintreten müssen, eine Aenderung; bald ist ein flattirender Affect, welcher das diesen punctirten Noten sonst eigene Trotzige nicht verträget, die Ursache, daß man bey dem Puncte etwas weniger anhält. Wenn man also nur **eine** Art vom Vortrage dieser Noten zum Grundsatze leget, so verliehrt man die übrigen Arten.

> In the notation of dotted notes generally, the needed precision is often lacking. Therefore one wished to advance a sure main rule regarding the execution of these notes, which, however, suffers many exceptions. According to this rule, the notes that follow dots should be played extremely short, and for the most part this rule is correct. Sometimes the disposition of certain notes in various parts, by virtue of which they must conjoin instantaneously, constitutes an exception. In other cases a flattering affect, which would not tolerate the characteristic defiance of these dotted notes, is the reason for dwelling somewhat less on the dot. Thus, if only **one** type of execution for these notes is established as the principle, one loses the other types.

Thus, Bach's main objection to "sure rules," such as Quantz's, is their apparent rigidity: he urges that both the texture and affect of a piece be considered before its rhythms are sharpened. Overall, he accepts the 'galant' overdotting of small note values (unless many smaller notes follow them); he is unclear about larger values (cf. points [2] and [6] on pp. 101–2 above); and he says nothing about Quantz's 'French' type of overdotting. Particularly noteworthy is his plea that performers advert to the disposition of part writing when contemplating rhythmic alteration. And we may note as well that, in partial agreement with Quantz, Bach associates overdotting with energizing or invigorating the performance. When he revised the first part of the treatise in 1787, Bach had been free from the Court of Frederick the Great for nearly twenty years; since he was no longer under any compulsion to endorse what was customary in Berlin, it would appear that he still found selective overdotting agreeable. Students do not always adhere strictly to the precepts of their teachers; nonetheless, it is worth noting that at the beginning of his autobiography, C. P. E.

Bach acknowledges that he never had any teacher other than his father in keyboard playing and composition.[30]

Just two years after the first part of Bach's treatise appeared, the Berlin theorist and journalist F. W. Marpurg published an introductory keyboard tutor in which he objects to the seeming irrationality of overdotting:

> Wenn der Punct recht scharf seyn soll, d. i. wenn die darauf folgende kurze Note mit mehrerer Lebhaftigkeit, als ihr Wehrt erfodert, vorgetragen werden soll: so muß man zuförderst **zwey Puncte hintereinander** gebrauchen, und alsdenn die darauf folgende Note um die Hälfte verkürzen. Zum Exempel Fig. 21. (b) soll gespielet werden, wie bey (c): so muß, wenn man nicht das Bindungszeichen gebrauchen will, solches geschrieben werden, wie bey (d) und so in andern Fällen. Ohne das ist man nicht verbunden, die Gedanken des Componisten zu errathen; und da dieser zwey Wege vor sich hat, sich dem Ausführer deutlich zu machen, nemlich, da er entweder das Bindungszeichen oder die zwey Puncte gebrauchen kann: so sehe ich nicht ab, warum man anders schreiben, und anders etwas vorgetragen wissen will, d. i. warum man nur einen Punkt hinsetzet, und denselben für anderthalb Punct gelesen haben will.[31]

FIG. 21

If the dot is to be quite sharp [*recht scharf*], that is, if the following short note is to be performed with more animation [*Lebhaftigkeit*] than its value would call for: then one must accordingly use **two dots, one after the other,** and also shorten the following note by one half. For example, fig. 21 (b) is supposed to be played as at (c): then if one doesn't wish to use the sign of the tie, such [a rhythm] must be written as in (d), and so on in other cases. Generally speaking, one is not required to divine the composer's thoughts; and since he has available two ways of making himself clear to the performer, namely, that he can use either the tie or the two dots: I do not see why one would write something one way, and intend it to be performed another way, i.e., why one puts only one dot and intends it to be read as a dot worth half again as much.

As noted previously, there are echoes of Quantz's terminology here (and of C. P. E. Bach's as well). In the short example of notation Marpurg cites, only small values are present, indicating that he objects to the 'galant' strain of unwritten overdotting. But we should note that his quarrel is logical rather than stylistic: he censures the inconsistency between notation and performance, not sharply dotted rhythms per se; if precisely notated, the mannerism would be quite acceptable. Marpurg's silence about the 'French' type of overdotting is striking, for he had been to France, written keyboard pieces in the French idiom, become well versed in French musical literature, and generally favored French style over Italian. But neither does he mention *notes inégales*. Following his arrival in Berlin (1749), Marpurg was strongly influenced by C. P. E. Bach and the prevailing Prussian tastes in music; accordingly, he dropped or modified many practices he had learned in France, as Hays has shown.[32] Given that Bach also says nothing about *inégalité* and concomitant overdotting, these may have been among the French customs Marpurg abandoned.

But Marpurg was not a member of Frederick the Great's ensemble, and his objection to overdotting is idiosyncratic: besides Bach and Quantz, four later writers from the Berlin circle endorse aspects of the practice. The earliest of these is J. F. Agricola, a student of both J. S. and C. P. E. Bach's, and also a pupil of Quantz's. In 1759 Agricola succeeded Graun as director of the Opera in Berlin, and he became an influential teacher as well: Burney later claimed he was "regarded as the best organ player in Berlin, and the best singing master in Germany."[33] As table 5-1 shows, Agricola's instructions about overdotting are virtually identical to Quantz's 'galant' type. And they are even less flexible: in Agricola's view, it is actually an error not to elongate dotted notes, and he spells things out in almost schoolmasterly fashion:

> Die kurzen Noten, welche hinter einem Puncte stehen, absonderlich Sechzehntheile oder Zwey und dreyßigtheile, auch im Allabreve die Achttheile, werden allezeit, es sey in langsamer oder geschwinder Tactbewegung, es mag ihrer eine oder mehrere seyn, sehr kurz, und ganz am äußersten Ende ihrer Geltung ausgeführt: die vor dem Puncte stehende wird dagegen desto länger gehalten. Z. E. diese:

> werden ausgeführet, als wenn sie so geschrieben wären:

> Die Note vor dem Puncte wird verstärkt, die nach dem Puncte aber schwächer angegeben.

> Wenn die kurze Note voran, und der Punct hinter der zweyten steht, so ist die erste Note so kurz als möglich, das übrige wird der Note zugelegt, die den Punct hinter sich hat. Z. E.

Ausführung.

Bey diesen Figuren aber wird die erste Note stark, und die vor dem
Puncte, welche allezeit an jene geschleifet wird, schwächer angeben, aber
wohl ausgehalten, und wenn Zeit dazu ist wieder verstärket.[34]

The short notes that come after a dot—particularly sixteenths and
thirty-seconds, and also eighths in alla breve—are always performed, be
it slow or quick tempo, and be there one or several of them, very short,
and at the outermost limit of their value: the notes that stand before the
dot are, on the contrary, held proportionately longer. For example these:
[see above]

are performed as though they were written thus: [see second example
above]

The note before the dot is strengthened, but those after it are rendered
weaker.

When the short note comes first, and the dot is after the second note,
then the first note is as short as possible, and the left over [time] is
assigned to the note that has the dot after it. E. g.: [see third example
above]

Performance: [see fourth example above]

In such figures, however, the first note is strong, and that before the dot,
which is always slurred to it [i.e., to the first note], is rendered weaker,
although well sustained; and when there is time, it is strengthened again.

Thus Agricola eschews the ambiguity of language that lingers in some of
Quantz's comments on overdotting. And although he does not mention
French music, Agricola's specific elongation of the dotted quarter in ₵
partially coincides with Quantz's discussion of French dance music
(XVII/vii/58—cf. table 5-1). One notes as well that he anticipates and
rejects the self-contradictory qualifications C. P. E. Bach later added to the
1787 edition of his keyboard treatise (see p. 102, items [5] and [6]); apparently former teacher and pupil already disagreed on these matters (as well

as several others). Concerning the execution of Lombardic rhythms, Agricola also follows Quantz's practice.

LEOPOLD MOZART

In 1754 Marpurg lamented that, despite the excellent examples of Quantz for the flute and Bach for the keyboard, nothing comparable had been written for violinists. Within two years, Leopold Mozart responded with the eighteenth century's most influential work on violin playing.[35] But unlike Marpurg, Mozart endorses the 'galant' manner of overdotting; and like Quantz, he introduces overdotting in a rudimentary section entitled "Of the Duration or Value of the Notes, Rests, and Dots, together with an Explanation of All Musical Signs . . .":

> Es giebt in langsamen Stücken gewisse Passagen, wo der Punct noch etwas länger gehalten werden muß, als die bereits vorgeschriebene Regel erfordert: wenn anders der Vortrag nicht zu schläferig ausfallen soll. Z. E. wenn hier

> der Punct in seiner gewöhnlichen Länge gehalten würde, würde es einmal zu faul und recht schläferig klingen. In solchem Falle nun muß man die punctirte Note etwas länger aushalten; die Zeit des längern Aushalten aber muß man der nach dem Puncte folgenden Note, so zu reden, abstehlen.

> . . . Der Punct soll überhaupt allezeit etwas länger gehalten werden. Denn nicht nur wird dadurch der Vortrag lebhafter; sondern es wird auch dem Eilen, jenem fast allgemeinen Fehler, Einhalt gethan . . . . Es wäre sehr gut, wenn diese längere Aushaltung des Puncts recht bestimmet und hingesetzet würde. Ich wenigstens habe es schon oft gethan, und meine Vortragsmeinung habe ich mit zween Puncten nebst Abkürzung der darauf folgenden Note also zu Tage geleget:

> Es ist wahr, anfangs fällt es fremd in die Augen. Allein was verschlägt dieß? Der Satz hat seinen Grund; und der musikalische Geschmack wird dadurch beförderet.[36]

> In slow pieces there are certain passages where the dot must be held somewhat longer than the aforementioned rule [i.e., 3:1] indicates, if the execution is not to seem too sleepy. For example, if here [see first example]
>
> the dot is held for its usual length, it would sound both too lazy and quite sleepy. In such cases therefore one must sustain the dotted note somewhat longer; and the time of this longer sustaining must, so to say, be stolen from the note after the dot.
>
> . . . The dot should generally always be held somewhat longer; for not only does the performance thereby become livelier [*lebhafter*], but hurrying, that almost universal error, is squelched. . . . It would be good if this longer sustaining of the dot were properly determined and set forth. I at least have often done so, and clarified my intention for performance with two dots, plus the shortening of the note that follows: [see second example]
>
> It is true that at first this seems strange to the eye. But what does that matter? There is good reason for it, and thereby musical taste is promoted.

The first portion of this passage broadly resembles Quantz's instructions to ripieno violinists in XVII/ii/13: it opens with a discussion of lengthening the dot in slow tempo, and an admonition about hurrying; then follows a more general advocacy of overdotting to make the performance more lively—the same reason given several times by Quantz. In the latter part of the passage, Mozart is clearly responding to Marpurg's call for double-dotted notation, and perhaps also to Emanuel Bach's remark that "it would be best if everything were indicated precisely"; nevertheless, he does not reject overdotting as an unwritten performance practice. Later in the *Violinschule* (VII/ii/2–4), Mozart also advocates rhythmic sharpening for the performance of smaller note values, and for the Lombard rhythms as well (see table 5-1), much as Quantz had done.[37]

Mozart's treatise went through four German editions. A complete Dutch translation appeared in 1766, and an abridged French version, including the passages on overdotting, was issued four times.[38] Thus, his views on rhythmic alteration must have been widely known.

During the five years from 1752 to 1757, the first five German discussions of overdotting were published. The latter four all stem from the first—that of Quantz, earliest chronicler of overdotting per se, whose teaching is rooted in the mixed musical style of Dresden in the 1730s. Both French and Italians were active in Dresden's musical life, and it seems probable that Quantz's instructions about French overtures and dance music reflect Parisian practice. From Dresden, too (and likely also from Celle), J. S. Bach probably became familiar with overdotting and contraction of pickups, which are notated in his revision of the keyboard overture BWV 831. His son Emanuel, followed by Marpurg and Mozart, acknowledges the incongruity between dotted notation and overdotted performance; and C. P. E. stresses further (especially in the 1762 volume of his treatise) that textural and expressive exigences require exceptions to the "main rule." Neither Emanuel Bach nor Marpurg, Agricola, or Mozart mentions the 'French' type of overdotting. Nor is this especially surprising: French style was on the wane, and none of these composers took much stock in it, save for the young Marpurg, who subsequently abandoned much of his French training when he moved to Berlin. Yet as regards 'galant' overdotting, all these authors, like Quantz, write as though this sort of rhythmic alteration had been common practice, certain differences in their accounts of it notwithstanding. (Marpurg's objections, it will be recalled, were on logical rather than stylistic grounds.)

Various treatise writers continued to discuss overdotting throughout the remainder of the eighteenth century, as table 5-1 shows: these accounts are the focus of the next chapter. But while they yield additional moments of insight into the practice of rhythmic alteration, they add little substance to the teachings of Quantz and C. P. E. Bach, with which the later authors were clearly familiar.

CHAPTER SIX

ॐ

Later Sources
on Overdotting

BERLIN (II): KIRNBERGER/SCHULZ,
REICHARDT, RELLSTAB

In 1773 J. A. P. Schulz, formerly a student of Kirnberger's and C. P. E. Bach's, returned to Berlin after three years of extensive travel in France, Italy, and Poland. Kirnberger, who had studied with J. S. Bach and held his master's music in highest esteem, immediately engaged Schulz's assistance in preparing the musical articles for Sulzer's *Allgemeine Theorie der schönen Künste*. Schulz and Kirnberger worked jointly on the entries from "Modulation" up to "Präludieren," while Schulz wrote virtually all of the remaining entries himself.[1] One of their joint contributions is the article "Ouvertüre," which is among the most detailed discussions of that genre to appear during the eighteenth century. Kirnberger and Schulz note that the term *Ouvertüre* is French (meaning an opening or introduction), and that Lully, who was among the first important writers of overtures, used them in both operas and ballets. Such pieces were customary until the rise of Italianate *Symphonien*, which dislodged overtures from fashion; yet in France, they report, the opening of an opera is still known as an overture, even if it is not of the older [Lullian] style.

> Weil diese Stücke Einleitungen zur Oper waren, so suchte man natürlicher Weise ihnen viel Pracht zu geben, Mannigfaltigkeit der Stimmen, und beynahe das Aeußerste, was die Kunst durch die Instrumentalmusik vermag, dabey anzubringen. Daher wird noch izt die Verfertigung einer guten Ouvertüre nur für das Werk eines geübten Meisters gehalten.

> Because these pieces served as introductions to operas, one naturally sought to give them much majesty [*viel Pracht*], to bring to them a multiplicity of parts, and virtually the utmost of which art through instrumental music was capable. Therefore the making of a good overture is still considered a task only for an experienced master.

The character of the overture should be adjusted to the nature of the piece it introduces; those for church music, opera, tragic opera, and pastorale all require different treatment. The authors continue:

> Zuerst erscheinet insgemein ein Stük [sic] von ernsthaftem aber feurigem Charakter in $\frac{4}{4}$ Takt. Die Bewegung hat etwas stolzes, die Schritte sind langsam, aber mit viel kleinen Noten ausgeziehret, die feurig vorgetragen...müssen...werden.... Die Hauptnoten sind meistentheils punktirt, und im Vortrag werden die Punkte über ihre Geltung ausgehalten. Nach diesen Hauptnoten folgen mehr oder weniger kleinere, die in der äußersten Geschwindigkeit und so viel möglich, abgestoßen müssen gespiehlt werden, welches freylich, wenn 10, 12 oder mehr Noten auf einen Vierteltakt kommen, nicht immer angeht.

> First of all there generally appears a section of serious yet fiery character in $\frac{4}{4}$ time. The movement has something proud about it, the steps [beats] are slow, but embellished with many little notes that must be played in a fiery manner.... The main notes are mostly dotted, and in performance the dots are held out beyond their value. After these main notes follow more or fewer smaller ones, which must be played with extreme rapidity, and insofar as possible, articulated (which of course does not always work when 10, 12, or more notes come in a quarter of a measure).

As noted above (p. 190–91, n. 12), Kirnberger and Schulz here advocate contraction of pickups without specific reference to their value—i.e., a brace of either sixteenths or thirty-seconds should be shortened, whereas Quantz mentions only thirty-seconds. (J. S. Bach, it will be recalled, contracted the sixteenths in his revision of BWV 831.)

The authors continue with a description of the fugal and quicker sections of the overture, and note that it is often followed by a group of dances in balleto and concert music. The following remarks conclude the entry:

> Die Ouvertüren sind in den neuern Zeiten selten geworden; weil sowol die Fuge, als die verschiedenen Tanzmelodien, mehr Wissenschaft, Kenntnis und Geschmak [sic] erfodern, als der gemeine Haufe der Tonsezer besizet. Hiedurch aber ist der gute Vortrag, der jedes Stük vor dem andern unterscheiden sollte, und zu dessen Uebung die Ouvertüren sehr vortheilhaft waren, an manchem Orte sehr gefallen.

> Im vorigen Jahrhundert hat man die besten Ouvertüren aus Frankreich erhalten, wo sie wie gesagt worden, zuerst aufgekommen sind. Nachher wurden sie auch anderwerts nachgeahmt, besonders in Deutschland, wo außer dem großen Bach, noch andre seines Namens, ingleichem Händel, Fasch in Zerbst und unsre beyden Graun, besonders aber Teleman sich hervorgethan haben.[2]

In recent times overtures have become rather rare, because both fugue
and the various dance melodies require more knowledge, familiarity, and
taste than the general run of composer possesses. But owing to this, good
performance (style), which is supposed to differentiate each piece from
the other, and for the practicing of which overtures were very beneficial,
has declined considerably in many locations.

In the previous century one obtained the best overtures from France,
where, as noted, they originated. Subsequently they were also imitated
elsewhere, especially in Germany, where, besides the great Bach, others
of his reputation have also distinguished themselves—likewise Händel,
Fasch in Zerbst, both of our Grauns, and especially Telemann.

Kirnberger may well have heard J. S. Bach's overtures while studying in
Leipzig between 1739 and 1741, during Bach's second stint as director of
the Collegium; in any case, three of Bach's orchestral suites (BWV 1066–
68) were in the library of Kirnberger's employer and student, Princess
Anna Amalia of Prussia, whom Kirnberger helped to obtain numerous
manuscript copies of Bach's works.[3] Johann Friedrich Fasch (1688–1758),
long active in Zerbst, maintained strong connections with the Dresden
Hofkapelle, where Pisendel performed his music.[4] We have already noted
Telemann's close acquaintance with French performance style (p. 42
above). The brothers Graun, trained in Dresden, had served many years at
the Court of Frederick the Great; Johann Gottlieb, who had just died in
1771, was among the last composers of French overtures. In the overture
quoted in example 6-1, it is only reasonable to assume that the composer,
who was also the concertmaster, overdotted the piece in performance;

EXAMPLE 6-1.   J. G. Graun, Suite in A minor, Overture.

and he would have done the same in the French overtures to his brother's operas.[5]

Schulz's article on dots and the dotted note ("Punkt; Punktierte Note") gives the usual rule of 3:1, but points out that "there are also cases where proper performance gives the dot a somewhat longer value, as already noted in the article 'Overture.' "[6] Similarly, in the entry for the loure (presumably by both Schulz and Kirnberger), we read that it is a dance "whose expression is earnestness, majesty, even sublimity."[7] The characteristic rhythm is ♪♩ | ♩· ♪♩ | to be executed thus:

> Um den Einschnitt nach dem ersten punktirten Viertel jedes Takts im Vortrag fühlbar zu machen, muß auf der Violin die Achtelnote wie ein Sechszehntheil hinauf, die darauf folgenden zwey Viertel aber stark herunter gestrichen und besonders das punktirte Viertel schweer [*sic*] angehalten werden.[8]

> In order to make the incise after the first dotted quarter of each beat palpable in performance, on the violin the eighth note has to be like a sixteenth, upbow, but the following two quarters are strongly stroked downbow, and in particular the dotted quarter must be arduously sustained.

All of this is much in keeping with what Quantz had written: the majestic, proud, earnest style of the French overture and the loure are linked with overdotting. Such rhythmic alteration may have been concomitant with *notes inégales,* as evidently it was for Quantz. (Yet as we have seen, *inégalité* was not responsible for J. S. Bach's B-minor revision of his keyboard overture.) In any case, Kirnberger must surely have been familiar with the 'French' overdotting described by Quantz: in 1751, well after his tutelage under Bach (1739–41), Kirnberger studied the violin in Dresden, whereafter he spent seven years in Prussia as a violinist, first in the service of Frederick the Great, then later in the chapel of Prince Heinrich. During the same period that he coauthored articles for Sulzer's encyclopedia, Kirnberger was deeply engrossed in his major theoretical work, *Die Kunst des reinen Satzes in der Musik* (1771–79): in it he strives to represent the teaching of J. S. Bach, repeatedly citing examples of Bach's music, and largely rejecting the harmonic theory of Rameau because, as C. P. E. Bach advised him, "You can loudly proclaim that mine and my late father's principles are anti-Rameau."[9] And as noted above, Kirnberger played a major part in establishing the important collection of Bach manuscripts in the library of Princess Anna Amalia (now known as the Amalienbibliothek). All things considered, it appears doubtful that he would sanction overdotting if it were utterly at variance with the practice of J. S. Bach—particularly since the "Ouvertüre" article lists "the great Bach" at the head of distinguished composers in this genre. And we have already noted that Bach himself incorporated overdotting into the revision of his keyboard overture BWV 831.

Schulz, on the other hand, had recently visited Paris: if overdotting were no longer current there in loures and overtures of the older [Lullian] style, it seems unlikely that he and Kirnberger would have underscored the practice for these genres yet overlooked it in other contexts; for in most respects, their articles evince accurate historical and national perspective. In Paris, to be sure, treatise writers were still discussing *inégalité* around the time of Schulz's visit, just as they had for nearly eighty years; and among them was Père Engramelle (1775), one of the four authors who explicitly discuss the overdotting that is concomitant with *notes inégales*. It must also be recalled that musical style at the Court of Frederick the Great had long since stagnated: as Burney noted during his visit of 1772, the names of Quantz and Graun "are religion at Berlin, and more sworn by, than those of Luther and Calvin."[10] Frederick would have nothing to do with more modern music, which he considered degenerate. Accordingly, between 1763 and 1786 his opera presented only three "new" works, which were composed by Agricola in the style of Graun, under the direct supervision of the king; all other performances were reruns of operas by Graun and Hasse written before the outbreak of the Seven Years' War (1756).[11] A similar recycling of works by Quantz and Frederick himself constituted the staple instrumental repertoire; as Burney observed of Quantz, "His taste is that of forty years ago," and indeed, Burney heard the king perform Quantz concertos that were twenty and forty years old.[12] Thus, it is scarcely surprising that overdotting, a manner of performance evidently dating back to Dresden in the 1730s, was still common in Berlin when Schulz and Kirnberger penned their articles of 1773–74.

Moreover, both Reichardt and Rellstab confirm that it was. When Reichardt published his treatise for the orchestral violinist in 1776, he had just been appointed Kapellmeister to Frederick the Great; prior to this he had traveled widely, studying briefly in Berlin with Kirnberger, and in Dresden with Homilius, a pupil of J. S. Bach's. Reichardt comments as follows about dotted values:

Die punktirten Noten erfordern einen genauen und bestimmten Vortrag.
Sind sie eine um die andere punktirt w. z B.

so hat man dabey nur besonders zu merken, daß die verkürzte Note so kurz als möglich vorgetragen muß, um der längeren destomehr Gewicht zu geben.[13]

Dotted notes require a precise and well-ordered execution. If they follow one after the other, e.g., [see example]

one must only observe in particular that the short note has to be played as short as possible, so as to give the longer one proportionately greater weight.

Although Reichardt generally recommends the treatises of Quantz (particularly chap. XVII), Bach, and Mozart, he does not agree with them in all respects.[14] Nevertheless, his brief mention of overdotting seems to fit the 'galant' pattern.

Rellstab, who had studied with Agricola and C. F. C. Fasch (C. P. E. Bach's assistant harpsichordist in Berlin), writes in greater detail:

Punctirte Noten wie bey *a* werden wie bey *b* ausgeführt. In den meisten Fällen wird allemal der Punct als eine Pause angesehen, und die letzte Note kürzer ausgeführt, als es nach ihrer innern Geltung seyn sollte. Wenn über dem ganzen Stück oder einer Stelle das Wort *sostenuto* (unterhalten) sieht, als bey Kirchenmusiken, Ouverturen, welche mehr Ernst als Pracht ausdrücken, so werden die Puncte streng ausgehalten, obgleich die letzten Noten doch kürzer als nach ihrem innern Werthe ausgeführet werden. Zuweilen muß man aber doch die kurze Note der Eintheilung und des sehr geschwinden Zeitmaaßes wegen, nach ihrem innern Werthe aushalten [as at *c*], ist das Zeitmaaß mäßig, so werden die Baßnoten kürzer nachgeschlagen.

Schmeichelhafter Ausdruck und längere Noten machen auch hier Ausnahmen; folgende Stelle wird sowohl mit ganz aushaltenden Noten, als auch die kürzern Noten nach ihrem wahren Werthe, gespielt.[15]

Dotted notes such as those at *a* are to be performed as in *b*. In most cases the dot is to be regarded as a rest, and the following note is to be performed shorter than it should be according to its intrinsic worth. When the word *sostenuto* (sustained) appears over the whole piece or a portion of it, as in church music and overtures, which ought to express more earnestness than majesty, the dots are tenaciously held out, although the following notes are still performed shorter than according to their intrinsic value. But sometimes, on account of the disposition [of parts] and a very fast tempo, one must hold them according to their value [as at *c*]; but if the tempo is moderate, the bass notes [in *c*] are struck afterward, shorter [see first example].

Flattering expression and longer notes also constitute exceptions here: the following passage is played with fully sustained notes, while the short notes are also rendered according to their true value [see second example].

This advocacy of the 'galant' mannerism echoes several of C. P. E. Bach's qualifications concerning tempo, texture, and type of expression. But unlike Bach, Rellstab explicitly mentions the overdotting of overtures; while in his view the overture should convey more earnestness than majesty, he nonetheless links overdotting with bold and serious affect, as do Quantz, Kirnberger/Schulz, and (to some extent) C. P. E. Bach himself.

LEIPZIG

During the last thirty years of the eighteenth century, J. A. Hiller, a pupil of Homilius's in Dresden, became the most influential figure in the musical life of Leipzig. Although Hiller himself does not write about overdotting, three of his colleagues — Löhlein, Petschke, and Tromlitz — do advocate the practice. Influenced and supported by Hiller, Löhlein concentrated his career on teaching. His clavier treatise of 1765 and 1773, which is largely based on the precepts of C. P. E. Bach, recommends overdotting of both dotted eighths and dotted quarters (see also table 5-1):

Bey **Puncten**, wo kurze Noten drauf folgen, ist folgendes in Acht zu nehmen: man muß nämlich den Punct ohngefähr die Hälfte länger halten, als es der Schreibart nach seyn sollte. z. B.

Ein gleiches ist auch bey kurzen Pausen zu beobachten:[16]

Where **dots** are followed by short notes, the following is to be heeded: namely, one must hold the dot approximately half again longer than it should be according to the notation. E. g., [see first example]

Something similar is to be observed at short rests: [see second example]

Very little is known about A. F. Petschke, except that he spent his entire career in Leipzig; in any case, his keyboard tutor also provides a fairly broad prescription for overdotting. Having explained the traditional value of the dot, and double-dotted notation as well, Petschke observes:

> Punkte bei Noten werden insgemein länger gehalten, als es ihre Gel-
> tung erfodert, und die darauf folgenden kurzen Noten werden um soviel
> kürzer gemacht, nur im Adagio werden diese kurzen Noten nicht so kurz
> abgefertigt, man muß da mehr auf das unterhaltende denken.[17]

> Dots after notes are generally held longer than their value requires,
> and the short notes that follow are made proportionately shorter, except
> that in the Adagio these short notes are not dispatched so briefly — there
> one must be more concerned about the underlying [affect].

J. C. Tromlitz served as first flutist of Hiller's Grosses Konzert in Leipzig; he subsequently became well known as a soloist, then retired from the stage and devoted the latter years of his life to teaching. Tromlitz advocates double-dotting of dotted rhythms and Lombardic figures in fast and lively tempo, and suggests that in slow movements the rhythmic alteration be treated more gently than in quick ones.

> Alle diese Figuren werden beym geschwinden und lebhaften Satz so ge-
> spielet, als ob die Note mit dem Punkte, zwey Punkte hätte, damit die
> kurze recht kurz gemachet werden könne; oder man hält, wenn z. B.
> diese zwey Noten ein Viertel ausmachen, die erste beynahe so lange als
> ein ganzes Viertel aus, und in dem Augenblick, da sich das zweyte Viertel
> anfangen soll, läßt man die kurze nach vorhergegangener Regel hören, so
> wird man gewiß die gehörige Zeit, die beyden zukömmt, treffen. Eben
> dieses beobachtet man, wenn mehrere Noten hinter dem Punkte stehen,

außer daß man diese kurzen Noten nach dem Punkte nicht besonders anspricht, sondern sanft an die Note mit dem Punkte bindet; s. *n*)

ta_ a_a_ra_ a_a_ra_ a_a   ta_a_a_ra ta ta_a_a_ra ta

Beym langsamen Satz werden die ersten Noten zwar auch länger, und die kurzen kürzer gehalten, aber nicht so hart wie im geschwinden Satz, sondern sanfter und milder behandelt.[18]

All these [dotted] figures are played in a quick and lively movement as though the note with the dot had two dots, so that the short note can be made quite short; or if, for example, these two notes make up a quarter, one holds the first almost as long as an entire quarter, and in the moment where the second quarter ought to begin, one lets the short note sound according to the foregoing rule, one will certainly hit upon the proper time that belongs to both. One certainly observes this when there are several notes after the dot, except that one does not particularly address these short notes, but rather connects them gently to the note with the dot; see *n*). [see above]

In a slow movement, to be sure, the first notes are also held longer, and the short shorter; however, they are not treated so severely as in the quick movement, but rather more softly and gently.

Although Tromlitz seems chiefly concerned with the small note values of 'galant' overdotting, one of his examples includes dotted quarters as well.[19] Like the majority of German writers who treat of rhythmic alteration, Tromlitz makes no mention of French music or performance practice; but in other respects, his commentary on overdotting is largely congruent with that of Quantz, whose flute tutor he knew thoroughly.

HALLE

Given that overdotting was common at the Court of Frederick the Great, it is scarcely surprising that we should find traces of the practice in the Prussian city of Halle. G. F. Wolf first raises the issue in his singing tutor of 1784: after explaining both single and double dots, he observes that

die Note die einen Punkt neben sich hat, muß mit einiger Verstärkung ausgehalten, werden, und lieber zu lang als zu kurz; daher komt es, daß neuere Componisten zwei Punkte neben die Noten setzen, wo denn die Note mit den Punkten so lange als möglich ausgehalten und die drauf folgende ganz kurz abgefertiget werden muß.[20]

the note that has a dot next to it must be held out with a certain strengthening, and better too long than too short; from this it emerges that more modern composers place two dots next to the notes, whereby the note with the dots must be held as long as possible, and the following note dispatched very shortly.

Yet in the second edition of his clavier treatise, published in the same year, Wolf sides with Marpurg in demanding precise notation when 7:1 ratios are expected:

Man wil [sic] behaupten, daß bei kurzen Noten der Punkt ohngefähr die Hälfte länger müsse gehalten werden, als es der Schreibart nach sein solte; man müsse also einen Punkt so halten als ob zwei da stünden. So meint Löhlein in seiner Klavierschulen T.[eil] I. S. 67; das Gegentheil hiervon zeigt mit Recht Marpurg in seiner Anleitung zum Klavierspielen, S. 13. §. 14. — Wil also der Componist seine Stücke nicht durch einen ungeschickten Vortrag verderben lassen, so mus [sic] er schreiben, wie ers wil vorgetragen oder ausgeführt wissen.[21]

Some would assert that with short notes the dot ought to be held approximately half again as long as it should be according to the notation; thus one should hold a dot as though two were present. So says Löhlein in his *Keyboard Method*, pt. 1, p. 67; Marpurg rightly indicates the opposite of this in his *Introduction to Keyboard Playing*, p. 13, §14. — Thus, if the composer does not want his pieces spoiled by a bungling performance, he must write as he wants it executed or performed.

One of the most substantial and detailed accounts of overdotting appears in D. G. Türk's keyboard tutor of 1789: Türk, who was educated at the Kreuzschule in Dresden under Homilius and subsequently studied with Hiller in Leipzig, was active as a composer, violinist, conductor, keyboard player, and director of music at the University of Halle. As table 5-1 shows, Türk generally recommends the 'galant' strain of elongating dots worth less than one beat (one-half beat in slow tempo):

Man pflegt nämlich bey punktirten Noten größtentheils*) länger zu verweilen, (und also die folgenden kurzen Noten dafür geschwinder zu spielen,) als die Schreibart anzeigt. Z. B.

[Footnote:]*) Alle mögliche Fälle sind nicht zu bestimmen; indessen kann man hierbey als Regel annehmen, daß alsdann die Geltung des Punktes nicht verlängert wird, wenn die darnach folgende Note völlig die Dauer eines Takttheiles oder, in langsamer Bewegung, eines Taktgliedes hat....[22]

One is accustomed mostly*) to dwell longer on dotted notes (and thus to play the following short notes correspondingly quicker) than the notation indicates. For example: [see above]

[Footnote:]*) Not all possible cases can be determined; in the meanwhile one can hereby take it as a rule that the value of the dot is not lengthened when the note immediately following has fully the value of a beat, or, in slow tempo, of a division of the beat. ...

Although Türk's musical examples are notated at the rhythmic level of dotted eighths, his general rule as it stands also includes dotted quarters. Like C. P. E. Bach, whose clavier treatise he had studied years earlier, Türk is by no means doctrinaire in the application of overdotting, but rather emphasizes that various musical contexts require different approaches; a "singing" piece will need less rhythmic sharpening than a lively one, or an earnest or solemn one, such as an overture; on the other hand, the contrapuntal disposition of voices may require literal rendition of dotted values:

Die bey *b)* bemerkte Ausführung der punktirten Noten wählt man gewöhnlich, wenn der Charakter des Tonstückes ernsthaft, feyerlich, erhaben &c. ist; also nicht nur beym eigentlichen *Grave* selbst, sondern auch in Ouvertüren oder *sostenuto* überschriebenen Tonstücken u. dgl. Man trägt in deisem Falle die punktirten Noten schwer, folglich ausgehalten, vor. Bey dem Ausdrucke munterer, freudiger &c. Empfindungen muß der Vortrag etwas leichter seyn, ungefähr wie bey *c)*. Der Ausführung *d)* bedient man sich vorzüglich bey heftig, trotzig &c. vorzutragenden, oder *staccato* überschriebenen Tonstücken.*) Die Tasten werden stark angeschlagen, man hebt aber die Finger früher wieder ab, als bey solchen Stellen, welche mit einer gewissen feyerlichen Würde vorzutragen sind. Bey gefälligen singbaren &c. Gedanken, wie unten bey *e)*, verlängert man die punktirten Noten zwar ebenfalls ein wenig — wenn auch nicht eben so merklich —; doch werden sie sanfter (weniger accentuirt) vorgetragen. Besonders spielt man in solchen Fällen die kurzen Noten nach dem Punkte schwach und geschleift. Ist eine zweite Stimme, etwa wie bey *f)*, zu den punktirten Noten gesetzt, so bleibt man bey der vorgeschriebenen Eintheilung.[23]

One usually chooses the performance of dotted notes indicated at b) [see above] when the character of the composition is earnest, solemn, exalted, etc.; thus, not only in a *Grave* proper, but also in overtures or pieces marked *sostenuto,* and the like. In these cases one renders the dotted notes ponderously, and hence held out. In the expression of more lively, joyous, etc., feelings, the performance must be somewhat lighter, approximately as at c). One avails oneself of the performance at d) above all in pieces that are to be rendered vehemently, defiantly, etc., or are labeled *staccato.**) The keys are struck vigorously, but one lifts the fingers away again sooner than in such passages that are to be performed with a certain solemn dignity. For ideas that are pleasing, singable, etc., as at e) below [see above], one certainly also elongates the dotted notes — even if not so noticeably [as in the previous cases] — ; but they are performed more gently (less accented). In particular, one plays the short notes after the dots weakly and slurred in such cases. If a second voice is set against the dotted notes, perhaps as at f), then one adheres to the written-out distribution [of time].

In an intriguing footnote*) concerning Example d) in this paragraph, Türk mentions a case in which he deplores exaggerated articulation between dotted and short notes:

*) Aber äußerst schlecht und ganz wider den erforderlichen Ausdruck ist diese Art des Vortrages z. B. in dem Schlußchore aus Grauns Tod Jesu: Hier liegen wir gerührte Sünder &c. und doch hört man dieses vortreffliche Chor nicht selten so trotzig vortragen. —

*) But this sort of expression is extremely bad and entirely contrary to the required performance, for example, in the final chorus of [Carl Heinrich] Graun's *The Death of Jesus:* "Here we lie, sinners moved," etc., yet nevertheless one often hears this magnificent chorus performed defiantly [as at d above].

The beginning of this chorus is shown in example 6-2 (pp. 124–25). clearly the persistent dotting is suggestive of the singers' agitation. Yet for Türk, "defiantly" stressed articulation is the wrong approach for such a somber text. Apparently the dotted rhythms are still to be elongated — nothing in the note suggests otherwise; but the piece presents a problem of coordination that is taken up only in the next paragraph of the treatise.

Türk is one of the few treatise writers to discuss the practice of synchronization — adjusting superimposed dotted rhythms in various parts so that they coincide at the smallest level of rhythmic value present:

Hin und wieder verlängert man bey mehrstimmigen Stellen die punktirten Noten nur in Einer Stimme, und spielt die kurzen Noten beyder Stimmen zu gleicher Zeit, damit das Ganze mehr überein stimme. Z. B.[24]

EXAMPLE 6-2.   C. H. Graun, *Der Tod Jesu* (1755), final chorus (ed. Howard Serwer).

Occasionally in polyphonic passages one elongates the dotted notes in one part and plays the short notes of both parts at the same time, so that the whole coincides more. E. g.: [see above]

Like Löhlein, Türk favors the contraction of short pickups after rests that take the place of dots; his discussion of Lombardic rhythms advocates the same sort of moderation that C. P. E. Bach had suggested:

EXAMPLE 6–2   *continued*

[etc.]

Auch die kurzen Pausen, welche die Stelle der Punkte vertreten, werden in Tonstücken von lebhaftem &c. Charakter oft verlängert, wie hier bey *b*).

Allegro con spirito.

Die Figuren, wo die erste Note kurz und die zweite punktirt ist, werden ohne Ausnahme geschleift und größtentheils schmeichelnd vorgetragen. Den ersten (kurzen) Ton accentuirt man zwar, doch darf der Nachdruck nur sehr gelinde seyn.

Man übereile sich, besonders in langsamer Bewegung, bey der ersten
Note nicht; denn der Gesang kann leicht in das Freche ausarten, oder die
erforderliche Ründung verlieren, wenn man den ersten Ton zu kurz an-
giebt, und den Punkt wohl noch überdies in eine hier fehlerhafte Pause
verwandelt, wie bey b).[25]

Short rests that take the place of dots are also frequently elongated in
pieces whose character is lively, etc., as at b): [in the Allegro con spirito
example]

Figures in which the first note is short and the second is dotted are
without exception slurred, and for the most part performed flatteringly.
Of course one accents the first (short) note, but the emphasis should be
only very gentle. [see "Lombardic" example above]

Especially in slow tempo, one should not be in too great a hurry with
the first note; for the song can easily degenerate into insolence, or lose
the requisite roundness, if one renders the first note too short and, moreover, transforms the dot into a rest, which is here incorrect, as at b).

Later in the treatise Türk provides a description of the overture that
is well worth citing in full:

Ouvertüre (Intrade, Einleitung) heißt ein aus zwey oder drey Sätzen be-
stehendes Instrumentalstück, welches zur Eröffnung einer grossen Musik z. b. eines Oratoriums, einer Oper u. gebracht wird. Die Ouvertüre muß
viel Pracht, Größe und Mannigfaltigkeit haben, vorzüglich soll sie dem
Hauptcharacter der folgenden Musik entsprechen. Ehedem wählte man
zum ersten Satze einer Ouvertüre gewöhnlich ein Tonstück von ernsthaft feyerlichem Charakter, mit vielen punktirten Noten, alsdann folgte
eine gut gearbeitete Fuge, und nach dieser wohl noch ein etwas munterer
oder dem ersten ähnlicher Satz. Allein in den neuern Werken findet man
wenige Ouvertüren von dieser Art. Doch haben **Schweizer** (zur Alceste)
und **Rolle** (zum Lazarus u.) solche Ouvertüren geschrieben.[26]

Overture (Intrada, Introduction) means an instrumental piece consisting
of two or three movements, which is used for the opening of a large
musical work, for example an oratorio, an opera, etc. The overture must
have much majesty [*Pracht*], grandeur, and diversity, and above all it
should correspond to the main character of the following music. Here-
tofore one usually chose as the first movement of an overture a piece of
earnestly solemn character, with many dotted notes; then followed a
well worked-out fugue, and after this a somewhat cheerier movement, or
else one more similar to the first movement. Only in more modern works
does one find few overtures of this sort. But **Schweizer** (for *Alceste*) and
Rolle (for *Lazarus*, etc.) have written such overtures.

This is very similar to what Scheibe, Kirnberger/Schulz, Rellstab, and
Quantz wrote; in particular, one notes again that the slow introduction is

FIGURE 6-1.   A. Schweitzer, Overture to *Alceste* (1773).

Vienna, Österreichische Nationalbibliothek, Musiksammlung, Mus. Hs. 16.152; reproduced by permission.

associated with majesty, solemnity, and grandeur. But most interesting is Türk's reference to the overtures by Anton Schweitzer (1773) and J. H. Rolle (1778), reproduced as figures 6-1 and 6-2 respectively. Schweitzer had traveled widely in northern Germany and was employed at Weimar by Seyler's company when his opera *Alceste* was produced. Rolle had served seven years (1741–47) as a violinist in the orchestra of Frederick the Great, where he came to know the Grauns, Bendas, and C. P. E. Bach. Thereafter he became organist and then director of music in Magdeburg, where he wrote more than two dozen oratorios that made him famous throughout Germany. According to Türk's accounts, the Grave openings of these overtures should be overdotted, just as Quantz or Graun would have played them nearly fifty years earlier. As it happens, most of the dotted notes in these particular examples are eighths or sixteenths; yet the viola part of the Schweitzer overture contains the characteristic

FIGURE 6-2. J. H. Rolle, Overture to *Lazarus* (1778), piano reduction (Leipzig, 1779).

Reproduced through courtesy of the Library of Congress, Washington, D.C.

dotted-quarter–eighth pattern, which, according to Türk's comments on synchronization (see above), would need to be crispened to coincide with the upper voices.[27]

AUSTRIA AND FRANCE

In 1788 Franz Anton Schlegel, about whom little is known, published in Graz an abridged and modified version of Quantz's *Versuch*. Schlegel's volume contains two passages on overdotting;[28] the first of these, which concerns crispening small values (dotted eighths and sixteenths) and

Lombardic rhythms, is a slightly condensed version of what Quantz had written in chapter V, §§21 and 23 (cf. table 5-1). The second reproduces Quantz's commentary in XII/24 about the effect of Majesty (*das Prächtige*; cf. table 5-1 and pp. 91–92 above). Schlegel omits Quantz's discussion of French dance music as well as his advocacy of *notes iné-gales*, which were probably of relatively little significance for Austrian musical style of the late 1780s.

We have already noted that the French version of Leopold Mozart's treatise first appeared in 1770; nearly thirty years later Antoine Bailleux's violin method advocates the overdotting of dotted eighths in a simple marchlike piece:

> Quand une mesure est composée de quatre notes dont la première et la troisième sont pointées on les exprimes détachées chacune de son coup d'archet particulier, de façon que la double croche doit être passée très vivement et un peu plus tard qu'a l'ordinaire.[29]

> When a measure is composed of four notes of which the first and the third are dotted, one conveys them detached, each with its own bow stroke, in such a way that the sixteenth must be passed very quickly and a little later than is usual.

Perhaps Bailleux was responding to Mozart's instructions; but in any case, this source, published well after the Revolution, is probably of little relevance for music of the *ancien régime*.

ENGLAND: THE "HANDEL TRADITION"

It has long been alleged that in the British Isles a continuous tradition of performing Handel's music extends back to the composer himself, and that overdotting, especially in the openings of Handel's overtures, is central to that tradition. Watkins Shaw and Donington took this position, which has been argued more recently (and with qualifications) by Pont and Best.[30] Neumann, on the other hand, has raised several objections: chief among these is the fact that performance of Handel's music did indeed change radically during the eighteenth, nineteenth, and twentieth centuries. As early as the 1784 Handel centenary celebrations in Westminster Abbey, his oratorios were presented with more than five hundred performers — nearly ten times the number Handel himself ever used — and such colossal casts become customary whenever possible. There is also persuasive evidence that as the forces expanded, the tempos slowed; and it is only reasonable to assume that many other aspects of whatever performance traditions may have survived from Handel's day were lost in such renditions.[31]

But this does not eliminate the possibility that Handel, like other north Germans, overdotted his overtures. From about 1701 to 1703, while still a student in Halle, he was on close terms with Telemann (then in Leipzig), who was already well versed in French style. And during 1719 Handel spent several months in Dresden; thus he had ample opportunity to become familiar with French overtures and their performance. The year after Handel's death, Mainwaring reports the famous anecdote about Handel's rehearsing his overtures in Rome with Corelli as a concertmaster (ca. 1707):

> Corelli himself complained of the difficulty he found in playing his [Handel's] Overtures. Indeed there was in the whole cast of these compositions, but especially in the opening of them, such a degree of fire and force, as never could consort with the mild graces, and placid elegancies of a genius so totally dissimilar. Several fruitless attempts HANDEL had one day made to instruct him in the manner of executing these spirited passages. Piqued at the tameness with which he still played them, he snatched the instrument out of his hand; and, to convince him how little he understood them, played the passages himself. . . . [Corelli] ingenuously declared that he did not understand them; *i.e.* knew not how to execute them properly, and give them the strength and expression they required. When HANDEL appeared impatient, *Ma, caro Sassone* (said he) *questa Musica è nel stylo Francese, di ch' io non m'intendo.*[32]

This is striking information from several angles (and it seems apparent that it came from Handel himself, perhaps via J. C. Smith). It will be recalled that Scheibe and Kirnberger/Schulz also underscore the "fiery" character of the overture's opening (see above, pp. 97 and 113). The *stylo Francese* that Corelli professed not to understand would have involved well articulated bow strokes with frequent retaking of the bow, and very likely some measure of overdotting, as we have seen: the French themselves elongated their dots in proportion to the prevailing degree of inequality; Quantz recommends overdotting for French dance music and (apparently) overtures; and several later German writers advocate overdotting in the opening of a French overture.

But there is more to the story. In a footnote Mainwaring singles out one particular overture, as follows: "The Overture for IL TRIONFO DEL TEMPO [1707] was that which occasioned CORELLI the greatest difficulty. At his [Corelli's] desire therefore he [Handel] made a symphony in the room of it, more in the Italian style." And as Terence Best has shown, this is indeed what happened: the "Sonata del Overtura" in the autograph of *Il trionfo* is a three-part Italian sinfonia whose opening quick section is based on the fugue subject from the original French overture.[33] If Corelli could understand this sinfonia, he could certainly have managed the original fugue; thus it must have been the introduction to the French overture, shown in example 6-3, which occasioned the difficulty. As in many such works, the conjunct eighths are dotted: for the French, who typically write their introductions in 2 or ¢, this is the rhythmic level of *notes inégales*, whereby dotted quarters are lengthened in proportion to the inequality. According to Mainwaring, Corelli declared "ingenuously" that he did not understand how to play a French overture, and the adverb is apt: Corelli had written at least one French overture, complete with notated overdotting, which is found in his Opus 3 trio sonatas of 1689 – a collection Handel may well have known in 1707 (see example 6-4); moreovor, Corelli would draw upon the overture style to open three of his concerti grossi (Op. 6, nos. 3, 7, and 9). Evidently, then, the great Itallau master knew about the French overture: to claim he did not "understand" it suggests either that he was not fond of such music, or that he insisted on more precise notation of the intended rhythmic execution. Thus, Corelli may have been among the first to argue about French rhythmic alteration.[34]

The most notable evidence that Handel may have overdotted his overtures is found in sundry keyboard arrangements of them dating from the 1720s through the 1830s: the earliest, some of which are Handel's own, are found in manuscripts (ca. 1717–46) and Walsh prints (1726–47, and variously reprinted throughout the eighteenth century).[35] Later sources include a reissued Walsh print purportedly annotated by the English harpsichordist and composer Jonathan Battishill (ca. 1785), as well

EXAMPLE 6-3.   Handel, opening of Overture in B flat, HWV 336 (originally the
overture to *Il trionfo del tempo,* 1707) (ed. Best).

Reprinted by permission of Baerenreiter Music Corporation.

as published arrangements by J. Mazzinghi (ca. 1811), William Crotch (ca.
1815), and John Watts (ca. 1830).[36] Pont's detailed discussions of these
materials permit a rather summary treatment of them here; and because
the authority of the nineteenth-century versions by Mazzinghi, Crotch,
and Watts is doubtful at best, we shall be concerned only with the earlier
arrangements.

   Although dozens of Handel overtures were transcribed for keyboard
during the eighteenth century, Best has shown that probably only twenty
such arrangements were done by Handel himself. Several of these contain
sporadic, inconsistent notated overdotting not found in the orchestral
originals—while this is insufficient evidence to establish a general performance custom, it is suggestive nonetheless. The most persuasive cases
are the introductions to the overtures in *Alessandro* and *Lotario,* in
which just over half of the dotted quarters have been elongated to 7:1
ratios in the keyboard versions: given this hint, the performer could
readily alter the others if this were the custom. (Example 6-5a shows the
opening measures of *Alessandro* in orchestral score, while 6-5b presents
the same measures from the harpsichord arrangement, probably by Handel, that Walsh first published ca. 1728.)

   As we have seen, the keyboard treatises of Türk and Rellstab advocate
the orchestral practice of overdotting overtures—and presumably the keyboard player is to imitate the orchestral custom in performing transcriptions of overtures. It would appear that J. S. Bach adopted this convention
in the revision of BWV 831; perhaps Handel was also attempting to spell
out overdotting in his arrangements of the *Alessandro* and *Lotario* overtures. Yet the other instances of rhythmic alteration that crop up in these

EXAMPLE 6-4. Corelli, Op. 3, No. 10, 1st mvt., (a) mm. 1–5, (b) mm. 10–16 (ed. Joachim and Chrysander).

EXAMPLE 6-5.   Handel, Overture to *Alessandro*, (a) orchestral version (ed. Chrysander), (b) keyboard arrangement (Walsh, ca. 1728, ed. Best).

transcriptions are considerably less compelling; moreover, as Best, Pont, and Neumann have argued, in some cases the inconsistent notation of dotted rhythms may be intentional: like the numerous French harpsichord arrangements of Lully overtures, dances, and airs, these Handel overtures for keyboard contain much that is idiomatically conceived for the instrument. And as Neumann has pointed out, a great many sources containing transcriptions of Handel overtures, including those in the hand of Handel's copyist J. C. Smith, contain no rhythmic alteration whatever.[37]

Sixty-five keyboard arrangements of Handel overtures were reissued by Wright from Walsh plates in about 1785: a copy of this set, now in the Hamburg Staats- und Universitätsbibliothek, contains the following inscription: "N. B.—The additional notes and alterations to many in this Collection of Overtures, are by the pen of John Battishill, intending thereby to instruct his pupils how Handel (whom he had many times heard) rendered the playing of them." Twenty-five of these pieces begin with a broad French-style introduction, and Battishill has edited eleven of them to show overdotting, contraction of upbeats, and sharpening of iambic figures (⁷ ♩♩♩ becomes ⁷ ♩♩♩). These rhythmic alterations are not carried out consistently;[38] yet they are sufficiently frequent to suggest that Battishill was probably introducing his students to a custom of performance: like many teachers' markings today, these are almost certainly not complete, but would have been supplemented by verbal instruction and demonstrations at the keyboard. Figure 6-3 shows Battishill's editing of the overture to *Partenope*, while figure 6-4 reproduces an unmarked copy of the Wright print (according to Best, the keyboard arrangement is probably Handel's own).

It seems unlikely that Battishill's markings constitute precise notation of Handel's playing. These annotations were evidently written down no earlier than ca. 1785;[39] when Handel died in 1759, Battishill was only twenty-one years old, and he was merely fifteen when Handel became blind in 1753. Although Handel would occasionally perform an organ concerto from memory during his last six years, it seems improbable that Battishill could have heard him play eleven different overtures at the keyboard, especially in arrangements that Handel himself did not write.[40] And while Battishill's memory is reputed to have been exceptional, he was also severely alcoholic, which can only have impaired his faculties. All things considered, Battishill's annotations of Handel overtures probably represent the teaching of a fine musician who may have been generally familiar with Handel's playing; at the very least, they document rhythmic alterations of French overtures by an English composer, con-

FIGURE 6-3. Handel, Overture to *Partenope*, keyboard arrangement (London: H. Wright [ca. 1785]), with annotations by Jonathan Battishill.

Reproduced through courtesy of the Hamburg Stadt- und Universitätsbibliothek.

ductor, and harpsichordist who was an active professional from about 1756 to 1780.

But another documentary source shows that overdotting in Handel was not universally practiced in late eighteenth-century England: this is the barrel organ built by Holland, ca. 1790, and now in the Colt Collection, Kent, England. Two Handel concertos, Op. 4, Nos. 2 and 5, are among its repertoire, and the opening of No. 2, written in the style of an

FIGURE 6-4.   Handel, Overture to *Partenope*, keyboard arrangement (London: H. Wright [ca. 1785])

Reproduced through courtesy of The Fitzwilliam Museum.

entrée, would be a prime candidate for overdotting (see example 6-6). But although the pinning provides for a good deal of *silence d'articulation*, it does not perceptibly alter the ratio of the dotted notes.[41] As to the significance of this source, Fuller has observed that "for the moment one dare not say more than that this instrument plays in the style of Holland, Organ builder";[42] if overdotting were part of the "Handel tradition," Holland apparently did not know of it.

EXAMPLE 6-6.   Handel, Organ Concerto Op. 4, No. 2, as performed by the Holland barrel organ in the Colt Collection; ed. David Fuller in *G. F. Handel, Two Ornamented Organ Concertos.*

[etc.]

Still, the 1770 harpsichord tutor by Robert Falkener, a London publisher and instrument dealer, suggests that the 'galant' type of overdotting had made its way to England:

> You must take Notice; the Third Bar consists of Notes of this kind which must be played in the following manner, *viz.* touch the Semiquavers as quick; or make it as short as you possibly can, and stay upon the dotted Quaver as long as the Time will permit you; . . . and in playing these kind of Notes, you   must make the dotted Quaver as long as the time will permit, and the Semiquaver as short, which you will find to be the reverse of these Notes   of which you had an example in the last Tune. . . .[43]

The later accounts of overdotting, written after the influential treatises of Quantz, Bach, and Mozart, indicate that 'galant' elongation of relatively small notes (dotted eighths and lesser values) was widespread in northern Germany, and was also known to well-read musicians in Austria, Bavaria, and Holland; vestiges of the practice have surfaced from England and France as well. Kirnberger and Schulz, the most historically oriented of the German writers, advocate the 'French' strain of overdotting for the loure and the French overture, tracing the development of the latter genre from Lully through Telemann, Handel, and Bach. As late as 1789 Türk observes that although French overtures are uncommon in "more modern works," when they do occur (as in music by Schweitzer and Rolle) they are to be overdotted. And the following year (1790) Rellstab notes that "the dots are strongly held out" in overtures, confirming that the tradition of 'French' overdotting was still known in Berlin. Certain qualifications notwithstanding, these accounts are largely concordant with all or part of what Quantz and C. P. E. Bach had written, nearly forty years earlier than Rellstab.

The interconnections among the most important authors concerning overdotting are summed up in table 6-1. Treatise publications are printed boldface in this table; a solid line with an arrow indicates the influence of one treatise upon another. Teacher-student relationships are shown with broken lines, and geographical or collegial ties are indicated with dotted lines.

TABLE 6-1. Connections among the Principal Sources on Overdotting.

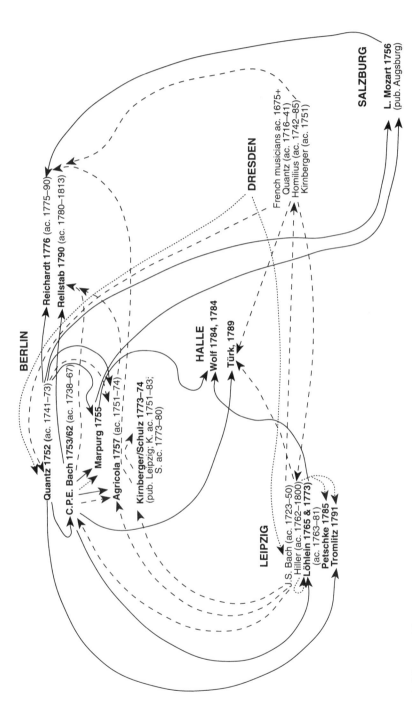

boldface = publication; ———— = geographical or collegial relationship; ·········· = influence of writings; – – – = teacher-student relationship; ac. = active

CHAPTER SEVEN

Summary Observations

In the preceding chapters we have critically examined documentary evidence concerning two significant (and controversial) practices of rhythmic alteration in seventeenth- and eighteenth-century music. Owing to the mass of data on these topics, our investigation has paid but scant attention to the interrelated matters of tempo, articulation, dynamic nuance, etc. In this brief closing section, I shall review what the foregoing information seems to imply, occasionally drawing on my twenty years' experience of performing baroque music on period instruments. Much that seems obscure in words becomes clear in the reconstructive process of interpreting old music: the effort to reestablish the *modi operandi* of seventeenth- and eighteenth-century musicians has taught us a good deal about what would then have been practicable, and what would not. In most types of ensemble music, all musicians must closely follow and imitate the leader (usually the first violinist), who ordinarily plays with the group: the result is that even a sizable orchestra functions essentially like a chamber ensemble. Quantz's discussion of ensemble leadership extends to thirteen paragraphs, wherein he recommends that the leader be a violinist, and stresses that he must develop and maintain uniform execution in the orchestra.[1] And J. S. Bach led his performers from the violin until the onset of old age, "and thus kept the orchestra in better order than he could have done with the harpsichord."[2] The violinist-leader is more effectual in guiding the playing of his colleagues (especially the string players) than a modern conductor can be. And the example set by his playing is more influential than the silent notes on the page.

Notes Inégales

While the custom of *notes inégales* will continue to pose problems in particular works and passages, on the whole it should not occasion major difficulties. The essential characteristics of French practice with respect to meter, conjunct motion, etc., are generally clear from about 1690 until the Revolution, as summarized in tables 1-1 and 1-2. And it is reasonable to suppose, on the basis of Muffat's testimony, that the rules distilled by the treatise writers largely reflect Lullian practice in the performance of opera and ballet. Today's performers can readily develop their taste by applying these precepts first to simple dances and characteristic airs, then gradually progressing to more refined and complex repertoire. The earlier French writings, from about 1660 to 1690, suggest that both vocal and instrumental soloists may have treated inequality more arbitrarily than the later, more formulaic tutors prescribe. And while such liberties were presumably the soloist's prerogative throughout the eighteenth century as well, the extensive evidence about *notes inégales* from ca. 1690 to 1790 indicates the practice was so well established in France that substantial deviation would indeed be exceptional.

To judge from the sources, French inequality was applied to passages moving predominantly in conjunct motion, and was virtually always trochaic (long–short). It was generally restricted to the half beat in triple time, and the fourth of a beat in duple time, eighths in meters **3** and **2** being the most commonly affected values (see tables 1-1 and 1-2). But as Saint-Lambert points out, taste provides "the freedom that musicians give themselves to transgress their own rules," and we have seen hints that all of these strictures were occasionally disregarded. Apparently the degree of rhythmic alteration was generally mild (probably 2:1 or less). But gradations from an almost imperceptible lilt up to a marked ratio of 3:1 are certainly possible; as Engramelle observes, a gay or vigorous piece needs more marked inequality than a gracious or tender one. Staccato articulation is largely incompatible with inequality, which "slurs the song and renders it more flowing," as Choquel puts it.[3] Soloists (particularly harpsichordists) can be intriguingly subtle in varying their *notes inégales,* but the larger the ensemble, the more likely that a consistent degree of alteration must needs prevail.

In practice, tempo is a limiting factor in ensemble music, particularly for string players; accordingly, a brief excursus may be in order. There is persuasive evidence that French overtures and dances were, on the whole, taken faster than many twentieth-century interpreters have played them.[4] According to writers such as L'Affilard, Pajot (Count D'Onzembray), Choquel, and Quantz, a courante, for example, should move in the vicinity of M.M. 80–90 to the beat; a gavotte should be taken somewhere between 97 and 152 to the half note; and the beat of a gigue should be about 100 to 120, perhaps even as fast as 160. Such tempo indications raise many issues that cannot be taken up here.[5] But my point is a fairly simple one: in ensemble playing, relatively quick speeds put practical limitations on the extent to which rhythmic alterations are performed — and perceived. Quick pieces seem to fall into natural patterns of inequality and concomitant overdotting, and the faster the pace, the less the listener is specifically aware of these features. In other words, for a substantial portion of the repertoire that calls for rhythmic alteration, the margin of variation is, practically speaking, not large; the altered rhythms should (and do) happen naturally (or not at all).[6] Very subtle inequality can be brought off only at a relatively moderate pace, while a stronger ratio of roughly 2:1 is manageable in quicker pieces. But at a certain point (particularly when sixteenth notes predominate), the bowing becomes too awkward for string players to project much more than the ordinary stress that distinguishes "good" and "bad" notes, and down-bow from up-. (See also below, p. 148–49.) Because a great deal of seventeenth- and eighteenth-century music is directly or indirectly related to the steps and gestures of French dancing, the ability to dance, even if only rudimentarily, is an indispensable point of reference in performing such repertoire, especially as regards tempo, accentuation, articulation, and phrasing. Needless to say, inequality that clashes with the elegant pulse of *demi-coupé* and *pas de bourée* is almost certainly inappropriate.

The relationship between *inégalité* and dotted notation at the same rhythmic level, although theoretically distinct according to several sources, remains problematic. Perplexing situations crop up in music ranging from Gigault and Muffat to Couperin, Rameau, and beyond; as late as 1782 Marcou noted that "among people of the art . . . there is not perfect agreement on this matter."[7] Just one case out of hundreds is shown in example 7-1, from *Les nations* by François Couperin. In the opening of this movement (7-1a), it would seem to me that the dotted notation in the second measure suggests a sharper rhythmic ratio than the eighth notes (*croches blanches*) in the third; these eighths, though notated equally, would customarily be rendered as *notes inégales*, and I like them played languidly, in a ratio perceptibly less than 2:1. Sixteen measures later in the same piece, however, we encounter (unequal) eighths above dotted eighths and sixteenths, as shown in example 7-1b (mm. 20–21). Earlier we noted at least one piece by Couperin—"La Raphaéle," example 2-10—in which he apparently distinguishes inequality from dotting. In this particular passage of "La piemontoise," however, I find it both fussy and unnatural to stress the difference in notation between bass and *dessus*; here, as in example 2-11 (Monteclair), synchronization seems appropriate. But others may prefer a different approach; the treatises provide no clear-cut guidelines for such problems, and individual cases must be decided with respect to the nature of the piece and the composer's habits of notation.

We have seen ample evidence that well-informed musicians in Germany, the Netherlands, and England must have known about *notes inégales;* unfortunately, to what extent they applied it is scarcely docu-

EXAMPLE 7-1.   François Couperin, *Les nations*, "La piemontoise" (1726), opening mvt., (a) mm. 1–4; (b) mm. 17–21.

mented. But the custom is French in origin, and today's performer who is thoroughly steeped in French music is not likely to commit serious *faux pas*. Telemann and J. S. Bach, as we have noted, were well acquainted with French style from early in their careers. A piece such as the first courante in Bach's A-major "English" Suite (BWV 806), for example, is so characteristically French that unequal eighths seem both natural and appropriate (see example 7-2). The courante of the C-major orchestral suite (BWV 1066) is a similar case, for larger forces (example 7-3).[8] On the other hand, many passages of intricate polyphony in Bach's so-called "French" Suites (BWV 812–17) for keyboard could hardly have been written in Paris, and several movements in that collection do not resemble French models: here circumspection would seem advisable. Then again, if the trio sonata from the *Musical Offering* (BWV 1079) was ever actually played at the Court of Frederick the Great, chances are Quantz (or the king) rendered it with *notes inégales* (e.g., the frequently recurring figure in m. 3 of the violin part, shown in example 7-4). But this work is far removed from French style, and we cannot assume that royal Prussian taste in performance always coincided with that of "old Bach." Here

EXAMPLE 7-2. J. S. Bach, "English" Suite No. 1 in A, BWV 806, first courante, opening (*BG*).

[etc.]

EXAMPLE 7-3. J. S. Bach, Orchestral Suite in C, BWV 1066, courante, opening (*BG*).

[etc.]

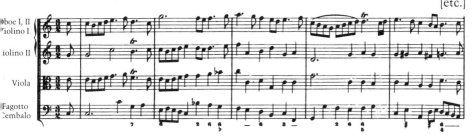

again, extensive familiarity with inequality in French music would seem to be the key—rather like accent in a language, *passer les croches* fits readily with pieces in appropriate style, and less well with others.

OVERDOTTING

Overdotting is not a delusion, as Neumann has claimed. But neither is the "French Overture style one of our best-attested conventions of baroque interpretation," as Donington would have it; and Dart's sweeping advocacy of overdotting from Monteverdi through Beethoven extends well beyond what the sources support.[9] Let us review first the more problematic 'French' strain of elongating dots in overtures and dances. There can be no question that overdotting did occur hand in hand with *notes inégales:* the degree of inequality determined the extent to which the dotted

EXAMPLE 7-4.   J. S. Bach, *Musical Offering*, BWV 1079, trio sonata, opening (*BG*).

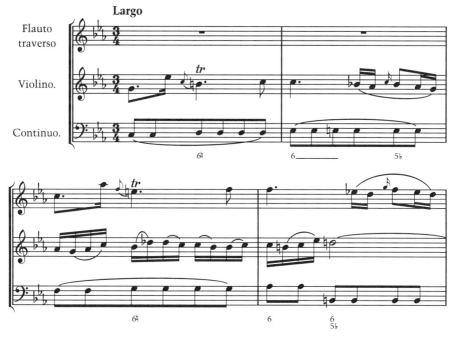

notes at the next higher rhythmic level were elongated. For Morel de Lescer (ca. 1760), this amounts to double-dotting quarters when eighths are unequal; but just as relatively mild inequality is an option, so too is less pronounced overdotting. Another passage from the opening *gravement* of Couperin's "La piemontoise" provides a case in point (example 7-5); if here, as I have suggested, the inequality is mild, so too will be the overdotting in the second *dessus* part (mm. 25–27).

According to Hotteterre (1738), one overdots in proportion to inequality even in a one-part piece, which would not require synchronization with other voices. Not surprisingly, this evidence is congruent with what we learn from experience in performance. To be sure, *notes inégales* and concomitant overdotting are easily achieved in ensembles both large and small: for example, in a piece in **3** the leader establishes the degree of inequality for the eighths, and players with dotted quarters lengthen them proportionately. But in any given bar, the dotted-quarter players do not wait to hear whether unequal eighths will actually be present: they simply overdot according to the expected degree of inequality. Hesitancy results in ragged ensemble: in Lully's band, such imprecision could win the offender a violin over the head.

It seems very probable that in just this way overdotting became a performance mannerism in its own right—an outgrowth of *notes in-*

EXAMPLE 7-5.   Couperin, "La piemontoise," first mvt., mm. 23–30.

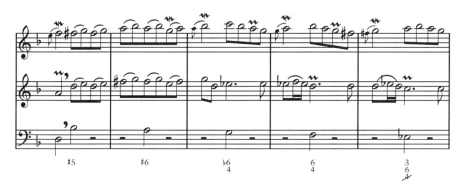

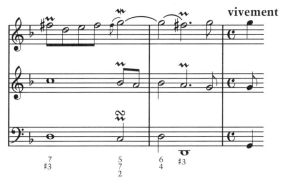

égales, yet no longer entirely dependent on that custom. Scattered bits of evidence from the Menetou manuscript (post-1689), Monteclair (1709 and 1736), and Roger North (1728) hint at this. As outlined above (pp. 40–61), acquaintance with French performance practices must have been considerably more extensive in northern Europe than has generally been supposed—particularly in Germany, but also in the Netherlands, England, and islands of northern Italy. In Berlin, Quantz (1752), describing practices that date from Dresden in the 1730s, writes as though overdotting were a matter of course in French dances, and (apparently) in the slow sections of French overtures as well; yet he does not link this practice to *notes inégales,* with which he was clearly familiar. To be sure, Quantz is the first writer who explicitly recommends contracting upbeat figures in overtures (although Muffat seems to hint at the practice). J. S. Bach rewrote the keyboard overture BWV 831 (1735) to include a good deal of both overdotting and contraction of upbeats. Kirnberger (a Bach pupil) and his collaborator J. A. P. Schulz were collectively familiar with musical style in Paris, Dresden, Berlin and *chez* J. S. Bach; they advocate (1771–74) overdotting of overtures and loures and upbeat contraction in overtures;

like Quantz, they draw attention to the majestic character of such pieces – and also like Quantz, they make no connection between overdotting and *notes inégales*. Türk (1789), who studied in Dresden and Leipzig, and Rellstab (1790), a product of the Berlin school, prescribe overdotting for the overture as well; yet again, neither mentions French *inégalité*. Thus there is reason to suppose that 'French' overdotting, originally concomitant with *notes inégales*, had become something of a separate custom. If, as the evidence indicates, Telemann, the Grauns, Fasch the elder, Rolle, Schweizer, and at least occasionally J. S. Bach were overdotting the main notes and contracting *roulades* in their overtures, it is likely that Handel knew of the custom as well. Overdotting is probably what brought about his argument with Corelli in 1707, and what is partially preserved in Battishill's inconsistently annotated copy of Handel overtures arranged for keyboard. Still, such rhythmic alteration was not universal: the organist J. G. Preller in Dortmund clearly did not know of it when he copied out Bach's overture BWV 831a; nor did Holland, builder of the Colt barrel organ, when he pinned Handel's Op. 4, No. 2 (see examples 5-3 and 6-6).

Today's performer must first consider what a work gains (or loses) through overdotting. Generally speaking, eighteenth-century sources regard it as a procedure that enlivens or invigorates. North associates the starts and leaps of an entrée with "the rage of an angry person"; for Quantz, overdotting is linked with liveliness or animation (*Lebhaftigkeit*) and boldness, plus sharp attacks on the long notes followed by very short little notes, and also with the more general affects of the majestic and sublime. C. P. E. Bach remarks that such rhythmic alteration yields "characteristic defiance," and observes that a flattering affect will not tolerate it; Rellstab says much the same thirty years later. Leopold Mozart (1756) also indicates that overdotting enlivens, and observes that slow pieces become too sleepy without it. For Kirnberger and Schulz, elongating dots in an overture is associated with the majestic, fiery, and yet serious character of the piece. Of course such characteristics are not achieved merely by rhythmic alteration: tempo, articulation, treatment of ornaments, and accentuation all contribute at least as much, and one can have a fairly fiery, majestic overture with no actual alteration of rhythmic ratios. Yet the evidence of overdotting is sufficiently widespread, both geographically and chronologically, that it must be considered an option for the performance of overtures and dances.

As in the execution of *notes inégales*, the feasibility and expressive impact of overdotting depends on the tempo of the music. Only one authentic tempo has been recorded for the opening of a French overture: Pajot's timing of ♩ = 64 for the overture to Collasse's *Thetis et Pélée* of

EXAMPLE 7-6.   Pascal Collasse, Overture to *Thetis et Pélée* (1689), opening.

1689 (example 7-6). (Not surprisingly, this tempo is nearly that given by de-La Chapelle — ♩ = 69 — for the entrée, which is closely related to the first section of the French overture.) Overdotting is certainly possible at this pace, but the extent of it depends upon the inequality of the eighth notes, which will probably emerge as approximately 2:1 in performance; consequently, the ratio between (over-)dotted quarters and eighths will be about 5:1.[10] On the other hand, in slower movements, more variety is possible; while a French sarabande may call for great subtlety, the over-dotting of a loure might be notably more pronounced.

Other important considerations are the precision of the composer's notation and the practicality of altering it in performance, particularly for ensemble pieces. J. S. Bach, for example, was known for relatively precise notation (although he too penned errors and inconsistencies); in the case of the keyboard overture BWV 831 he apparently took the trouble to notate the performance mannerism of overdotting before sending the work to press. Among his other works, the French-overture opening cho-rus of "Nun komm, der Heiden Heiland" (BWV 61) can be easily and effectively overdotted (example 7-7): the voices are confined to the cho-rale, and the strings and continuo can readily manage the alterations. Overdotting also works well in the overture to the B minor suite for flute and strings (BWV 1067). But the opening of the C-major orchestral suite (BWV 1066) is quite a different matter; unlike most French overtures, this one has flowing sixteenths running through two and three consecutive beats. It is exceedingly unlikely that Bach could have achieved the sort of rhythmic alteration advocated by John O'Donnell (see example 7-8b, p. 151) without heavily editing the parts.[11] The players could not know which sixteenths to contract and which to leave intact; even today's best early-music ensembles would have to resort to rewriting the rhythms. Such editing has not come to light in any of Bach's performance parts, or to any significant extent in the works of other composers. Moreover, no eighteenth-century source speaks of contracted sixteenths in a situation such as this — rather, to paraphrase C. P. E. Bach, it is a case where the

EXAMPLE 7-7. J. S. Bach, "Nun komm, der Heiden Heiland," BWV 61, opening
(*BG*).

disposition of parts requires precise rendition. And we know that in
Leipzig, where Bach *père* certainly performed the C-major overture, he
often had little rehearsal time and less than ideal performers; it is scarcely
imaginable that he would spend precious resources on such a convoluted
mode of performance when, had he wanted the "altered" rhythms, he
could have achieved them much more efficiently through more precise
notation in the new set of parts copied in Leipzig.[12]

The historically justified rule of thumb is that if an ensemble of
musicians familiar with the instruments and playing style of the period
cannot quickly absorb rhythmic alterations by following the leader, the
mannerism should be reconsidered, and probably dropped. The majority
of simple dance pieces and overtures, such as Lully's and Muffat's, pose
few difficulties; more complex works frequently present thornier problems.

If we accept that the renowned precision of ensembles such as those
in Paris and Dresden was considered exemplary, then the sort of sporadic

EXAMPLE 7-8. J. S. Bach, Overture to BWV 1066, (a) condensed score,
(b) O'Donnell's proposed interpretation.

rhythmic alteration inherent in Graham Pont's "paradigm of inconsistency" is utterly unworkable.[13] Notational discrepancies and inconsistencies of all sorts abound in seventeenth- and eighteenth-century scores: while it may be sound editorial practice to let them stand in print, in performance they should be dealt with in light of what we know about historical practice. As regards dotted rhythms, two such situations are common in overtures and dances as well as in other sorts of pieces: simultaneous dotting at two different rhythmic levels (e.g.,), and pickup notes that clash within a context of fairly consistent dotting (e.g.,). Today both of these rhythmic conflicts are frequently resolved according to the principle of "synchronization" or "assimilation," whereby the larger values are adjusted to fit with the smaller. As we have seen, seventeenth- and eighteenth-century discussions of such synchronization per se are relatively rare: Gigault mentions it briefly; C. P. E. Bach illustrates it in an example, yet without specific discussion; Türk states that now and gain one elongates dotted notes in one part so that the ensuing short notes coincide with those of another voice, e.g., becomes ; and Quantz stipulates that upbeats be shortened to fit with prevalent dotted rhythms.[14] But rhythmic assimilation is certainly inherent in overdotting concomitant with *notes inégales*. And when Türk recommends overdotting for overtures, such as those by Rolle and Schweitzer (figures 6-1 and 6-2 above), he surely intends that it result in synchronization as well. Here again, blanket generalizations cannot be made, and the possibility of intentional rhythmic conflicts should be seriously entertained. But when seemingly meaningless clashes can be assimilated easily by following the leader, it seems likely that this is the appropriate (and historically founded) solution;[15] the alternative is a ragged-sounding ensemble.

Handel's overtures are a notable case in point: try as one will to discern rational intent behind the barrage of inconsistent rhythms, it remains elusive; and when the notation is rendered precisely as written, it sounds as though the members of the band cannot play together. One such example is the overture to *Riccardo primo*. Figure 7-1 reproduces the opening of the autograph orchestral score; for clarity, example 7-9 presents Chrysander's edition; and figure 7-2 shows the same music in Handel's autograph keyboard arrangement. The first two measures in the orchestral score have crisp "overdotting" (7:1 ratios) and contracted pickups written out: Why should these be absent from the keyboard version? Yet by the twelfth measure the keyboard score also has contracted pickups, which continue through the first ending. Suppose the repeat is taken: Is the player then to resume the slower, duller sixteenth-note pickups? In the orchestral score, the upper part has dotted quarters and eighths in mm. 4 and 13–14; yet the deviance from the prevailing 7:1 rhythmic pattern here is puzzling, especially when the keyboard score shows the sharper rhythm in two of these three spots. And the last beat of m. 13 of the orchestral autograph shows an absurd clash between sixteenth- and thirty-second-note pickups in violas and basses (synchronized in Chrysander's edition). Most such problems are easily resolved through overdotting and synchronization; in view of all we have reviewed above, I suspect that is what Handel did.[16]

The two versions of the overture to *Riccardo* present instances of sixteenth-note *tirades* contracted to thirty-seconds—a controversial matter briefly touched upon in chapter 5 (n. 12). Quantz is the principal theoretical source on this issue—and as Neumann has emphasized, Quantz mentions only the hurrying of three or more *thirty-second* notes after a dot or rest (XVII/vii/58). But J. S. Bach contracted sixteenths to thirty-seconds in the revision of the keyboard overture BWV 831; Kirnberger and Schulz allow for contraction of "more or fewer smaller notes" after the main notes of the overture (which "are mostly dotted");[17] and in *Riccardo*, apparently, we find Handel shortening sixteenth pickups to thirty-seconds as well. At issue, of course, is musical gesture rather than jurisprudence; without having made an exhaustive study, I strongly suspect that sixteenth-note *tirades* are as common in overtures and entrées as thirty-seconds (possibly more so),[18] and that despite his minute thoroughness, Quantz may here have committed an oversight. (Perhaps he

FIGURE 7-1. Handel, overture to *Riccardo primo*, opening, autograph orchestral score (1727).

British Library, RM. 20. c. 2, reproduced by permission.

was thinking of such pickups in the rhythmic values corresponding most closely to how they would *sound*—namely, as thirty-seconds—rather than in the values by which they might actually be notated.) As always, blanket rules ought not to be made, and each piece must be evaluated individually. But on the basis of all we have seen, I think it generally reasonable and appropriate to contract sixteenth pickups in overtures and dances, provided that such notes are actually upbeat flourishes and not fragments of larger lines, such as the flowing sixteenths in the overture to Bach's C-major orchestral suite (example 7-8 above).

As regards the problem of inconsistent notation, let us consider one additional example: the overture to Handel's *Judas Maccabaeus* (1747), shown in figure 7-3 (p. 156). In the first two measures, the 7:1 ratios are clearly notated. But beginning in the fourth measure, the inner voices are written in simpler 3:1 values ($\sf J\cdot\ \sf J$), as is the upper part in mm. 9–13. Meanwhile, however, in the second half of m. 13 the viola notation is

EXAMPLE 7-9. Handel, Overture to *Riccardo primo*, opening, orchestral score
(ed. Chrysander, *G. F. Händels Werke*, vol. 74).

synchronized with the bass line, even through the upper part is not; in the
next bar, the situation is just the reverse (upper part "overdotted," viola
not). And note the inconsistencies in the next measure (15). Here again,
two possibilities emerge: (a) Handel wanted all these rhythmic clashes,
for reasons that remain obscure; (b) the notation of the first two measures
sets the pattern to be followed for the rest of the piece, and the inconsis-

FIGURE 7-2.   Handel, overture to *Riccardo primo*, opening, autograph keyboard
arrangement (1727–28).

Fitzwilliam Museum, Mus. MS. 257, reproduced by permission.

tencies are just careless notation. Option (a) strikes me as highly unlikely;
(b), however, quickly and simply solves the problems.

By and large, overdotting was a phenomenon of instrumental music.
Mattheson, who does not actually discuss rhythmic alteration, nevertheless makes the trenchant observation that

**die Vocal-Melodie kein solches reissendes, punctirtes Wesen zulasse,
als die Instrumental-Composition.** Wenn die Frantzosen, die ich für
grosse Meister im Instrumenten-Styl halte, sich der Puncte bey den Noten begeben sollten, würden sie, wie Köche ohne Saltz, bestehen. Gewiß
ist es dennoch, daß dergleichen geschärffte *rhythmi,* so schön und mun-
ter sie auch bey Instrumenten fallen, im Halse eines Sängers gar keine
artige Wirckung thun, und gewisser maassen für Fremdlinge in der
Vocal-Melodie zu achten sind, auch als solche nur, dann und wann er-
scheinen; . . .[19]

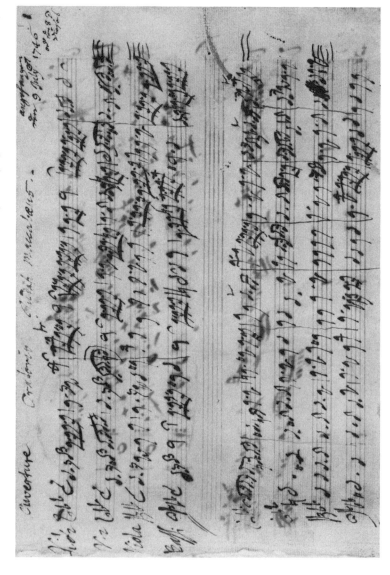

FIGURE 7-3. Handel, overture to *Judas Maccabaeus*, opening, autograph orchestral score (1747).

vocal melody does not admit of such a snapping, dotted character as instrumental composition. If the French, whom I regard as great masters in instrumental style, had to forgo the dots beside the notes, they would be like cooks without salt. For it is certain that such sharpened rhythms, so beautiful and cheerful for instruments, make no such agreeable effect in the throat of a singer, and are to be regarded, so to say, as foreigners in vocal melody (and only as such) when they occasionally appear; . . .

To be sure, as inequality affects French vocal music, so too does overdotting. And among the German writers cited above, Agricola insists upon 'galant'-type overdotting for singers. But passages such as Agricola's examples are more likely to be encountered in arias written after about 1730 than in earlier music, and they are not characteristic of choral writing. Thus, for example, to overdot "Worthy Is the Lamb" from *Messiah* (example 7-10) seems questionable not only on historical grounds, but also because the text declamation becomes curiously distorted, without appreciable gain in grandeur: "*thul*hamb" makes little sense; it is "the *Lamb*" that is worthy.[20]

What we have termed 'galant' overdotting—the exaggeration of dotted rhythms at the level of eighth notes and smaller values—poses few difficulties. The earliest witness to this custom is Quantz; it bears no apparent relation to French inequality. The affective range of such alteration extends from the pleasing to liveliness and boldness, depending upon the tempo, melodic contour, and articulation of the music to which

EXAMPLE 7-10.   Handel, *Messiah* (1741), "Worthy Is the Lamb," opening.

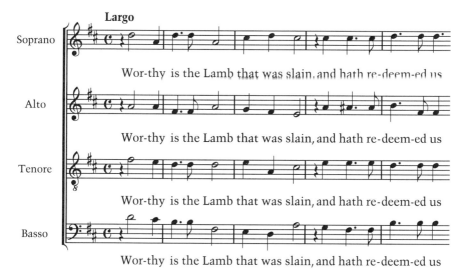

it is applied. And it is easily adopted in ensemble music when desired. There is little reason to suppose 'galant' overdotting was very common outside Germany, or that it was in use there much before 1730; to develop taste in its application, one need only study the music of Quantz, C. P. E. Bach, and their contemporaries. Although Quantz and Agricola write as though this mannerism were essential, Emanuel Bach, Türk, and Rellstab introduce qualifications, among which are a flattering or singing affect, the presence of ornaments, or the contrapuntal disposition of the parts. One example where overdotting strikes me as particularly effective is the slow movement of C. P. E. Bach's first "string" symphony, Wq 182/1, in which the melodic figures of the opening measures (example 7-11) recur frequently. Only Emanuel Bach would write such a piece—by turns elegant, weird, witty, and poignant, its special poise is enhanced by elongation of the dots, without which (in Leopold Mozart's words) the movement seems too sleepy.

Outside the contexts of overtures and dances, synchronization, and the 'galant' heightening of small-scale dotted rhythms, we know little else about overdotting. Several writers who mention it—Löhlein, Wolf, Petschke, and Tromlitz—provide accounts so vague as to be of little use today, except to confirm that something of the practice was widely known in Germany during the latter half of the eighteenth century. Given the propensity of German treatise writers to read the works of their forebears before commencing their own, it seems doubtful that there was much more to be said on the subject beyond what has been reviewed in part II above.

We cannot here pursue a detailed investigation of the extent to which overdotting might apply to works of the classical period; this is, in any case, an issue to be decided chiefly on the basis of style, composers' habits of notation, and practicability.[21] To be sure, Türk and Rellstab were writing during Mozart's last years; Haydn regarded C. P. E. Bach's treatise as "the school of all schools," and Beethoven taught young Czerny from it. Yet as Mozart reportedly said of Emanuel Bach's music, "We can no longer do as he did; but the way in which he did it places him beyond all others."[22] Style had greatly changed. By the 1780s Haydn and Mozart had moved well beyond French overtures and suites, or the musical milieu of Quantz and the Grauns, or even the more progressive oeuvre of Emanuel Bach—so much so that Frederick the Great deemed the new style degenerate. As regards rhythmic notation, Mozart, for example, used the double dot from his early years, apparently in conformity with his father's precepts;[23] thus it seems unlikely that he expected exaggeration of his dotting, except perhaps for some 'galant' figures such as those for which Leopold had advocated intensification. And in the case of suave, "sing-

EXAMPLE 7-11.   C. P. E. Bach, Sinfonia in G. Wq. 182/1 (1773), 2d mvt. mm.
1–8 (ed. Traugott Fedtke).

ing" melodies like those shown in example 7-12, nothing in the treatise
sources would particularly suggest overdotting if 7:1 ratios were not already notated; indeed, the commentary of C. P. E. Bach, Türk, and Rellstab might seem to discourage it.

Perhaps these pages will mitigate some of the "useless embarrassment" concerning rhythmic alteration that J.-J. Rousseau noted more

EXAMPLE 7-12.   Mozart, (a) Symphony No. 29, K. 201/186a (1774), Andante;
                 (b) Symphony No. 41, K. 551 (1788), Andante cantabile.

than two centuries ago, which has only increased in performance practice
scholarship during the past forty years. Although additional data will
doubtless be uncovered in future (particularly in scores themselves), it is
difficult to envision what would substantially alter the main points that
emerge from the evidence reviewed here. Not surprisingly, many details
concerning the customs of inequality and overdotting cannot be established with utter certainty. The task remaining for scholars and performers is to cease polemicizing, absorb what we now know about rhythmic
alteration, and continue the process of historical reconstruction and ar-
tistic realization through informed performance and critical observation.

N O T E S

Preface

1. Jean-Jacques Rousseau, *Dictionnaire de musique* (Paris, 1768), 380.

2. Bénigne de Bacilly, *Remarques curieuses sur l'art de bien chanter . . .* (Paris, 1668), 232; Georg Muffat writes of *pointer alternativement* in the preface to his *Florilegium Primum* (Augsburg, 1695; modern ed. in *Denkmäler der Tonkunst in Österreich* I/2 [1894]).

3. E.g., Michel L'Affilard, *Principes tres-faciles pour bien apprendre la musique . . .* (Paris, 1694ff.); la Ferté, *Premier livre de sonates pour le violon* (Paris, 1707); Jacques Hotteterre-le-Romain, *Principes de la flute traversiere, ou flute d'allemagne . . .* (Paris, 1707; reprinted, Amsterdam [1710]), and idem, *L'art de préluder sur la flûte traversiere . . .* (Paris 1719); François Couperin, *L'art de toucher le clavecin . . .* (Paris, 1717). As noted below (pp. 18–19), this term is problematic because it can also mean "to dot," i.e., to add dots to the rhythmic notation.

4. Michel de Saint-Lambert, *Les principes du clavecin . . .* (Paris, 1702).

5. Or *passer plus vite la deuxieme croche;* e.g., Michael Corrette, *L'ecole d'Orphée* (Paris, 1738) and *Méthode théorique et pratique pour apprendre en peu de tems le violoncelle . . .* (Paris, 1741); Charles Buterne, *Méthode pour apprendre la musique vocale et instrumentale* (Paris, Lyon, and Rouen, 1752); Alexandre de Villencuve, *Nouvelle methode tres courte . . .* (Paris, 1733 and 1756); Rollet, *Méthode pour apprendre la musique* (Paris [1760]).

6. E.g., Michel Pignolet de Monteclair, *Nouvelle methode pour apprendre la musique . . .* (Paris, 1709); P. F. C. X. Vion, *La musique pratique et theorique . . .* (Paris, 1742); Pierre Denis, *Nouveau systeme de musique pratique . . .* (Paris, [1747 and 1757]). *Croches* (eighth notes) refers to the rhythmic value most frequently affected by the custom.

7. Erwin Bodky, *The Interpretation of Bach's Keyboard Works* (Cambridge: Harvard University Press, 1960), 189ff.

8. This term was introduced by Ralph Leavis, "Double-Dotting and Ultra-Dotting," *Early Music* 6 (1978): 309.

9. E.g., recently, David Wulstan, "Glorious Uncertainty," *Early Music* 14 (1986): 406–9.

10. For more extensive accounts see *The New Grove*, s. v. "Notes Inégales" by David Fuller, and Frederick Neumann, "The French *Inégales*, Quantz, and Bach," reprinted in his *Essays in Performance Practice* (Ann Arbor: UMI Research Press, 1982), as well as idem, "Facts and Fiction about Overdotting," *Essays*, 111–12.

11. Dolmetsch, 84–87 and 62.

12. Thurston Dart, *The Interpretation of Music* (London, 1954; reprinted, New York: Harper & Row, 1963), 80–81, 116.

13. Dart, 81–82.

14. Robert Donington, *The Interpretation of Early Music* (New York: St. Martin's Press, 1963), chaps. 43–45, esp. pp. 396–97 and 375 (where the quoted passage appears).

15. Neumann, "The French *Inégales*, Quantz, and Bach," *Essays*, 17–54, and "La note pointée et la soi-disant 'manière française,' " *Revue de musicologie* 51 (1965): 66–92; trans. Edmund Shay and Raymond Harris as "The Dotted Note and the So-called French Style," *Early Music* 5 (1977): 310–24, and reprinted in Neumann, *Essays*, 73–98.

16. "The Dotted Note and the So-called French Style," *Essays*, 82, and 98 (where the quoted passage appears).

17. David Fuller, "Dotting, the 'French Style,' and Frederick Neumann's Counter-Reformation," *Early Music* 5 (1977): 517–43, and idem, *The New Grove*, s. v. "Notes Inégales," 13: 424.

18. See R. G. Collingwood, *The Idea of History*, ed. T. M. Knox (Oxford, 1946; reprinted, New York: Oxford University Press, 1956); cf. also Louis O. Mink, "Collingwood's Dialectic of History," *History and Theory* 7 (1968): 3–37; Leon J. Goldstein, "Collingwood's Theory of Historical Knowing," *History and Theory* 9 (1970): 3–36; Bernard Lonergan, *Method in Theology*, 2d ed. (New York: Seabury Press, 1973), chap. 9, "History and Historians"; and Leo Treitler, "History, Criticism, and Beethoven's Ninth Symphony," *19th Century Music* 3 (1980): 193–210. For rather different views on the foundations of historical performance practice see, e.g., Laurence Dreyfus, "Early Music Defended against Its Devotees: A Theory of Historical Performance in the Twentieth Century," *Musical Quarterly* 69 (1983): 297–322, and Richard Taruskin, "The Pastness of the Present and the Presence of the Past," in *Authenticity and Early Music: A Symposium*, ed. Nicholas Kenyon (New York: Oxford University Press, 1988), 137–207.

19. *The Music Forum* 6/1 (1987): 93–127; reprinted in Frederick Neumann, *New Essays on Performance Practice* (Ann Arbor: UMI Research Press, 1989), 35–64. For additional references on this topic see chap. 4, n. 9 below.

Chapter 1.   Conventional Aspects of French Inequality

1. Loys Bourgeois, *Le droict chemin de mvsique* . . . (Geneva, 1550), chap. 10. The semibreve is the basic unit of tactus for Bourgeois (chap. 6), and the breve becomes the tactus under the "diminished signs" of *proportio dupla* (chap. 11).

2. Tomás de Santa Maria, *Libro llamade arte de tañer fantasia* . . . (Valladolid, 1565), 45v–46v.

3. "Tengase auiso, que el detenimiento en las Corcheas no ha de ser mucho, sino solamente quanto se señale." See also Newman W. Powell, "Rhythmic Freedom in the Performance of French Music from 1650 to 1735" (Ph.D. diss., Stanford University, 1959), 52–56.

4. Giovanni Battista Bovicelli, *Regole, passaggi di musica* . . . (Venice, 1594), 11; Giulio Caccini, *Le nuove musiche* (Florence, 1602), [viii]; trans. and ed. H. Wiley Hitchcock (Madison, Wis.: A-R Editions, 1973), 51–52.

5. Pedro Cerone, *El melopeo y maestro* . . . (Naples, 1613), 541–42; Girolamo Frescobaldi, preface to *Toccate e partite d'intavolature di cimbalo* (Rome, 1615); reprinted in the facsimile of the 1637 ed. (Florence: Studio per Edizioni Scelti, 1980).

6. Domenico Puliaschi, *Musiche varie a una voce* (Rome, 1618); preface reprinted in Gaetano Gaspari, *Catalogo della biblioteca del Liceo musicale de Bologna* (Bologna, 1893; reprinted, Bologna: Forni Editore, 1961), 155–56.

7. This is a complex issue that cannot be pursued further here; a useful discussion of articulation in the *passaggi* tutors is found in *Italienische Diminutionen: die zwischen 1553 und 1638 mehrmals bearbeiteten Sätze*, ed. Richard Erig and Veronika Gutmann, Prattica musicale, vol. 1 (Zürich: Amadeus Verlag/ Bernhard Päuler, 1979): 9–58; cf. also Howard Brown, *Embellishing Sixteenth-Century Music* (London: Oxford University Press, 1976).

8. Jean Saint-Arroman, "Les inégalités," in *L'interprétation de la musique française aux XVIIe et XVIIIe siècles*, ed. Edith Weber (Paris: Éditions du Centre National de la Recherche Scientifique, 1974), 70.

9. Guillaume-Gabriel Nivers, *Livre d'orgue contenant cent pieces . . .* (Paris, 1665), preface. Nivers indicates this is appropriate for a fugue (on p. 14) in which the meter signature is C and the motion is primarily in eighth notes, with no sixteenths present: as we shall see, inequality at this metric level in C is not common in later French practice.

10. *Livre d'orgue des huit tones de l'eglise* (Paris, 1675).

11. *Livre d'orgue contenant la messe et les hymnes d'eglise* (Paris, 1667); modern ed. Norbert Dufourcq (Paris: Schola Cantorum, 1956), 37, 61–63, 72, 75. Each of these pieces is in ¢ or **2**. This notation is not found in the 1665 collection (as mistakenly reported by Fuller, s. v. "Dotted Notes," *The New Harvard Dictionary of Music,* 238).

12. Bacilly, (1668), 235–36; quotation from p. 232. The first words of this passage suggest previous mention of this practice in the treatise, but I have been unable to locate it.

13. The examples are conveniently provided in Caswell's English translation of Bacilly, *A Commentary upon the Art of Proper Singing* (Brooklyn, N.Y.: Institute for Mediaeval Music, 1968), 118, but the translation itself is questionable.

14. Michael Collins ("A Reconsideration of French Overdotting," *Music and Letters* 50 [1969], 116–17, 123) attempts to see these remarks as the primordial source for the "jerky style" of performing French overtures, a view briefly entertained again by John O'Donnell ("The French Style and the Overtures of Bach," pt. 2, *Early Music* 8 [1979]: 336); such an interpretation stretches the passage well out of context, as already pointed out by Neumann ("Facts and Fiction about Overdotting" and "The Overdotting Syndrome: Anatomy of a Delusion," *Essays in Performance Practice,* 130, 178). But Bacilly's comments do suggest that gigues were performed in a sprightly manner, and that certain situations might call for strong inequality.

15. Perrine, *Pieces de luth en musique* (Paris [ca. 1680]), 9: "Il faut en fin observer, pour trouuer le veritable mouuement de toutes sortes de pieces de Lut, que les premieres parties, ou premieres parties de parties des temps de la mesure soient plus-longues que les autres."

16. Gigault, *Livre de musique pour l'orgue* (Paris, 1685), preface: "On poura aussi pour animer son jou plus ou moins en adjoutant des points ou l'on voudra." (Modern ed. by Alexandre Guilmant and André Pirro, Archives des maîtres de l'orgue des XVe, XVIIe, XVIIIe siècles . . . , vol. 4 [Leipzig: B. Schott's Söhne, 1902].)

17. Gilles Jullien, *Premier livre d'orgue . . .* (Paris, 1690), preface: "Je n'ay mis les points apres les premieres croches, que dans la piece, quy Est au folio 51 pour

Servir d'Exemple apointer les autres de mesme, plus ou moins legerement selon le mouvement, quy y Sera marqué." Here again, unequal eighths in **C** are contrary to the rhythm-inequality relationships set forth by many later writers.

18.

Il faut remarquer que ces ce pointement qui donne la grace le mouvement et la beaute et lagrement aux piece, sans cela les pieces sont plate sant gout ny mouvement et ne paroisse rien. . . .

. . . Voisy dont la manierre de pointer le prelude et toutte les autre piece generallement parlants exemples 8. ou huit croses plus ou moins qui sois pair faire la premierre crose longue comme cy il lyavet un point avec la crose et la suivante fort breve comme si cettoit une double croce la suivante longue comme la premierre et lautre suivante breve comme la segonde ainsi de touttes les autres. . . .

It is necessary to remark that it is this pointing which gives grace, *mouvement,* and beauty and agreeableness to the piece. Without it the pieces are flat, without taste or tempo, and appear to be as nothing. . . .

Here is the way to point the prelude and all the other pieces, generally speaking; for example, for 8 eighth notes more or less, which are even, make the first eighth long as though it had a dot with it, and the following one notably short as though it were a sixteenth; the next one long like the first, and the ensuing one short like the second; and so forth for all the others. . . .

Anon., "Maniere de toucher lorgue dans toute la proprete et la delicatesse qui est en usage aujourdhy a Paris," *F-Pa*, MS. 3042, fols. 100–19 [ca. 1685], printed in William Pruitt, "Un traité d'interprétation du XVIIe siècle," *L'orgue* 152 (Oct.–Dec. 1974): 104; see also idem, "A Seventeenth-Century French Manuscript on Organ Performance," *Early Music* 14 (1986): 240–41.

19.

Le trio ce touche hardiment mais fort lentement et on ne peut aller trop doucement le principal du trio est de le bien pointer mais il faut que ce pointement ce face avec grand feu et grande hardiesse . . . on ne peut dont pas trop le pointer. . . .

. . . Il faut etremement pointer le duo car ces en cela ou est sa beauté. . . .

Il faut jouer le cornet fort viste et vivement sans pointer. . . .

The trio is played boldly but very slowly and one may not proceed too sweetly; the principle of the trio is to point it well, but it is necessary that this pointing be done with great fire and great boldness . . . one cannot point it too much. . . .

. . . The duo must be pointed extremely, because therein consists its beauty. . . .

. . . The cornet must be played very fast and lively without pointing. . . .

Pruitt, *L'orgue* 152 (1974): 106–7, 109; *Early Music* 14 (1986): 247, 250. The treatise is the work of two different authors, and the statement concerning the *cornet* is by the second of them.

20. Jean Rousseau, *Traite de la viole* . . . (Paris, 1687), 114:

Au Signe de quatre Temps [**C**] les Croches doivent estre touchées également;
c'est à dire qu'il n'en faut pas marquer une: Mais au regard des doubles Croches il
faut un peu marquer la premiere, troisiéme, &c.

Aux Signes de deux Temps [**2, ₵**], dans les Airs de Mouvement sur des Croches,
il faut un peu marquer la premiere, troisiéme, &c. de chaque Mesure; mais il faut
prendre garde de les marquer trop rudement.

Aux Signes de trois Temps sur des Croches, il faut un peu marquer la premiere
de chaque Mesure, & suivre les autres également: Il faut observer la mesme chose
au triple double [$\frac{3}{2}$] sur les Noires, aux Airs de Mouvement.

Under the signature of four beats [**C**] the eighths must be touched equally;
which is to say that it is not necessary to mark any of them: but as regards the
sixteenths, it is necessary to mark a little bit the first, third, and so on.

Under the signatures of duple meter [**2, ₵**], in *airs de mouvement* with eighth
notes, it is necessary to mark a bit the first, third, etc. [eighth note], of each
measure; but it is necessary to take care not to mark them too roughly.

Under the signatures of triple time with eighths, it is necessary to mark the
first of each measure, and for the others to ensue equally: It is necessary to observe
the same thing in three-two with the quarters, in *airs de mouvement*.

The bracketed meter signatures are to be inferred from Rousseau's previous discussion of bowing and from the *Exemple* on pp. 114–15. *Airs de mouvement* are
characteristic pieces, chiefly dances, of French seventeenth- and eighteenth-century music; see Jean Saint-Arroman, *L'interprétation de la musique française
1661–1789*, vol. 1: *Dictionnaire d'interprétation* (Paris: Librarie Honoré Champion, 1983), 27.

21. "The French *Inégales*, Quantz, and Bach," *Essays*, 24–25.
22. See also Saint-Arroman, "Les inégalités," 71–74.
23. Neumann has contended that the nature of inequality "predestines its
use by soloists . . . [it] would create confusion in an orchestral section and would
make for difficulties in chamber music" ("The French *Inégales*, Quantz, and
Bach," *Essays*, 30). But Muffat's *Florilegium Primum* and *Florilegium Secundum*
(Passau, 1695, 1698; modern ed. in *DTÖ* I/2, II/2), in which he expects *notes
inégales*, are orchestral works, and many French treatise writers use musical
examples from operatic works in discussing *mesure* and *notes inégales*. Only one
case will be cited here: Michel Corrette writes that "dans la musique françoise on
passe la deuxieme croche de chaque tems plus vite, comme dans la Chaccone de
Phaëton de M^r. de Lully." [*Méthode théorique et pratique pour apprendre en peu
de tems le violoncelle . . .* [1741], 5).
24. *L'art de toucher le clavecin* (Paris, 1717), 39–40.
25. Vague, *L'art d'apprendre la musique . . .* (Paris, 1733), 54: "On peut observer que les nottes en Dégres-disjoints sont ordinairement égales en quelle
mesure que se soit [One may observe that notes in disjunct intervals are ordinarily
equal in whatever the measure may be]."
26. Michel Pignolet de Monteclair, *Nouvelle methode pour apprendre la
musique . . .* (Paris, 1709), 15: "Quand le chant procede par intervalles disjoints,
les croches sont ordinairement égalles dans le Triple $\frac{3}{4}$."
27. *L'ecole d'Orphée* (1738), 4 and 30; see also Muffat, *Florilegium Secundum* (1698), preface, examples QQ and RR, and Engramelle's treatment of the

"Romance de Mr. Balbastre" in Dom François Bedos de Celles, *L'art du facteur d'orgues* (Paris, 1778), plates CXIX–CXXVIII.

28. See Étienne Loulié, *Elements ou principes de musique* . . . (Paris, 1696), 33–34 (reprinted, Amsterdam, 1698, 38–39); la Ferté, *Sonates* (1707), 16–18, 34; and Caix d'Hervelois, *Deuxiéme recueil de pieces pour la flute-traversiere* (Paris, 1731), 20–21.

29. Neumann, "The French *Inégales,* Quantz, and Bach," *Essays,* 23–28.

30. Loulié, *Elements* (1696), 62 (1698 ed., 71–72).

31. Manuscript additions from *F-Pn,* f. fr. n. a. 6355, printed in Loulié, *Elements or Principles of Music,* trans. and ed. Albert Cohen (Brooklyn, N.Y.: Institute for Mediaeval Music, 1965), 67.

32. *Pieces de clavecin . . . premier livre* (Paris, 1713), 75.

33. Pierre-Claude Fouquet, *Les caracteres de la paix* . . . (Paris [1749]), 5; Frederick Wilhelm Marpurg, *Pieces de clavecin* (Paris [ca. 1741–48]), "Les remouleurs," 17. See also n. 39 below.

34. In Dom Bedos de Celles, *L'art de facteur d'orgues* (Paris, 1778), plate CXI.

35. Cf. *Le dictionnaire de l'Académie françoise* (Paris, 1694), 1: 47.

36. Bacilly (1668), 232; Marin Marais, *Pièces de viole* [2d book] (Paris, 1701), preface; Dupont, *Principes de musique par demande et par reponce* (Paris, 1718), 42; Anon., *Nouvelle methode pour apprendre à jouer du violon et à lire la musique* (n. p., [ca. 1760]), 29; Dard, *Nouveaux principes de musique* (Paris [1769]), 8; Jacob Roussier, *Méthode de musique sur un nouveau plan* (Paris, 1769), 57.

37. It is worth noting that Monteclair was apparently on close terms with Couperin, to whose daughters he taught music, and to whom he dedicated the 1709 *Nouvelle methode.*

38. *Essai d'une methode pour apprendre à jouer de la flute traversiere* . . . (Berlin, 1752), 107–8; Quantz's remarks on *notes inégales* are discussed below, pp. 43–48.

39. Neumann believes that Couperin's use of *couler* in his short description of the slur-and-dot "refers to nothing but the slurred notes" ("The French *Inégales,* Quantz, and Bach," *Essays,* 27). Yet the term would seem to suggest a relation to French *tierces coulées* (descending thirds with an ornamental passing note between them), and such was apparently Engramelle's interpretation of the symbol (*secondes coulées;* the difference is that in *secondes coulées* the passing note falls on the beat). Virtually every time Couperin uses this marking in his *Premier livre,* the first of the two pitches is an onbeat upper-neighbor note (i.e., accented passing tone); he does not use it in his later works. Fouquet employs the slur-and-dot notation twice in the first piece of his *Second livre de pieces de clavecin* (Paris [1750/51]), 1; neither spot is particularly informative.

40. Dupuit's *Principes pour toucher de la viele* (Paris [1741]), VIII, introduces a dot-and-slur notation in which the dot occurs above the first rather than the second of the paired notes:

Dans un air marqué, s'il y a deux notes liées ensemble, il faut donner un coup de poignet sur la second, et non pas sur la première comme dans le Vivace page 13 pourvû quil y ait un point dessus. Fig. 53.

> In a marked piece, if there are two notes slurred together, it is necessary to give a stroke of the wrist to the second, and not to the first, as in the Vivace, p. 13, provided that there be a dot above. Fig. 53.

Dupuit's musical illustration is not entirely clear, but it seems to indicate that the notation means short–long inequality. The dot-and-slur does not appear, however, in the Vivace on pp. 12–13, or anywhere else in the volume.

For C. P. E. Bach the sign ⌒ indicates that the note over which the dot appears is detached (*Versuch über die wahre Art das Clavier zu spielen* [Berlin, 1753], chap. 3, §21). Marpurg follows suit in his *Anleitung zum Clavierspielen* (Berlin, 1755), 66 and table VII, figure 17: thus he apparently contradicts his earlier use of the slur-plus-dot in the *Pieces de clavecin* [ca. 1741–48], which are strongly influenced by Couperin. This may be another of several instances whereby Marpurg rejected customs he had learned in France in favor of the prevailing taste in Berlin (see Elizabeth Loretta Hays, "F. W. Marpurg's *Anleitung zum Clavierspielen* (Berlin, 1755) and *Principes du clavecin* (Berlin, 1756): Translation and Commentary," [Ph.D. diss., Stanford University, 1976], vol. 2, chap. 3, esp. 177–85). In any case, his explanation of the symbol in the *Anleitung* has nothing to do with *note inégales;* Collins, in "Three Further Views on Notes Inégales," *Journal of the American Musicological Society* 20 (1967): 481–82, provides a misleading account of the matter based on misinterpretation of Valentin Roeser's French translation of Marpurg (*L'art de toucher le clavecin . . . Par M. Marpourg . . . mis au jour par M. Valentin Roeser . . .* [Paris (1764)], 3).

41. Cf. also Fuller, *The New Grove,* 13: 422.

42. de La Feillée, *Méthode nouvelle pour apprendre parfaitement les regles du plain-chant et de la psalmodie,* 3d ed. (Poitiers, 1777), 99, 101–2; a similar but less precise discussion is found in the first edition (Poitiers, 1748), 108–11. I am grateful to Professor Lenora McCroskey for drawing my attention to this source. Musical notation reproduced through courtesy of the Sibley Library, Eastman School of Music, Rochester, N.Y.

43. *Elements* (1696), 39. Loulié's use of *lourer* to mean mild inequality is reflected in later definitions by Brossard (*Dictionnaire de musique . . . ,* 2d ed. [Paris, 1705], 274), Demotz de la Salle (*Méthode de musique . . .* [Paris, 1728], 181; see below, chap. 2, n. 6), Walther (*Musikalisches Lexikon . . .* [Leipzig, 1732], 372; see below, chap. 3, n. 24), J. J. Rousseau (*Dictionnaire* [1768], 269), the *Dictionnaire universel françois et latin, vulgairement appelé dictionnaire de Trévoux* (Paris, 1771), 5: 651, Pierre Duval (*Méthode agréable . . .* [Paris (1775)], 13), and Azaïs (*Méthode de musique sur un nouveau plan . . .* [Sorèse par Revel (1776)], 167). But the term need not mandate *notes inégales;* according to David, for example (*Méthode nouvelle ou principes généraux pour apprendre facilement la musique . . .* [Paris (1737)], 28), *notes lourées* are triplets that replace the ordinary duple division of the beat (and which are often bracketed with a slur); for Boüin (*La vielleuse habile . . .* [Paris (ca. 1761)], 12), *louré* means simply "notes carressées & coulées"; and Meude-Monpas's rather confusing definition (*Dictionnaire de musique . . .* [Paris, 1787], 86) makes no mention of rhythmic inequality (see also Saint-Arroman, *Dictionnaire d'interprétation,* 206–8, as well as Fuller, s. v. "Notes Inégales" in both *The New Grove,* 13: 421, and *The New Grove Dictionary of Musical Instruments* [London: Macmillan, 1984], 2: 777). Occasionally *louré* appears in situations where inequality is simply not an issue, as in Antoine Forqueray, *Pieces de viole . . . Livre Ier.* (Paris [1747]), 10, and Dandrieu,

Pièces de clavecin ... (Paris, 1724), 43. O'Donnell's discussion of the term is quite misleading ("The French Style," pt. 2: 338), and Houle confuses matters by taking *lourer* and *notes inégales* to be synonymous (*Meter in Music, 1600–1800* [Bloomington: Indiana University Press, 1987], 88).

44. Printed in Cohen's edition (1965), 67.

45. *Elements* (1696), 39: "... le premier demi-temps doit avoir un point." The manuscript annotations are printed in Cohen's edition (1965), 67.

46. Jean Rousseau (1687), 114; Jean-Pierre Freillon-Poncein, *La véritable manière d'apprendre à jouer en perfection du haut-bois* ... (Paris, 1700), 17; Monteclair (1709), 15; idem (1736), 21; Alexandre de Villeneuve, *Nouvelle méthode* ... (Paris, 1733 and 1756), 5; Rollet (1760), 27 and 29; Henri-Louis Choquel, *La musique rendue sensible par la méquanique,* 2d ed. (Paris, 1762), 106; J.-J. Rousseau (1768), 381; Antoine Bailleux, *Méthode pour apprendre la musique* ... (Paris [1770]), 23; C. Torlez, *Methode de musique* ... (Paris [ca. 1775]), 23; Azaïs (1776), 15; Mercadier de Belesta, *Nouveau systeme de musique* ... (Paris, 1777), 67; and Pierre Marcou, *Elémens théoriques et pratiques de musique* (London and Paris, 1782), 35. Mercadier de Belesta's comments are curious, however: "... deux notes de valeur égale qui composent un tems, se passent d'ordinaire fort inégalement, la première étant un peu plus longue que la seconde."

47. Vague, *L'art* (1733), 54: "... il faut distinguer cette inégalité dont nous venons de parler, de celle que demande le Point, laquelle est plus grande."

48. Jacques-Alexandre de-La Chapelle, *Les vrais principes de la musique* ... (Paris [1736–52]), 5.

49. Rollet, *Méthode* [1760], 29: "... on doit observer qu'il faut passer un peu la seconde des deux croches sans pourtant les chanter par saccade."

50. Neumann writes inaccurately of "the monotonous refrain not contradicted by a single theorist, that *inégalité* was a gentle lilt ... and nothing more...." ("Facts and Fiction," *Essays,* 120).

51. Saint-Lambert, *Principes* (1702), 26.

52. L'Abbé Joseph Lacassagne, *Traité général des élémens du chant* ... (Paris, 1766), 44:

> De la Mesure Simple marquée par 2 ou ₵ ... Les croches se passent inégales, c'est-a-dire que la 1.ere est beaucoup plus longue que la 2.de à proportion du mouvement que l'on exécute.
>
> In the non-compound measure marked by 2 or ₵ ... the eighths are rendered unequal, which is to say that the first is much longer than the second, in proportion to the tempo that one executes.

53. David, *Méthode* [1737], 22–23; the mathematics ("au quart de la valeur de la premiére") are slightly awry here. In "The Overdotting Syndrome," *Essays,* 176, Neumann incorrectly asserts that "the maverick François David" is the only theorist who lists 3:1 inequality.

54. Dupuit, *Principes* [1741], IV–V.

55. L'Abbé Duval, *Principes de la musique pratique, par demandes et par reponses* (Paris 1764), 43.

56. Théodore-Jean Tarade, *Traité du violon* ... (Paris [ca. 1774]), 26.

57. Cleret *fils,* "Principes de musique vocale ou l'art du musicien mis en pratique" (MS. *F-Pn* Rés 2327, 1786), 36:

Pour faire comme il faut deux croches qui suivent une noire, il faut pointer la premiere (c'est à dire lui donner la moitié de plus que la valeur et passer vite la 2ᵉ).

To execute properly two eighths that follow a quarter, it is necessary to point the first (which is to say give it half again its value, and pass quickly the second).

58. "Facts and Fiction," *Essays*, 119–21.

59. E.g., Muffat, *Florilegium Primum* (1695), DTÖ I/2:20; idem, *Florilegium Secundum* (1698), DTÖ II/2: 53, Ex. QQ and RR; Monteclair, *Nouvelle methode* (1709), 15; idem, *Petite methode pour apprendre la musique* . . . (Paris [ca. 1735]), 42; idem, *Principes* (1736), 30.

60. ". . . la premiere doit être presqu'aussy longue que si elle etoit pointée." *Nouvelle methode* (1709), 15. Monteclair's *Petit methode* [ca. 1735], 42, is slightly more specific:

la premiere croche dure presqu'autant que si elle etoit suivie d'un point, et la Seconde passe presqu'aussi vitte qu'une Double-croche.

the first eighth lasts almost as long as if it were followed by a dot, and the second passes almost as quickly as a sixteenth.

61. *Principes* (1736), 21, 30.

62. Denis, *Nouveau systeme* (1747) and *Nouvelle methode* [1757], 5: ". . . les doubles croches y doivent être inégalles comme si elles etoient pointées, scavoir, la premiere de chacque temps longue la seconde brêve. . . ."

63. J.-J. Rousseau, *Dictionnaire* (1768), 380–81.

64. Couperin, *Pieces de clavecin* . . . *premier livre* (Paris, 1713), 18.

65. Antoine Dornel, *Pieces de clavecin* (Paris [1731]); modern ed. by Catherine Caumont (Paris: Éditions Musicales Transatlantiques, 1982), 24.

66. "*Pointer* se dit improprement pour faire les croches inégalles." Duval, *Méthode* [1775], 15. O'Donnell ("The French Style," pt. 2: 338) mistakenly insists that "*pointer*, according to Gigault, Jullien, l'Affillard, Montéclair and David, is synonymous with dotted notation, and consequently qualifies for Loulié's category of vigorous inequality." As we have seen (p. 6), Gigault and Jullien are by no means so specific. Moreover, Monteclair's commentary is severely misinterpreted by such a statement; we shall examine l'Affilard presently.

67. Marcou, *Flémens*, 35.

68. In the fourth volume of this treatise Dom Bedos, Engramelle, and Balbastre collaborated in meticulous notation for barrel organ of a "Romance" by Balbastre, "selon le vrai goût de son exécution" (596n). This is discussed and recorded (through computer synthesis) by David Fuller, *Mechanical Musical Instruments as a Source for the Study of Notes, Inégales* (Cleveland: Divisions, 1979), with accompanying LP disc.

69. *La tonotechnie ou l'art de noter les cylinders* . . . (Paris, 1775), 3–30, 212–32, and plates III–V; these examples are discussed and recorded (through computer synthesis) by Houle, *Meter in Music*, 110–22 and accompanying cassette.

70. ". . . laquelle [i.e., inequality] est souvent dans le cas de varier dans le même air, si l'on veut exprimer certains passages d'une manière plus intéressante. . . ." *La tonotechnie*, 33; see also 30–31, 34, 230, and cf. his comments in Bedos de Celles (1778), 602, cited below, p. 20.

71. On the basis of Hans-Peter Schmitz's *Die Tontechnik des Père Engramelle* (Kassel, 1953), Neumann ("Facts and Fiction," *Essays,* 120–21) inaccurately states that Engramelle uses a ratio as sharp as 2:1 only in an assimilation to triplets in the Balbastre "Romance" (= Bedos de Celles, vol. 4, plate CXIX). Neumann's later discussion of Engramelle in "The *Notes inégales* Revisited," *Journal of Musicology* 6 (1988): 145, still ignores the strong inequality prescribed for the "Marche du roi de Prusse" and the "petit menuet Trompette."

72. *La tonotechnie,* 34: ". . . la différence la moins marquée, comme dans beaucoup de menuets, est comme de 3 à 2, de 7 à 5, &c." This is reconfirmed and qualified in Bedos de Celles (1778); see p. 20 below.

73. *La tonotechnie,* 33–34; no musical notation.

74. Bedos de Celles (1778), 602. *Notage* is Engramelle's term for his system of notation for mechanical organs.

CHAPTER 2.   The Negation of Inequality, Discrepancies among the Sources, and Related Matters

1. Duval, *Méthode* [1775], 9: "Il n'y a d'exception à cette régle, que quand on est averti, soit par des points soit par des petites lignes perpendiculaires aux croches."

2. Writers who specify this include Marais (1701), preface; Giovanni Antonio Piani, *Sonate a violino solo* . . . (Paris, 1712), 2; Jean-Baptiste Cappus, *Etrennes de musique* . . . (Paris [1730]), 16–17; Toussaint Bordet, *Méthode raisonnée* . . . (Paris [1755]), 5; Rollet (1760), 57, 62; L'Abbé Duval (1764), 43; Lacassagne (1766), 55, 57; Dard [1769], 17; P. Duval [1775], 8–9; Tarade [ca. 1774], 15, 29; Torlez [ca. 1775], 31; Mercadier de Belesta (1777), 69.

3. Loulié (1696), 39; A. D. Philidor, *I.er livre de pieces pour la flute traversiere* . . . (Paris, 1712), 20; Dupont (1718), 42f.; Demotz de la Salle (1728), 167; Boüin, *La vielleuse* [ca. 1761], 12; Hotteterre, *Methode pour la musette* . . . (Paris, 1737), 35; Choquel (1762), 105, 107.

4. Demotz de la Salle (1728), 167, and Torlez [ca. 1775], 31.

5. ". . . ce qui lie le Chant, & le rend plus coulant." Choquel, *La musique* (1762), 106.

6. E.g., Hotteterre, *Premier livre de pieces pour la flûte-traversiere* . . . (Paris, 1715), 16; Dandrieu (1724), 1; Dornel ([1731]/1982), 4; Corrette (1738), 4, 30; Anon. [ca. 1760], 33–34; Boüin, *La vielleuse* [ca. 1761], 7, 10; Engramelle, *La tonotechnie* (1775), 228 and plate IV; Azaïs [1776], 36. Among the *Concerts royeaux* of Couperin's third volume is a "Courante a L'italiéne" marked "Pointé-Coulé" ([Paris, 1722], 24). Demotz de la Salle (1728), 181, defines *lourer* as follows:

> . . . C'est éxprimer les notes qui sont liées de deux en deux par cette figure⌢en les coulant, caressant, & roulant de telle sorte que les Sons soient continus, liez & conjoins . . . en marquent sensiblement la premiere Note de deux en deux. . . .

> . . . It is to render the notes tied in pairs by this figure⌢through slurring, caressing, and rolling them in such a way that the sounds are continuous, tied, and conjoined . . . marking perceptibly the first note of the pair. . . .

Azaïs defines the term similarly as well ([1776], 167).

Torlez ([ca. 1775], 30) seems to speak against inequality when slurs are present:

> Quand les croches sont lieés de deux en deux, par un petit croissant qu'on appelle liason, il faut les passer egales c'est a dire les lourer.

> When the eighths are bound two by two by a little crescent that one calls the slur, it is necessary to pass them equally, that is to say, to tie [*lourer*] them.

But the example he gives is in **3** with conjunct motion: since all prerequisites for inequality are present, one suspects a misprint (viz., "egales" should read "inegales"). As we shall see below, Quantz (alone) states that inequality does not apply when there is a slur over more than two notes (1752, chap. XII, §12): this much-read passage may be the source of the fairly common belief that slurs cancel *notes inégales*. Fuller (*The New Harvard Dictionary of Music*, s. v. "Notes Inégales," 549) mistakenly asserts that Lacassagne (1766, 51, 57) takes the slur to mean negation of inequality; but Lacassagne is clearly referring to triplets and sextuplets, marked ♪♪♪ , etc., which are always equal in ordinary French practice.

7. Brossard, *Dictionnaire* (1705), 56.

8. Saint-Arroman, *Dictionnaire d'interprétation* (1983), 212–14.

9. Ed. Cohen (1965), 67.

10. E.g., Corrette, *Methode pour apprendre aisèment à joüer de la flute traversiere* . . . (Paris [ca. 1742]), 5; Cappus, *Etrennes* [1730], 13; see also Saint-Arroman, loc. cit.

11. ". . . parce que le mouvement est marqué." *Sçience de la musique vocale* . . . (Paris [ca. 1760]), 11.

12. *La vielleuse* [ca. 1761], 6: ". . . dans des airs d'un caractere grave & picqué comme dans des marches ou ouvertures . . . Les croches sont toujours inégales & marquées. . . ." (The dots preceding "Les croches" are Boüin's.)

13. *Quatrième livre de pieces de clavecin* (Paris, 1730), 2.

14. Lacassagne, *Traité général* (1766), 55, 57. A. J. Dumas's *L'art de la musique* . . . (Paris [1753]), 200, contains an exercise (in $\frac{12}{4}$) wherein "Noires Egales" (♪♪♪) are contrasted with dotted patterns (♪·♪♪) marked "piqué"; thus he uses the term in conjunction with a 3:1 rhythmic ratio, but also notates all the dots. (Cf. also idem, 238.)

15. *Dictionnaire* (1705), 174.

16. 1705, 114.

> STACCATO. ou *Stoccatò*. veut dire à peu prés la même chose que *Spiccato*. C'est à dire que, sur tout les Instrumens à Archet, doivent faire leur coups d'Archet *secs, sans traîner*, & bien *détachez* ou *separez* les uns des autres, c'est presque ce que nous apellons en François, *Picqué* ou *Pointé*.

> STACCATO or *Stoccatò* means almost the same thing as *Spiccato*. That is to say that particularly the bowed instruments must make their bow strokes dry, without drawing-out, and well detached or separated one from another; it is almost what we call in French *Picqué* or *Pointé*.

The influential *Dictionnaire Trévoux* adopted Brossard's definition almost verbatim (1771, 6: 793); according to Patricia Ranum, "*Piquer ou Pointer:* A Word Changes Meaning, 1690–1770" (unpublished paper [1980]), this definition first appears in the 1752 edition of the dictionary.

17. *Dictionnaire* (1768), 372–73:

PIQUÉ, *adj. pris adverbialement.* Manière de jouer en pointant les Notes & marquant fortement le Pointé.

Notes *piquées* sont des suites de Notes montant ou descendant diatoniquement, ou rebattues sur le même degré, sur chacune desquelles on met un point, quelquefois un peu allongé pour indiquer qu'elles doivent être marquées égales par des coups de langue ou d'Archet secs & détachés, sans retirer ou repousser l'archet.

PIQUÉ, *adj. used adverbially.* Manner of playing by dotting the notes and strongly marking the dotted one.

Notes that are *piquées* are rows of notes ascending or descending diatonically, or restruck on the same pitch, above each of which one places a dot (which is sometimes a bit elongated [i.e, a stroke]) to indicate that they must be equally marked by tongue strokes or by dry and detached bow strokes, without redrawing [or "hooking"] the bow.

18. 1787, 147, 152.
19. André Campra, *Cantatas françoises . . . livre premier* (Paris, 1708), 32, 36.
20. *L'art de préluder* (1719), 58, 60. Cf. also Hotteterre's comments about $\frac{2}{4}$ (p. 60):

. . . les croches simples y sont egales, pour l'ordinaire, et les doubles pointées. Elle convient aux Airs legers et piqués.

. . . the eighths are equal, ordinarily, and the sixteenths pointed. This meter suits airs that are light and detached [*piqués*].

21. *La vielleuse* [ca. 1761], 6; for the French text see n. 12. On p. 9 Boüin identifies the character of $\frac{6}{8}$ as

vif & piqué . . . quand pour un tems il se rencontre une croche pointée, une double croche & une croche. . . .

brisk and piqué . . . when one finds a dotted eighth, a sixteenth, and an eighth per beat. . . .

—which is a description of the characteristic gigue rhythm. In the previous paragraph he had already noted that eighths are equal in this meter, and sixteenths unequal; hence *piqué* again seems to mean staccato (the inconsistent spellings appear in the original). In the little overture to "Vos beaux yeux" from Boüin's *Les amusements d'une heure et demie* (Paris [ca. 1761]), the opening "Grave et Piqué" in ₵ contains only two eighth notes that would ordinarily be subject to inequality; here, too, staccato is apparently intended.

22. *Méthode raisonnée* [1755], 6.
23. *Nouveaux principes* [1769], 17.
24. *Méthode* [1775], 15: "égalles et bien marquées."
25. Pp. 9 and 29; for direct quotations see n. 71 below.
26. Dandrieu, *Second livre de pièces de clavecin . . .* (Paris, 1728), 5; modern ed. by Pauline Aubert and Brigitte François-Sappey (Paris: Éditions de la Schola Cantorum, 1973), 86. Fuller's suggestion ("Notes and *inégales* Unjoined: Defending a Definition," *Journal of Musicology* 7 [1989]: 27) that " 'staccato' is ruled out

by written overlapping" in this piece is unconvincing; in the first measure (and similar spots) the offbeat eighths can certainly be shortened, as could the quarters if this seemed warranted. Related situations occur in "Les tendres reproches," "L'impérieuse," and "L'éclatante" of this collection.

27. (Paris, 1753), 84ff. Similar passages occur in Elizabeth Jaquet de la Guerre, *Cantates françoises* . . . (Paris, 1708), 43, and Gaumey, *Cantates,* "Borée," "Air, vif. et piqué" (MS, *Recueil de cantates, US*-Wcm, n.d.).

28. The same is true of the *Rondeau* by P. D. Philidor (1717) cited by Saint-Arroman (*Dictionnaire d'interprétation,* 275). There are of course occurrences of the term where the intended meaning is less than certain—e.g., Boismortier, *Quatre suites de pieces de clavecin* . . . Op. 59 (Paris, 1736; modern ed. by Erwin R. Jacobi, Munich: Leuckart, 1960), 13, and Dutartre, *La volupté* . . . (Paris, 1738), 1. A truly puzzling case is the "Dacapella Fugue" in P. D. Philidor's *Trio premier oeuvre contenant six suites* (Paris [1718]), marked "un peu piqué louré."

29. I am indebted to the unpublished paper of Patricia Ranum [1980] for numerous musical references to this term. Saint-Arroman (*Dictionnaire d'interprétation,* 274) declares that *piqué* corresponds to the verb *pointer,* and that it means to dot the notes strongly; he admits that contemporary definitions of this sort are rare, yet claims that this meaning is to be derived from musical contexts in which the term occurs. But Saint-Arroman's references do not unequivocally support sharp inequality. His most telling example (p. 274) is a pair of parallel passages said to be from the "second edition" of Lagarde's *Aeglé* (Paris, 1748), where the first is marked "Piqué" and the second is written in dotted note values; but neither *piqué* nor dots appear in the first print of the work ([1751], 56–57, copy at *US*-Wcm), which raises questions about the significance of this case; as in his other citations, *piqué* could here just as well mean staccato. Fuller's assertion (*The New Grove,* 13: 421) that " 'Piqué' usually meant sharply dotted, but one or two writers used it to mean equal and staccato" is inaccurate, as is O'Donnell's unsupported conjecture that the word's "application to the 'piquant' dance style led to its equation with *pointer,* to dot" (The French Style," pt. 2: 338).

30. Thurston Dart (*The Interpretation of Music* [London: Hutchison and Co., 1954], 81) and Betty Bang Mather (*Interpretation of French Music from 1675 to 1775* [New York: McGinnis & Marx, 1973], 3) are but two of several modern writers who claim this meaning for *mesuré,* yet cite no source.

31. *Dictionnaire* (1768), 273

32. 1717, 60: "Il faut que ceux qui auront recours à ces Préludes-réglés, les joüent d'une maniere aisée sans trop s'attacher à la précision des mouvemens; à moins que je ne l'aÿe marqué exprés par le mot de, **Mesuré.**"

33. E.g., "La mézangére," *Second livre de piéces de clavecin* (Paris, 1717), 56, and "Le rossignol en-amour" and its *double, Troisiéme livre* . . . (Paris, 1722), 11–12.

34. "*Mesuré,* indique plus de précision dans chaque tems de la mesure." *Méthode* [1775], 13; see also Saint-Arroman, *Dictionnaire d'interprétation,* 218–20.

35. Apparently Arnold Dolmetsch (*The Interpretation of Music of the Sixteenth and Seventeenth Centuries* [London: Novello, 1915; new ed. 1946], 75–76) established this notion by misunderstanding the references in Marais and Couperin cited below; it was then passed on by Dart (*Interpretation of Music,* 81) and later writers, including Neumann ("Facts and Fiction about Overdotting," *Musical Quarterly* 63 [1977]: 165, 166, n. 24, expurgated from *Essays,* 119).

36. *Les principes du clavecin* (1702), 26.

37. Corrette, *L'ecole d'Orphée* (1738), 4; *Methode pour la flute traversiere* [ca. 1742], 4; *La belle vielleuse* [ca. 1783], 5; Hotteterre, *L'art de préluder* (1719), 57; Vion, *La musique* (1742), 22.

38. *Traité général* (1766), 51.

39. "The French *Inégales*, Quantz, and Bach," *Essays*, 30–31 and table 1 above.

40. 1722, 27: ". . . dans quelque Mesure que ce soit, lorsqu'une espece de Note est inegale, il s'ensuit que les especes inferieures le sont aussi." Other writers who take this position include Demotz de la Salle (1728, 160), de-La Chapelle ([1736–52], 1: 5 and 2: 38–39), Vion (1742, 25, only for the meter $\frac{3}{2}$), Buterne (1752, 11), Anon. ([ca. 1760], 9, 29, 31–32), Morel de Lescer ([ca. 1760], 7 and 9), L'Abbé Duval (1764, 43ff.), and Dard ([1769], 11–12, for triple meters **3**, $\frac{3}{2}$, $\frac{3}{8}$, and $\frac{3}{16}$ [but not $\frac{3}{4}$]).

41. Azaïs [1776], 42. Other writers who advocate descending inequality include Corrette (1741, 4–5, only for meter **3**), Dupuit ([1741], VI), Bordet ([1755], 8), Dumas ([1753], 73–74 [for **C**] and 91–93 [for $\frac{3}{2}$ and $\frac{3}{4}$]); Bordier ([1760], 39), Boüin ([ca. 1761], 6–7), Lacassagne (1766, 55, 57), Cajon ([1772], 8–9), and Mercadier de Belesta (1777, 69). Fuller's accounts of cumulative and descending inequality (*The New Grove*, 13: 422; *The New Harvard Dictionary*, 549) slightly confuse the issues.

42. Corrette, *Methode pour la flute traversiere* [ca. 1742], 4; Denis (1747/ [1757]), 6; Rollet (1760), 29. In his earlier *L'ecole d'Orphée* (1738, 4), however, Corrette observes that

> le trois quatre $\frac{3}{4}$ Sert dans les Courantes des Sonates il faut jouer les Croches Egales et passer la deuxieme Double Croche plus viste.
>
> three-quarter time $\frac{3}{4}$ is used in the courantes of sonatas; it is necessary to play the eighths equal and render the second sixteenth more quickly [i.e., unequally].

Pollet (*Methode pour . . . cistre ou guittare* [Paris (1775), 5]) declares that eighths are equal in $\frac{3}{4}$ but says nothing of sixteenths in this meter.

43. E.g., Fuller, *The New Grove*, 13: 421.

44. In addition to the sources listed in table 1-1, the following suggest that eighths are equal in $\frac{3}{4}$: de-La Chapelle ([1736–52], 2: 19); Morel de Lescer ([ca. 1760], 14, 16); Boüin ([ca. 1761], 10); Dard ([1769], 12, 41); Tarade ([ca. 1774], 14, 20–21); Duval ([1775], 9); Torlez ([ca. 1775], 49). Mussard (*Nouveaux principes pour . . . la flütte traversiere* [Paris (1779), 12]) writes of "les croches quelquefois inegales [the eighths sometimes unequal]" in $\frac{3}{4}$; and Cappus ([1730], 14) suggests similarly that "souvent les croches sont egalles [often the eighths are equal]."

45. [1776], 41; see also his comments cited above, p. 27.

46. *Nouvelle methode* (1709), 15. His musical example here shows unequal eighths in **2**, and unequal sixteenths in **C** and **3**. Rollet ([1760], 27) also notes that "il n'est presque pas possible de donner des principes pour ces sortes de regles parce que c'est selon la fantaisie des compositeurs [it is almost impossible to give principles for these sorts of rules, because it depends on the fancy of the composers]."

47. *Méthode de musique* (1728), 166.

48. *L'art de la musique* [1753], 73–75, 201.

49. See above, pp. 6–7. Vion (1742) appears self-contradictory on the matter of inequality in 𝄴. On p. 18 he states that "Chaque Tems de la *Mesure à quatre*, est rempli d'une Noire ou de l'équivalent, les doubles-Croches inegales [Each beat of quadruple meter consists of a quarter note or the equivalent; the sixteenths are unequal]," which is the normal meter-inequality relationship; but on pp. 21–22 he writes "La Mesure à quatre se bat *Lentement*; elle a les Croches inégales [quadruple meter is beater *slowly*; it has unequal eighths]," with no mention of sixteenths. The treatise contains a similar discrepancy (or misprint?) concerning eighths in 𝄵 (pp. 18, 23).

50. [ca. 1760], 11: "les croches sont quelque fois Egales. mais les doubles croches toujours inegales, a moins qu'elles ne soient marquées."

51. Cappus ([1730], 13), Villeneuve (1733/56, III), and Rollet ([1760], 29) all suggest 𝄵 should be taken in four when many sixteenths are present. But Cajon claims it makes no significant difference (*Éléments* [1772], 8):

> Mais cela ne doit absolument rien changer ni au mouvement de cette mesure, ni à la maniére d'y passer les croches, les différentes façons de la battre n'en changeant pas la nature.

> But that absolutely may not change anything concerning either the *mouvement* of this meter, or the manner of inequalizing the eighths; the different ways of beating it do not change its nature.

52. *La vielleuse* [ca. 1761], 7: "Il se trouve quelquefois des airs de Musique marqués par un 𝄴 simple, qui demandent à être joués comme les airs de Musique marqués par un 2, dans lesquels il ne se rencontre pas de doubles croches, surtout lorsque les airs, dont je veux parler ici, sont d'un mouvement gai ou léger, & lorsque dans ces airs il ne s'y rencontre pas de doubles croches. . . ." He adds, however, that "les croches sont toujours égales. . . ."

53. *Méthode raisonnée* [1755], 8: "Il y en a qui battent deux fois dans les mesures de 𝄴 & de $\frac{12}{8}$, mais c'est un mauvais usage qui est contre le principe. . . ."

54. *Traité du violon* [ca. 1774], 21.

55. *Ballet royal d'Alcidiane* (1658); modern ed. in *Oeuvres complètes de J.-B. Lully, Les ballets*, vol. 2, ed. Henry Prunières and André Tessier (Paris: Éditions de *La revue musicale*, 1936), 56, 183.

56. Dieupart, *Six suittes de clavessin* . . . (Amsterdam [1701]); modern ed. by Paul Brunold (Paris: Éditions de l'Oiseau Lyre, 1934). The Babell keyboard manuscript (*GB*-Lbm Add. mss. 39569, dated 1702) is described in Bruce Lester Gustafson, *French Harpsichord Music of the Seventeenth Century* (Ann Arbor: UMI Research Press, 1979), 1: 68–73; the overtures in question are 24-Babell #18, 25, 101, and 109 in Gustafson's catalogue. Gustafson considers the manuscript "an important and excellent source of French harpsichord music," and has shown that Charles Babell must have been in contact with "the inner circles of the Parisian harpsichord world, since the works of Louis Couperin are found in few manuscripts in France and in no foreign sources other than 24-*Babell*." The connection may have been through Dieupart himself (pp. 71–72). Neumann, evidently unaware of the Babell manuscript, contends that *notes inégales* are to be excluded from Dieupart's overtures ("Rhythm in the Two Versions . . .," *Essays*, 103).

57. [ca. 1774], 18: ". . . $\frac{12}{8}$. Ces trois Croches sont toujours égales entr'elles ou que l'Auteur ne fasse exception à la Régle en Crochant doublement celle du

Milieu et mettant un Point entre la Premiére et la Seconde pour donner plus de Valeur de Moitié à la premiére. . . ." Cf. Also Demotz de la Salle (1728), 167; Torlez [ca. 1775], 34; and table 1.

58. [1730], 25–26.

59. *Principes* (1772), 11: "*Nota.* Le goût du Chant éxige très-souvent que les croches soient inégales, la prémière longue, la seconde brève, & la troisième longue." It will be recalled that Bacilly (1668) had obscurely hinted at this practice as well (see above, p. 6).

60. Charles-François-Alexandre Pollet, *Méthode pour apprendre a pincer du cistre ou guittare* . . . (Paris [1775]), 5.

61. *Nouveau systeme* (1777), 68.

62. 1702, 25: ". . . la liberté que se donnent les Musiciens de transgresser leurs propres regles. . . ."

63. See esp. Neumann, "*Notes inégales* Revisited," and Fuller, "Notes and *inégales* Unjoined."

64. See also the following spots in the *DTÖ* editions: vol. I/2: 23, 45–46, 61; vol. II/2: 74, 155.

65. *Second livre* (1717), 56.

66. This occurs in the second half of the piece as well; concerning Couperin's unorthodox usage of extra beams (sixty-fourths in this case), see below, pp. 66–67.

67. Monteclair, "Ariane et Bacchus," *Cantates a une et a deux voix* . . . , bk. 3 (Paris, 1728; facs. ed., New York: Garland, 1990), 30–31; modern ed. in *Cantatas for One and Two Voices,* ed. James R. Anthony and Diran Akmajian, Recent Researches in the Music of the Baroque Era, vol. 29/30 (Madison, Wis.: A-R Editions, 1978): 48–49. Cf. also Fuller, "Notes and *inégales* Unjoined," 27, n. 13.

68. Neumann, "The French *Inégales,*" *Essays,* 34–41; cf. also Fuller, *The New Grove,* 13: 423.

69. See also Houle, 78–84.

70. Jacob Roussier, *Méthode de musique* . . . (Paris, 1769), 55ff.

71. Mercadier de Belesta (1777, 66–67) discusses *tems forts et foibles* (strong and weak beats) and *passer inégalement deux notes de valeur égale qui composent un tems* (rendering unequally two notes of equal value that constitute a beat) in immediate succession, but he does not really conflate the concepts, as Fuller seems to suggest ("Notes and *inégales* Unjoined," 28, n. 15). Similarly, the anonymous author of *Nouvelle methode pour apprendre à jouer du violon* ([ca. 1760], 9, 29) discusses "les notes détachées en fortes et foibles, et les notes articulées en longues et breves [notes detached as strong and weak, and notes articulated as long and short]" on the same page (29), yet has already distinguished between two rhythmic levels to which these apply (p. 9): in meter **2**, for example, the *notes détachées* are the quarters, while *notes articulées* (i.e., long–short) are the eighths and sixteenths. The author further clarifies (p. 29) that

> il faut appuyer un peu plus sur les fortes que sur les foibles, en employant pour les unes et pour les autres la même quantité de temps: on employe au contraire plus de temps pour les longues que pour les breves.

> it is necessary to *lean* a little more on the *strong* notes than on the weak, in employing for the one and the other the same quantity of time; on the contrary, one employs *more time* for the *long* notes than for the short [emphasis added].

72. Houle's statement that *notes inégales* "enhances meter through lengthening good notes and shortening bad notes" (p. 86) should be qualified by the considerations set forth above.

CHAPTER 3.   Notes Inégales Outside France

1. Brossard (1705), 5:

> ANDANTE. du Verbe *Andare*. ALLER, *cheminer à pas égaux.* veut dire sur tout pour les Basses-Continuës, qu'il faut faire toutes les Nottes égales, & en bien séparer les Sons.

> ANDANTE. from the verb *Andare*, TO GO, *to walk with equal steps;* it means especially for continuo-basses that it is necessary to make all the notes equal, and to separate the sounds well.

Brossard motet cited by Eugène Borrel, *L'interprétation de la musique française de Lully à la revolution* (Paris: Librairie Félix Alcan, 1934), 157:

> Andante, ou à notes égales. Le mot andante indique que c'est de la musique à l'italienne non pointée.

> Andante, or with equal notes. The word andante indicates that it is Italiante music, and not pointed.

2. *L'art de toucher* (1717), 39–40; see above, p. 12.
3. *L'art de preluder* (1719), 58: "Les croches y sont presque toujours pointées dans la musique françoise."
4. *Principes* (1736), 50, 53.
5. [1737], 25: "selon l'usage des François."
6. *Dictionnaire* (1768), 380–81.
7. "Il faut . . . distinguer sur tout les phrases qui sont dans le goût François, d'avec celles qui exigent le goût Italien."
8. Modern ed. by Barbara Garvey Jackson, Recent Researches in the Music of the Baroque Era, vol. 20 (Madison, Wis.: A-R Editions, 1975).
9. 1741, 4–5: ". . . dans chaque mesure les croches se jouent également dans la musique italienne; comme dans la Courante de la 7ᵉ. Sonate du 5ᵉ. Oeuvre de Corelli." [1748], 13–14:

> Aux mouvemens de 2. et de 3. tems dans la musique françoise, comme Opera ou Motets, il faut pointer les croches de deux en deux; . . . Mais dans la Musique Italienne les croches se joüent également.

> In pieces in duple and triple meter in French music, such as opera or motets, it is necessary to point the eighth notes two by two; . . . But in Italian music the eighths are played equally.

10. *L'ecole d'Orphée* (1738), 4–5, 27, 30. "Voyez les Opera italiens de Mʳˢ. Handel, Bononcini, Pepuseh, Scarlatti, Porpora, et toutes les Sonates Composées par nos illustres françois. . . . Il faut joüer les Croches égales et passer la deuxieme Double-croche plus viste" (p. 5).
11. *Methode pour la flute* [ca. 1742], 4–5:

Il faut joüer les Croches Egales et pointer les Doubles-Croches de deux en deux. On les joüe aussi quelque fois également dans les Allegro, et Presto des Sonàtes et Concerto.

. . . Les Anglois Composent beaucoup de Vaudevilles, et Contredances sur cette mesure. Voyez Bartholomew Fair, Hunt the Sanerel, Lilibulero, Hooptpetty-coat, dans les Chansons Angloises.

It is necessary to play the eighths equal and to point the sixteenths two by two. One sometimes also plays them equally in the allegros and prestos of sonatas and concertos.

. . . The English compose many vaudevilles and contradances in this measure [$^6_4$]. See "Bartholomew Fair," "Hunt the Sanerel," "Lilibulero," and "Hooptpetty-coat" in the *Chansons Angloises.*

Corrette refers here to his own collection of *Les plus beaux vaudevilles, chansons et contredances anglois* (1740), of which no copies are known to survive.

12. Paris [1782], 4.

13. Vion, *La musique* (1742), 22, 25, 26, 29. In 1721 Hotteterre published an arrangement of Valentine's "op. 5," which is very likely the source of Vion's acquaintance with this music; according to *The New Grove* (s. v. "Hotteterre, Jacques[-Martin]" by Jane M. Bowers), the pieces in question are actually from Valentine's opp. 4 and 6.

14. [1776], 41–42: ". . . tous les étrangers se servent unanimement du signe $^3_4$ et n'en font pas moins les croches inégales dans la mesure ordinaire à trois tems." See also above, p. 27.

15. *Nouveaux principes* [1779], 12.

16. (Schwednitz, 1678), 56.

17. Collins ("Three Further Views," 483), who claims Printz to be certain evidence of French inequality in Germany, omits the second line of the example.

18. *DTÖ* I/2: 11, 20; II/2: 24, 48, 52.

19. Muffat, *Auserlesene Instrumental-Music* (Passau, 1701), preface; modern ed., *DTÖ* XI/2 (Vienna, 1904): 2.

20. In the preface to this collection Kusser writes that

j'ay crû n'y pouuoir mieux paruenir, qu'en m'attachant a jmiter ce fameux BAP-TISTE . . . Je me suis reglé a suiure sa Methode, et a entrer dans ses manieres delicates, autant qu'il m'a esté possible. . . .

I believed it not possible to make my way better than by applying myself to imitate the famous Baptiste. . . . I have required myself to follow his method and enter into his delicate manners in so far as possible. . . .

21. *MGG* 5: 1471; Georg Philipp Telemann, "Lebens-Lauff . . . 1718," in Johann Mattheson, *Grosse General-Baß-Schule . . .*, 2d ed. (Hamburg, 1731), 172–76; p. 176:

Monsieur Pantlon, sage ich / hatte / nebst der Erfahrung auf vielerley Instrumen-ten / zugleich in der Französischen Music und Composition eine ungemeine Ge-schicklichkeit / woraus ich mehr Vortheil geschöpfet / als ich hier anzuführen vermögend bin.

> Mr. *Pantlon*, I say, had in addition to practical experience on various instruments, also unusual adroitness in French music and composition, from which I obtained more advantage than I am here able to adduce.

Hebenstreit had visited Paris and performed before Louis XIV in 1705.

22. Georg Linnemann, *Celler Musikgeschichte bis zum Beginn des 19. Jahrhunderts* (Celle: Schweiger & Pick [Ernst Pfingsten], 1935), 57–65.

23. Christoph Wolf, "Johann Sebastian Bach," *The New Grove Bach Family* (New York: W. W. Norton, 1983), 51; Gustav Fock, *Der junge Bach in Lüneburg, 1700 bis 1702* (Hamburg: Merseburger, 1950), 44–46, 53–54; C. P. E. Bach (with J. F. Agricola), "Obituary of Bach" (1754) in *The Bach Reader*, ed. Hans T. David and Arthur Mendel (New York: W. W. Norton, 1966), 217, where the material in quotation marks appears.

24.

> *Lourer* [gall.] bestehet darinn: daß man unter 2 gleichgeltenden Noten, bey der ersten ein wenig mehr hält, und derselben mehr Nachdruck giebt, als der zweyten, jedoch so, daß man sie nicht punctiret oder abstösset. s. *Brossards* Diction. pag. 293 sq.

> *Lourer* (French) consists of holding the first of two equal-value notes a little longer, and giving it more stress than the second, yet in such a way that one does not dot it or make it staccato. See Brossard's *Dictionary*, p. 293f.

Cf. the discussions by Loulié and Brossard on pp. 16 and 22 above. Walther's definition of *andante* is also very close to Brossard's; but whereas Brossard's reason for requiring equality in an Andante is clarified by a remark in one of his unpublished motets (see above, p. 37), it is unclear that Walther held the same view on this issue.

25. This information comes from quantz's "Lebenslauf" (1755), cited with useful commentary in Reilly's translation of the *Versuch*, xii–xix; see esp. xii–xv. Telemann also comments on the mixture of French and Italian styles in the Dresden Hofkapelle ("Lebens-Lauff" [1718], 173–74).

26. 1752, esp. chap. XI, §12.

27. *Solfeggi pour la flute traversiere* . . . (MS. *DK*-Kk); modern ed. by Winfried Michel and Hermien Teske (Winterthur: Amadeus, 1978). Michel and Teske suggest that this volume was compiled for the instruction of Frederick the Great ca. 1730–40, before Quantz moved to Berlin. But according to Horst Augsbach (*Johann Joachim Quantz: Thematisches Verzeichnis der musikalischen Werke, Werkgruppen QV 2 und QV 3*, Studien und Materialien zur Musikgeschichte Dresdens, vol. 5 [Dresden: Sächische Landesbibliothek, 1984], V–VI), both the content and watermarks of this source indicate that it was written out much later, probably between 1775 and 1782, by Quantz's pupil Augustin Neuff. As early as 1782 the collection was attributed to Quantz, who died in 1773; accordingly, the provisional date of ca. 1770 for the content of the *Solfeggi* has been adopted here.

28. Pp. 38, 40, 55, and passim. In example 3-5 the syllables below the notes identify various tongue strokes.

29. P. 89, no sixteenths present; cf. the discussion of this issue on pp. 27–30 above.

30. One of Quantz's examples of inequality does show a three-note slur, however: Table IX, fig. 1, *m*), cited below, p. 47.

31. Chap. XI, §12; trans. Reilly, *On Playing the Flute*, 123–24 (here modified).

32. Reilly, *Quantz and His Versuch: Three Studies* (New York: Galaxy Music, 1971), 38; idem, preface to Quantz, *On Playing the Flute*, xv.

33. Moritz Fürstenau, *Zur Geschichte der Musik und des Theaters am Hofe zu Dresden* (Dresden: Verlagsbuchhandlung von Rudolf Kunze, 1861–62), 1: 201 and 2: 85; Ortrun Landmann, "Französische Elemente in der Musikpraxis des 18. Jahrhunderts am Dresdener Hof," *Der Einfluß der französischen Musik auf die Komponisten der ersten Hälfte des 18. Jahrhunderts*, Studien zur Aufführungspraxis und Interpretation von Instrumentalmusik des 18. Jahrhunderts, vol. 16, Konferenzbericht der IX. Wissenschaftlichen Arbeitstagung, Blankenburg/Harz, 26. Juni bis 28. Juni 1981 [n.p., 1982], 48–50; idem, "The Dresden Hofkapelle during the Lifetime of Johann Sebastian Bach," *Early Music* 17 (1989): 20-23.

34. "Spielen nicht Quantz, Benda, Graun sehr französisch?" *Der critische Musicus an der Spree*, no. 27 (2 Sept. 1749; reprinted, Berlin, 1750): 218.

35. Ernest Eugene Helm, *Music at the Court of Frederick the Great* (Norman: University of Oklahoma Press, 1960), chap. 3.

36. See Reilly, *Quantz and His Versuch*, chap. 2; concerning the ossification of musical style in Berlin, see also below, pp. 83 and 116.

37. Christoph Wolff goes so far as to suggest that "French performing practice became predominant in instrumental music . . . virtually throughout central and north Germany, especially after about 1680. . . ." (*The New Grove*, 7: 273).

38. Johann Mattheson, *Der volkommene Kapellmeister* (Hamburg, 1739), 86: ". . . denn Franckreich ist und bleibet doch die rechte Tanz-Schule. . . ."

39. Meredith Little, "French Court Dance in Germany at the Time of Johann Sebastian Bach: *La Bourgogne* in Paris and Leipzig," in International Musicological Society, *Report of the Twelfth Congress Berkeley 1977*, ed. Daniel Heartz and Bonnie Wade (Kassel: Bärenreiter/The American Musicological Society, 1981), 730–31; an additional tutor not cited by Little is Carl Pauli, *Elémens de la danse* (Leipzig, 1756). See also Walter Salmen, "Der akademische Tanzmeister," International Musicological Society, *Atti del XIV congresso della Società Internazionale di Musicologia* (Torino: Edizioni di Torino, 1990), 1: 83–88, as well as Meredith Little and Natalie Jenne, *Dance and the Music of J. S. Bach* (Bloomington: Indiana University Press, 1991), ix–15.

40. Telemann, "Lebens-Lauff" (1718), passim; Mattheson, *Der volkommene Kapellmeister*, 225; Scheibe, *Critischer Musicus* (1745), 146–47, 673.

41. Charles Sanford Terry, *Bach's Orchestra* (London: Oxford University Press, 1932), 6; see also n. 39 above, and figure 3-1.

42. *Bach-Dokumente. Supplement zu Johann Sebastian Bach: neue Ausgabe sämtlicher Werke*, vol. 3: *Dokumente zum Nachwirken Johann Sebastian Bachs 1750–1800*, ed. Hans-Joachim Schulze (Kassel: Bärenreiter 1972/Leipzig: VEB Deutscher Verlag für Musik 1972), 4.

43. Walther, *Musikalisches Lexikon* (1732), 109, 114, 319, and passim; see also n. 24 above.

Neumann has suggested that in the case of the *Domine Deus* in the B-minor *Missa*, which was written for the Dresden Hofkapelle, Bach used the Lombardic rhythm (   ) at the beginning of the (autograph) obbligato flute part to prevent the French flutist Buffardin from playing this piece with French inequality ("The French *Inégales*," *Essays*, 52–53). But as Gerhard Herz has shown, the same rhythm appears at crucial points in the second violin and viola parts (both autograph) as well (*Essays on J. S. Bach* [Ann Arbor: UMI Research Press, 1985], 223–27). This suggests that Bach intended Lombardic rhythm, and not cancellation of *inégalité*, throughout the *Domine Deus*.

44. Mattheson, *Der volkommene Kapellmeister*, 22, 133, 136, 173, 233; Adlung (Erfurt, 1758), 244–45, 606, 613, 616.

45. Collins ("Three Further Views," 481–82) and Fuller (*The New Grove*, 13: 423; *The New Grove Instruments*, 2: 779) claim that inequality is indicated in Christoph Bernhard's *Tractatus Compositionis Augmentatus* (MS ca. 1657; printed in *Die Kompositionslehre Heinrich Schützens in der Fassung seines Schülers Christoph Bernhard*, ed. Joseph Müller-Blattau [Kassel: Bärenreiter, 1963]). But the passage in question (chap. 27, p. 76) concerns treatment of prolonged passing dissonance (*prolongatio in transitu*), and the dotted notation in Bernhard's example is purely coincidental: he could and did use other note values to illustrate the concept in his *Ausführlicher Bericht* (chap. 17, 1963, 150; for quick comparison see Walter Hilse's trans., "The Treatises of Christoph Bernhard," *Music Forum* 3 [1973]: 101–2). Both of these composition treatises are virtually devoid of information about performance: Bernhard had written on that subject in his earlier *Von der Singe-Kunst*, yet there too he says nothing about rhythmic alteration.

Although Leopold Mozart's *Versuch einer gründlichen Violinschule* (Augsburg, 1756) has occasionally been cited as a source for *inégalité*, Mozart was clearly not advocating the French convention, as Neumann has already shown ("The French *Inégales*," *Essays*, 38–39). Houle's suggestion (*Meter in Music*, 88) that *notes inégales* "is defined and discussed in a number of German instruction books" is misleading, as is his assertion (p. 91) that D. G. Türk mentions *notes inégales* in his *Kalvierschule* ([Leipzig and Halle, 1789], 323–24): in a brief section on ornamental variations ("Die Veränderungen sind auf verschiedene Art möglich . . ."), Türk suggests that such ornamentation may involve adding or reducing the number of notes in a passage, or "das so gennante Verrücken der Noten" – lengthening some while shortening others. The interpolation of dotted rhythms is but one of three sorts of *Verrücken der Noten* Türk illustrates: this is not French *inégalité*.

46. E.g., Parran (1646), Cousu (1658), Fleury (1660), Millet (1666), Borjon de Scellery (1672), Danoville (1687), Berthet (1691), Jean Rousseau [ca. 1710], Grandval (1732), Moyreau (1753), Berard (1755), Blanchet (1756), Mahaut [1759], de Lusse (1761), Bethizy (1764), Lécuyer (1769), Biferi [1770], Carpentier [1771], Bemetzrieder [1771, 1778], Bailleux [1773], Corbelin (1779), Cupis le jeune [1772], Lemoine (n. d.), Azaïs [ca. 1775], Dellain [1781], Despréaux (1785), Cardon [ca. 1786], Borghese (1786), Cousineau [ca. 1790]; Fuller ("Notes and *inégales* Unjoined," 25, n. 8) also lists [Nivers], 1666ff, "Principes de musique" for students at Saint-Cyr, MSS. *F-V*, and Francoeur, 1772; and there are probably others. (None of these items is included in the bibliography for this study; see *RISM* BVI$^{1-2}$ for full citations.) Neumann ("The *Notes inégales* Revisited," 140–41) is mistaken in suggesting that "all French texts without exception" take up the topic.

47. Telemann, "Lebens-Lauff" (1718), 172, 177; p. 172: "Wie nöthig and nützlich es sey / diese Arten in ihren wesentlichen Stücken unterscheiden zu können /

solches erfahre noch biß auf den heutigen Tag / und sage / es könne niemand / ohne solches zu wissen / hurtig und glücklich im Erfinden seyn." Marpurg, *Des critischen Musicus* (1750), 218: "In allen Arten der Music, in den Musicken aller Nationen giebt es schlechtes Zeug und auch wieder etwas schönes. Dieß ist der Ausspruch des alten Bachs in Leipzig, der gewiß in der Music gelten kann." Quantz, XVIII/87–89, and index, s. v. "Geschmack"; see also XVII/vii/56.

48. Johann Friedrich Agricola, *Anleitung zur Singkunst* . . . (Berlin, 1757); Marpurg, *Anleitung zum Clavierspielen* (Berlin, 1755 and 1765), and *Anleitung zur Musik überhaupt, und zur Singkunst besonders* (Berlin, 1763); Carl Philipp Emmanuel Bach, *Versuch über die wahre Art das Clavier zu spielen* (Berlin, 1753–62); Johann Friedrich Reichardt, *Ueber die Pflichten des Ripien-Violinisten* . . . (Berlin and Leipzig, 1776).

49. *Grond-beginselen over de behandeling van de dwars-fluit,* trans. Abraham Moubach (Amsterdam, 1728); the section on inequality is found on pp. 32ff. Another edition of Brossard was published in Amsterdam by Mortier (ca. 1710).

50. *Grondig onderwys van den aardt en de regte behandeling der dwarsfluit,* trans. Jacob Wilhelm Lustig (Amsterdam, 1754), 83–84.

51. *Gedagten over de beginselen en onderwyzingen des clavicimbaals* (Amsterdam, 1758), 52; English trans. by Jaap Schröder.

52. *Cursory Notes of Musicke* [ca. 1698–1703], ed. Mary Chan and Jamie C. Kassler (Kensington: Unisearch/University of New South Wales, 1986), 213; *Roger North on Music,* ed. John Wilson (London: Novello, 1959), 350 and 301; see also 25 and 299ff.

53. Facs. ed. by Robert Spencer (Leeds: Boethius Press, 1974); reproduced by kind permission of Boethius Press. For further information on this source see Spencer's preface as well as Dart's study and transcription, "Miss Mary Burwell's Instruction Book for the Lute," *Galpin Society Journal* 11 (1958): 3–7, 46–47. The tuning assumed in the transcription given above is that suggested by Spencer.

54. *Roger North on Music,* 295.

55. Ibid., 223–24 (ca. 1710). North mentions acquaintance with two French violinists, Messrs. Porter and Farinell (p. 351).

56. See Gustafson, *French Harpsichord Music of the Seventeenth Century,*1: chap. 4; see also chap. 2, n. 56 (p. 175) above. Here and later, the sigla that identify manuscripts of French harpsichord music are adopted from Gustafson's catalogue.

57. Hotteterre, *The Rudiments or Principles of the German Flute* . . . (London [1729]), 17: "You must observe that Quavers are not always to be play'd equally, but that you must in certain movements make one long, and one short, which is also regulated by their number when they are even. You make the first long, the second short, and so on. when [sic] they are odd, you do quite the reverse, that is call'd pointing; the movements in which 'tis most commonly used is Duple, or Common Time, Triple Time and Jigg Time or $\frac{6}{4}$." Peter Prelleur, *The Modern Musick-Master* (London, 1731), pt. 3, *The Newest Method for Learners on the German Flute,* 7, is virtually identical to this, although Prelleur's minor modifications suggest he understood what he was copying. (Concerning the plagiarism from Hotteterre, see also A. H. King's notes to the facsimile ed. of Prelleur [Kassel: Bärenreiter, 1965].) Yet it is noteworthy that the other sections of Prelleur's volume—instructions for singing, violin, harpsichord, etc.—do not mention inequality.

58. Terence Best, "Interpreting Handel's Rhythmic Notation—Some Reflections on Modern Practice," *Handel Tercentenary Collection,* ed. Stanley Sadie

and Anthony Hicks (Ann Arbor: UMI Research Press, 1987), 280. Concerning the Holland barrel organ see David Fuller, "Analyzing the Performance of a Barrel Organ," *Organ Yearbook* 11 (1980): 109, and Stephen Hefling, review of *G. F. Handel, Two Ornamented Organ Concertos*, transcribed with commentary by David Fuller, *Early Keyboard Journal* 1 (1982–83): 88–89.

59. *A Practical Treatise on Singing and Playing* (London, 1771), 55–56.

60. Graham Pont (communication to the *Journal of the American Musicological Society* 19 [1966]: 438) and Fuller (*The New Grove*, 13: 424; *The New Grove Instruments*, 2: 780) inaccurately assert that Bayly advised unequal quavers as possible in an anthem by Greene. What Bayly advocates for this and other pieces is either (1) Tosi's "stealing of time in the *pathetick*," known as "gliding" or "dragging" (43–45 and 96–97; see below, pp. 54–58), or (2) sporadic adjustments of rhythm to improve the accentuation of the text setting (95–97); neither practice is the same as French inequality.

61. *The Works of Henry Purcell*, vol. 29: *Sacred Music, Part V: Anthems*, rev. ed. Anthony Lewis and Nigel Fortune (London: Novello, 1967), 94, 88–89.

62. Tosi, *Opinioni de' cantari antichi e moderni . . .* (Bologna, 1723), 114; trans. J. E. Galliard as *Observations on the Florid Song*, 2d ed. (London, 1743), 178.

63. *Anleitung zur Singkunst* (1757), 234:

Ich würde die Beschreibung des **Tosi** hier gern durch Noten deutlicher machen, wenn ich nur seinen eigentlichen Sinn vollkommen errathen könnte.

I would gladly here make **Tosi**'s description clearer through notes if I could just completely divine his actual meaning.

64. *Roger North on Music*, ed. Wilson, 151–53.

65. *A Practical Treatise* (1771), 43–45.

66. Greene, *Six Solo Anthems Perform'd before His Majesty at the Chapel Royal . . .* (London: Walsh [1747]).

67. 1771, 95–98.

68. Donington's account of "dragging" is misleading ("A Problem of Inequality," *Musical Quarterly* 53 [1967], 509), and his claim that it is equivalent to the French *inégalité* (*The Interpretation of Early Music*, new version [New York: St. Martin's Press, 1974], 665) is untenable.

69. *Saggio per ben sonare il flautotraverso . . .* (Venice, 1779), 81. Lorenzoni's footnote (ww) read as follows: "(ww La ragione è quella, che abbiamo accennato alla nota (hh) [The reason is the one we have indicated in note (hh)]." Note (hh), p. 58, amplifies the recommendation that the flutist not breathe after a "bad" note:

La nota cattiva, quando è di qualche prestezza, non viene dalli Compositori nel basso fondamentale considerata; perciò dee essere sempre più presta della nota buona, come si vedrà a suo luogo. Ora la nota cattiva, dovendo essere più presta della buona, sarebbe sempre più lunga, se vi si prendesse fiato dopo.

The bad note, when it is of some rapidity, is not considered by composers in the fundamental bass; therefore it ought always to be quicker than the good note, as will be seen in its place. Now the bad note, having to be quicker than the good, would always be longer, if breath were taken afterward.

Collins ("Three Further Views," 484) mistranslates the phrase "non per altro quanto . . ." from p. 81 as "just as if they were dotted."

70. Reilly, *Quantz and His Versuch*, 87. The nature of Lorenzoni's borrowing becomes clearer when one compares the lines cited above from p. 81 of this text to the French edition of Quantz (1752, 107), which Lorenzoni knew:

> Les notes capitales doivent toujours, s'il est possible, être plus relevées que celles qui ne sont que passer. Suivant cette régle il faut que dans les piéces d'un mouvement temperé ou même dans l'Adagio, les notes les plus vites soient jouées avec quelqu'inégalité . . . quoiqu'il ne faille pourtant pas les soutenir aussi longtems que si elles étoient pointées.

> The main notes must always, if it is possible, be in greater relief than those that are only passing. According to this rule it is necessary that in pieces of temperate movement or even in the Adagio, the quickest notes should be played with some inequality . . . although it would not, however, be necessary to hold them as long as if they were dotted..

71. Collins ("Three Further Views," 484) and Fuller (*The New Grove*, 13: 424; *The New Grove Instruments*, 2: 780) provide misleading accounts of Lorenzoni.

72. Reilly, *Quantz and His Versuch*, 81–89.

73. P. 4: "PONTATO, annonce qu'on doit marquer fortement le Pointé, savoir, bien faire sentir l'inégalité des proportions alternativement longues & brèves entre les Notes. *Pointé.*"

74. *The New Grove*, s. v. "Bach, Johann Christian" by Ernst Warburton (works-list), and s. v. "Ricci, Francesco Pasquale" by Ronald R. Kidd.

75. See William Klenz, *Giovanni Maria Bononcini of Modena* (Durham: Duke University Press, 1962), 18, 20, 28–30, and passim.

76. François Raguenet, *Paralèle des Italiens et des Français . . .* (Paris, 1702); Jean-Laurent Le Cerf de La Viéville de Fresneuse, *Comparaison de la musique italienne et de la musique française . . .*, 2d ed. (Brussels, 1705 [–6]); portions of both trans. in Oliver Strunk, *Source Readings in Music History* (New York: W. W. Norton, 1950), 473–507.

77. Donington, "A Problem of Inequality," 509–17.

78. Fuller, "The 'Dotted Style' in Bach, Handel, and Scarlatti," in *Bach, Handel, Scarlatti: Tercentenary Essays*, ed. Peter Williams (Cambridge: Cambridge University Press, 1985), 99–117.

CHAPTER 4.   The Value(s) of the Dot

1. *Principes de musique par demande et par reponce . . .* (Paris, 1718), 11. The dedication to the king includes the line "ce seroit le comble de ma gloire, si Vôtre Majesté y prenoit les premiers principes de la musique [it would be the summit of my glory if Your Majesty would take from here the first principles of music]. . . ."

2. "l'aduertis aussi qu'il y a des notes qui ont vn point esloigné de leur caractere que je n'employe que pour vn quart de leur valeur; c'est pour sauuer vne note & vne liaison qu'il faudroit pour le signifier. . . ."

3. Cohen, ed., 67. Abgedruckt mit Erlaubnis des Institutes für Mittelalterliche Musikwissenschaft.

4. *Démonstration des principes de musique* . . . (Paris, n. d.), 17. The last two clauses seem to refer to *notes inégales,* although it is difficult to suppose that time permitted inequality in most of these *traits.*

5. *Livre de musique pour l'orgue* (Paris, 1685; modern ed. Alexandre Guilmant and André Pirro, Archives des maitres de l'orgue des XVIe, XVIIe, XVIIIe siècles . . . , vol. 4. [Leipzig: B. Schott's Söhne, 1902]), preface: "jl ne faut pas que les croches barrées plusieurs fois les effrayent, d'autant qu'ils les faut regarder comme si elles n'estoient que doubles croches."

6. For examples see Neumann, "The Dotted Note and the So-Called French Style" and "Facts and Fiction," *Essays,* 93, 131; see also Fuller, *The New Harvard Dictionary,* 238.

7. Johann Peter Sperling, *Principia musicae* . . . (Budissin, 1705), 55–56.

8. Simpertus Schmelz, *Fundamenta musica cantus artificialis* . . . (Yresee, 1752), 31–32.

9. Quantz (1752, chap. V, §22) insists that when dotted eighth-plus-sixteenth figures appear against triplets, "you must not strike the short note after the dot with the third note of the triplet, but after it." Agricola (1769; reprinted in *Bach-Dokumente* 3: 206) claims that this was also J. S. Bach's teaching. But C. P. E. Bach permits the synchronization of the sixteenth and the last triplet (1753, chap. 3, §27), and there are cases in J. S. Bach's music where this meaning seems indisputable (see e.g., Neumann, "External Evidence and Uneven Notes" and "Facts and Fiction," *Essays,* 60, 121–22). For reviews of the issue, which leads beyond our immediate concerns here, see the articles "Über die Angleichung nachschlagender Sechzehntel an Triolen" by Eta Harich-Schneider and Erwin R. Jacobi, respectively, in *Musikforschung* 12 (1959): 35–39, and 13 (1960): 268–81; Jacobi, "Neues zur Frage 'Punktierte Rhythmen gegen Triolen' und zur Transcriptionstechnik bei J. S. Bach," *Bach-Jahrbuch* 49 (1962): 88–96; and esp. Neumann, "Conflicting Binary and Ternary Rhythms: From the Theory of Mensural Notation to the Music of J. S. Bach," *Music Forum* 6/1 (1987): 93–127, reprinted in idem, *New Essays on Performance Practice* (Ann Arbor: UMI Research Press, 1989), 35–64.

10. Gigault, *Livre de musique pour l'orgue* (1685), preface: "Lors qu'il y aura vne double croche au dessus d'vne croche jl les faut toucher ensemble. . . ." For examples, see pp. 6, 49, 95–98, 122, 132, 153, 173, 201, 203 in the edition by Guilmant and Pirro; cf. also O'Donnell, "The French style," pt. 2: 337. In "Facts and Fiction," *Essays,* 123, Neumann mistakenly reports that "not a single such instance occurs in the music of this book."

11. A number of examples are reproduced in Neumann, *Ornamentation in Baroque and Post-Baroque Music* (Princeton: Princeton University Press, 1978), 88–89, 281–84, 470, and passim; see also Raparlier, *Principes de musique* . . . (Lille, 1772), 26, and Marcou, *Elemens* (1782), 53.

12. *Methode pour la musette* . . . (Paris, 1737), 35. It should be noted that elsewhere Hotteterre explicitly identifies *pointer* as the verb for rendering *notes inégales* (1707, 1719): therefore this passage is *not* "a description of exact double dotting" as asserted by O'Donnell, who also mistranslates it ("The French Style," pt. 2: 337).

13. *Sçience de la musique vocale* [ca. 1760], 8.

14. *Démonstration* [n. d.], 17: "Quand les croches sont inégales, le Point qui est après la Noire doit être de la Valeur d'une croche longue, et celle qui est après le Point est toujours breve."

15. *La tonotechnie* (1775), 217: "... cette noire doit être prolongée de la valeur d'une *premiere* croche que ce point indique, & qu'en conséquence la croche qui suit ce point étant une *seconde tactée,* doit être marquée à sa place entre les chiffres 2 & 3 du *cadran....*" See also Engramelle's plate III and passim.

16. Ibid., 217, 212, and plates. There is a hint of the same procedure in Saint-Lambert's much earlier treatise (1702, 25–26), but his remark is less than explicit:

> Si le nombre des Croches qui se suivent sans interruption est pair, la premiére est longue, la seconde bréve, la troisiéme longue, la quatriéme bréve.... Si le nombre en est impair, la premiére au contraire est bréve.... Une Croche seule est toùjours bréve....

> If the number of eighths that follow without interruption is even, the first is long, the second short, the third long, the fourth short.... If the number is uneven, the first, on the contrary, is short.... A single eighth by itself is always short....

The eighth after a dotted quarter would be "a single eighth by itself."

17. Neumann, esp. "The Dotted Note," *Essays,* 95–98, cites only Hotteterre in conjunction with this issue, and underplays the implications of even that source by claiming that the situation could occur only when isolated dotted quarters are linked to a series of continuous eighths (e.g., ♩♪♪♪♪), or when synchronization is necessary (e.g., as illustrated above, p. 68); Neumann further insists that inequality "very rarely attains the 3:1 ratio of an actual dotted note." Considered collectively, the evidence from Hotteterre, Metoyen, Morel de Lescer, and Engramelle just cited, plus that concerning the variable degree of inequality, would seem to render his position untenable.

18. "Dotting, the 'French Style,' and Frederick Neumann's Counter-Reformation," *Early Music* 5 (1977): 533.

19. Pont, "Rhythmic Alteration and the Majestic," *Studies in Music* (Australia), no. 12 (1978): 87–89.

20. Louis-Nicolas Clérambault, "Leandre et Hero," *Cantates françoises ...,* bk. 2 (Paris, 1713; facs. ed. New York: Garland, 1990), 33, 37; Hotteterre, *L'art de préluder* (1719), 20; Georg Muffat, *Apparatus Musico-Organisticus ...* (Salzburg, 1690), first and sixth toccatas, and *Nova Cyclopeias Harmonica.* The double-dotting in the first Muffat toccata is also found in an earlier version of the piece (ca. 1683–85); on the relationship between the Salzburg and earlier prints see Craig A. Monson, "Eine neuentdeckte Fassung einer Toccata von Muffat," *Musikforschung* 25 (1972): 465–71.

21. See also chap. 2, n. 51 (p. 175) above.

22. Neumann ("The Dotted Note" and "Facts and Fiction," *Essays,* 85–87, 115) has also drawn attention to Raison's careful distinction between single and double dots. Fuller claims "this applies to perhaps three pieces out of the body of Raison's work.... Fewer than ten per cent have any double dots at all" ("Dotting, the 'French Style,' " 525). But in the 1688 *Livre d'orgue* alone, more than 20 percent of the pieces contain both single and double dots, and both notations are found in the *Second livre d'orgue* (Paris, 1714) as well. O'Donnell's conjecture that "the distinction between dotted crotchets and double-dotted crotchets in the same piece is not one of rhythmic ratio, but of the amount of silence between the

long and short notes" ("The French Style," pt. 2: 339) is not based on any historical documentation known to me; nor has his announced development of this hypothesis been forthcoming.

23. 32-Oldham is an inaccessible, privately owned manuscript, but incipits of its harpsichord music are quoted in Gustafson, *French Harpsichord Music;* Dart cites several of its readings in his edition of *Pièces de clavecin de Louis Couperin . . .* (Monaco: Éditions de l'Oiseau-Lyre, 1959); and two pieces from the manuscript have been published in Alan Curtis's edition of *Pièces de clavecin,* Le Pupitre no. 18 (Paris: Heugel, 1970). 24-Babell contains double dots only in the portion copied from the print of Muffat's *Apparatus Musico-Organisticus . . .* (1690). 5-Munich-1503*l* and 20-Ch-Ch-378 also include concordances with the sources cited above, but do not contain double dots. Other manuscripts containing no double dots include 40-Rés-476, 44-LaPierre, 48-LaBarre-6, 23-Tenbury, and 8-Hintze.

24. A minor difference occurs in m. 8 of the double, where Parville reads ♩· ♪. Although 36-Parville contains a good many double dots, there is at least one other instance of a single-dotted quarter followed by a sixteenth (see #14); clearly this notation is to be interpreted according to the precepts set forth by Loulié and Metoyen, whereby the dot is sustained in proportion to what follows it (see above, pp. 66–67). Gustafson dates Bauyn after 1676, and Parville after 1686 (*French Harpsichord Music* 1: 96, 105, 123, plus personal communication to the present author). In general, the readings in 35-Bauyn and 36-Parville are very similar, suggesting that "they may have been derived in part from the same original manuscripts" (Gustafson 1: 99).

25. Cf. Chambonnières, "Allemande la loureuse," m. 4, 35-Bauyn-I #30, 32-Oldham #23, 62 Chamb I (1670), #11, and 24-Babell #184; "Allemande Couprin," 3 mm. before the end, 35-Bauyn-II #82, 36-Parville #88, 33-Rés-89ter #33, 47-Gen-2356, #5, and 24-Babell #252.

26. *Les pieces de clavessin,* 2 vols. (Paris, 1670) (= 62-Chamb-I and 63-Chamb-II in Gustafson's catalogue).

27. See e.g. the courantes 62-Chamb-I #3, penultimate measure (co. 35-Bauyn-I #116; 38-Gen-2348/53 is different in many respects), and 63-Chamb-II #28, mm. 1 and 14 (co. 35-Bauyn-I #91, 36-Parville #91; 38-Gen-2348/53 #33 has single dotting, and 33-Rés-89ter #35 differs from the other sources in several respects).

28. Gustafson, *French Harpsichord Music* 1: 114–15, 124; Alan Curtis, "Musique classique française à Berkeley," *Revue de musicologie* 56 (1977): 129–33.

29. Neumann inaccurately describes the double-dotting of the *Persée* overture in 46-Menetou as "some spotty rhythmic alterations," and relegates the matter to a footnote ("The Overdotting Syndrome," *Essays,* 170, 298, n. 35), wherein he claims "some notes are doubledotted for keyboard-idiomatic reasons." But as figure 4-4 shows, there are fully thirteen double-dotted quarters, and only five single-dotted. Whether the latter are inadvertent or intentional is a matter for conjecture, given that the notation is slightly careless in other respects: three of the double-dotted quarters are followed by eighths (rather than sixteenths; yet this notation crops up in 36-Parville as well [#97], a source in which double dotting is commonplace). As to "keyboard-idiomatic reasons" for the rhythmic alteration, I submit that anyone who plays through figure 4-4 will find it just as easy, and perhaps easier, without the double dotting. Neumann also

reproduces (plate 8, pp. 168–69) the harpsichord arrangement of the *Persée* over-ture from 24-Babell, which differs from the Menetou version in several respects, and contains no double dots; but as noted above (n. 23), for whatever reasons, Babell is practically devoid of this notation, even when it occurs in concordances of works specifically for harpsichord by identifiable composers.

I have not yet encountered double dots in any Italian sources from ca. 1600–1750. In two modern publications of eighteenth-century Italian music – Carl'Ambrogio Lonati, *Die Violinsonaten: Mailand 1701*, ed. Franz Giegling (Winterthur: Amadeus, 1981), 369, and Janet K. Page, "The Hautboy in London's Musical Life, 1730–1770," *Early Music* 16 (1988): 363, example 1 (Giuseppe Sammartini) – the printed double dots are editorial errors (personal communications from Professor Giegling and Ms. Page to the present author).

30. *Elements* (1696), 14: "La Croche pointée ⸗ vaut trois doubles Croches." P. 16: "La premiere & la troisiéme Double Croche de chaque Temps sont longues." Loulié's general discussion of inequality is found on pp. 34–35 of his treatise.

31. P. 16: "Quand le Point est du mesme Temps que la Croche qui le precede, il faut tenir en chantant cette Croche un peu plus long temps, & passer viste la Double Croche suivante, dans un mesme Temps sans remuer la main." P. 17: "Il faut concevoir & étudier le Point d'une seconde Croche, comme si c'estoit une Notte double croche."

32. Vion (1742, 37) uses similarly informal language about the performance of ordinary (downbeat) dotted rhythms, yet there can be no doubt that he means a 3:1 ratio:

> L'on met souvent des Points à côté des Notes, pour en augmenter leur valeur de la moitié. Cette augmentation de durée se prend d'ordinaire sur les Notes qui suivent immediatement celles qui sont pointées; & pour lors, après avoir soutenu la Note pointée, on passe vîte celle qui suit.

> One often places dots beside the notes to augment their value by one half. This augmentation of duration is ordinarily taken from the notes that immediately follow those that have dots; and therefore, after having sustained the dotted note, one passes quickly that which follows.

33. P. 22: "Leçon pour apprendre à chanter les Noires pointées. . . . Pour faire les Points comme il faut, on vous avertit que l'on suspend la Noire pointée, & que l'on passe viste la Croche qui suit." *Suspendre* is ambiguous here, but it probably means simply "to sustain"; if "to interrupt" is actually intended, then L'Affilard is apparently advising the student not to dwell too long on the dot.

34. See also n. 32 above, and Neumann, "Facts and Fiction" and "The Overdotting Syndrome," *Essays*, 130, 179–80, as well as Beverly Scheibert, "French Overdotting," *Early Music* 15 (1987): 443–44. Among those who have misinter-preted Loulié and L'Affilard are Collins ("A Reconsideration of French Overdot-ting," 117), Donington (*The Interpretation of Early Music*, 441–42), and Wulstan (communication to *Early Music* 15 [1987]: 141); O'Donnell ("The French Style," pt. 2: 337) misreads only L'Affilard.

35. See also Neumann, "The Overdotting Syndrome," *Essays*, 179–80. Col-lins ("A Reconsideration," 117) and O'Donnell ("The French Style," pt. 2: 337) insist upon interpreting this exercise as evidence of overdotting.

36. Monteclair, *Petite methode* [ca. 1735], 56–57; *Principes* (1736), 22–23.

37. *Roger North on Music*, 185, 350 (© 1959 Novello & Company Ltd. Reproduced by Permission of the Publisher; Sole Representative U.S.A. & Canada, Theodore Presser Company). North's other "mode of the Grave," the Stopp, is irrelevant to the issues of rhythmic alteration. In the second passage cited, North more properly characterizes Lully as "an Itallian frenchifyed."

38. Neumann's rejection of such an interpretation ("The Overdotting Syndrome," *Essays*, 177) is based on his insistent argument that 7:1 rhythmic sharpening *"had* to be specified in notation" (italics mine). But as we have seen in the case of overdotting concomitant with *notes inégales*, this is not necessarily so.

39. See Eugene Joseph Enrico, "Giuseppe Torelli's Music for Instrumental Ensemble with Trumpet" (Ph.D. diss., University of Michigan, 1970), 225–27, 231.

Chapter 5.   The Earlier German Sources on Overdotting

1. See above, pp. 43 and 47–48, and below, p. 116.

2. These examples (and that cited in XVII/ii/21) reveal as well that Quantz was aware of double-dotted notation, yet chose to rely upon performance tradition to achieve his desired effect.

3. Quantz's use of letter labels in this sentence assumes the identity of examples (c), (d), and (e), and the upper line in examples (f), (g), and (h). Reilly's translation (p. 67) tacitly clarifies the matter by referring only to the upper line of (f), (g), and (h).

4. As Reilly points out in his translation (p. 67, n. 1), although the German and French texts read literally "the notes with the dots," it is clear from the examples that the notes after the dots are meant.

5. VI/ii/3: "Bey Noten mit Puncten ist dieses **tiri** unentbehrlich; denn es drücket die punctirten Noten viel schärfer und lebhafter aus, als keine andere Art des Zungengebrauches vermögend ist."

6. "Je kürzer man die ersten Noten bey (a) (b) (c) (d) machet: je lebhafter und frecher ist der Ausdruck."

7. *Solfeggi*, ed. Michel and Teske (1978), 41, 47, 69.

8. Preface to *Florilegium Secundum* (1698), "First Observations," sec. II.

9. Cf. also Quantz's general discussion of French musical style in XVIII/ 65–67, 76, as well as his commentary on executing the Adagio in XIV, esp. §§11–13. (Further on French bowing style, see David D. Boyden, *The History of Violin Playing from Its Origins to 1761* [London: Oxford University Press, 1965], 256–63 and passim.) Neumann ("The Overdotting Syndrome" [1981], *Essays*, 172–73) argues unconvincingly that this passage in Quantz means only that the short notes after dots are to be sharply articulated, and that it excludes lengthening of the dot, which is "violinistically impossible" because "the bow *is not to be lifted*" before the short note. But Quantz does not say the bow is not to be lifted at all—"Den Bogen muß man nicht absetzen, als wenn anstatt der Puncte Pausen stünden"—he states that it must not be lifted "as though there were rests instead of dots." It must be retaken, but the character of the Adagio requires more sustaining of the dot than does the typical French dance style; see also below, pp. 94–97 and notes 11 and 16. As we shall see (pp. 121–23 and 117–18), the later writers Türk (1789) and Rellstab (1790) also indicate that varying degrees of articulation space are possible between the lengthened dotted note and the follow-

ing short note(s). Neumann further claims (loc. cit.) that Quantz's directive to hold dots to the outermost limit of their value (*bis zu dem aüßersten Ende ihrer Geltung*) "cautions against *shortening* the dot, but excludes its lengthening." Isolated from the context of Quantz's previous commentary on dotted notes, this phrase might seem ambiguous. But Quantz's student Agricola evidently perceived the ambiguity and clarified the meaning of the phrase as follows: "The short notes that come after a dot . . . are always performed . . . very short, and at the outermost limit of their value [*am aüßersten Ende ihrer Geltung*]: the notes that stand before the dot are, on the contrary, held proportionately longer." (Agricola's remarks are cited in full on pp. 107–8 below.)

Neumann first advanced his counterinterpretation tentatively in "Facts and Fiction" (1977; *Essays*, 125ff.), but there his paraphrase of Quantz conflates two separate sentences (*Essays*, 125, ¶3, lines 17–18). And Neumann obviously over-looks XVII/ii/13 when he claims that to associate Quantz's overdotting with *das Prächtige* is "a classical 'fallacy of the undistributed middle' " ("Once More: The 'French Overture Style,' " *Essays*, 144–45).

10. As Reilly notes in his translation, the French version of the treatise provides the better reading of this phrase: "un coup d'archet . . . marqué par un poids interieur qu'on lui donne."

11. Thus, as Quantz indicates earlier in the chapter (XVII/ii/26, a passage not specifically concerned with dotted notes), this section contains comments about the kind of bow stroke to be employed in French dance music, including partic-ular remarks about the loure (cited above), gigue, canarie, and minuet (not quoted here). But see also n. 16 below.

12. Neumann insists that "several modern authors seem to have ignored the limitation of this directive to thirty-second notes, and . . . have applied the same principle without hesitation to sixteenth-notes" ("The Dotted Note," *Essays*, 77–78; see also idem, "Rhythm in the Two Versions," *Essays*, 105). But short *tirades* of sixteenth-note pickups seem to be more common than thirty-seconds in overtures, especially in the works of Lully, Muffat, and Kusser, three of the earliest composers in the genre. And in the preface to the *Florilegium Secundum* (1698, *DTÖ* II/2: 26, 49) Muffat indicates that tirades are performed with extreme speed (two of the four languages in which he writes are reproduced here):

> Die *Incursion* oder *Tirada* (⤳ , oder ⤳) laufft Staffelweiß mit der grösten Schnelligkeit deß Bogens zu ihrer Noten. Mm. [see below]

> La Tirade, ou Course (⤳ , ou ⤳) court à la note, ou elle butte par plusieurs touches de suitte avec rapidité, & extreme vitesse de l'archet. Mm. [see below]

> The tirade or incursion . . . [symbol shown above] runs stepwise up to the note it aims at, with swiftness and extreme speed of the bow. Mm.

Although Muffat does not notate rhythmic contraction, his emphasis of running, swiftness, and speed raises the possibility of shortening the note values.

As we shall see below (p. 99), J. S. Bach contracted sixteenths in revising one of his overtures, and Bach's pupil Kirnberger allows for contraction of sixteenths in performing an overture (p. 113); see also chapter 7, pp. 152–53.

13. See e.g. Walther, *Musikalisches Lexikon* (1732), 226, and Mattheson, *Der volkommene Kapellmeister* (1739), 227.

14. "Eine edle Lebhaftigkeit, ein ernsthaftes, männliches und prächtiges Wesen, und überhaupt ein beständiges Feuer müssen ihn durchgehends erheben." *Critischer Musikus*, no. 73 (January 1740); new ed. (1745), 669.

15. *Anleitung zum Clavierspielen* (1755), 13; see also below, pp. 106–7.

16. *Anleitung zur Singkunst* (1757), 133–34; see also below, pp. 107–8.

Until 1981, Neumann also essentially accepted the interpretation of Quantz XVII/vii/58 set forth here, even with respect to the French overture (see e.g. Neumann, "Facts and Fiction" [1977], *Essays*, 126–27). But in "The Overdotting Syndrome" (1981; *Essays*, 170–73), he changed his position, insisting that Quantz's use of *kurz und scharf* with respect to the performance of French dance music describes only articulation, and does not indicate overdotting (see also n. 9 above). But Neumann does not advert to the fact that *kurz* describes the late execution of the short note after the dot in Quantz's very first mention of overdotting (V/21; see above, pp. 89–90), which even Neumann admits to be unambiguous; nor does he pay attention to Quantz's "sharp and lively" tonguing of dotted patterns in chapter VI. And Neumann also overlooks the use of "sehr kurz, und scharf gestoßen" in Quantz's *Solfeggi* (see example 5-1 above). Moreover, he avoids the implications of Quantz's associating majestic affect (*das Prächtige*) with overdotted performance (e.g., "The Overdotting Syndrome," 170–71). Although Neumann has never denied that Marpurg and Agricola are writing about overdotting, neither has he acknowledged that their terminology so closely parallels Quantz's.

As pointed out above (p. 93 and n. 11), in XVII/ii/26 Quantz tells us that "an account of the kind of stroke to be employed in French dance music is found in §58 of Section VII of this chapter": although §58 does contain a few comments about bowing, §56 (cited above, pp. 94–95) provides a much fuller description of the bow stroke used in French dance music, which suggests that Quantz may have made a mistake in his cross reference (cf. also the incorrect cross reference in VI/i/9, cited above, p. 43, as well as the one in VII/3 [corrected in Reilly's trans., p. 86, n. 1]). According to Neumann, however, ("The Overdotting Syndrome," 171 and 173), "We are thus explicitly told" that the fourth and fifth "key" sentences from XVII/vii/58 (as cited above, pp. 95–96) "deal with *bowstroke*, hence with articulation, not with rhythm." But of course we have been told nothing so explicit: §58 is, above all, concerned with the character and tempo of French dances; it speaks as well of meter, bowing, and — read in light of all that precedes it — overdotting. In Neumann's view, "This passage has deceived everyone, including myself, into believing that it prescribes strong overdotting of the quarter notes in French dances" (loc. cit.). But perhaps "everyone" arrived at that interpretation because it is the simplest, and accords with what Quantz (and Marpurg, Agricola, and others) wrote elsewhere.

Neumann also rejects the possibility that Quantz's overdotting of dance music might possibly stem from the French tradition of inequality (see e.g. "Facts and Fiction," 118–19; "The Overdotting Syndrome," 154–55), because he insists that "*inégalité* was a gentle lilt . . . and nothing more, proving conclusively that the idea of vigorous inequality, equivalent to and occasionally exceeding a dotted note, is based on misunderstanding" ("Facts and Fiction," 120). But as we have seen (pp. 16–20 above), this is not necessarily the case at all.

17. Unacceptable, however, is Neumann's contention ("The Overdotting Syndrome," 170, 172) that Quantz's 'galant' overdotting is only for soloists: XVII/ii/13 and XVII/iv/10 are explicitly instructions for orchestral string players. And flutists, to whom the earlier portions of the *Versuch* are directed, would also be called upon to perform in orchestral and chamber music. Cf. also C. P. E. Bach's comments about overdotting in keyboard accompaniment (pt. 2 [1763]: XXIX/15), cited below, pp. 104–5; thoroughbass accompaniment is needed in orchestral and chamber works as well as solos. And the discussion of overdotting in Türk's *Klavierschule* (1789) makes reference to the final chorus of C. H. Graun's oratorio *Der Tod Jesu* — clearly not a work for solo keyboard (see below, p. 123 and example 6-2). For a listing of additional writers who prescribe overdotting for various media, see table 5-1; see also chap 6, n. 27 below.

18. See *NBA* V/2, *Kritischer Bericht*, 15, 48, 52, 58; both versions of the overture are included in *NBA* V/2, and the *KB*, 87–88, prints the opening of the overture as it appears in the Preller manuscript. Cf. also the facsimile editions of *Zweyter Theil der Clavier Ubung . . .* (Leipzig, 1735) by Christoph Wolff (Leipzig and Dresden: Edition Peters, 1984) and David Kinsela (Godstone, England: Gregg International, 1985). Concerning Preller, see Hans-Joachim Schulze, "Wie entstand die Bach-Sammlung Mempell-Preller?" *Bach-Jahrbuch* 60 (1974): 104–22. For reviews of possible explanations for Bach's transposition from C minor to B minor, see *KB* 49–50 and Neumann, "Rhythm in the Two Versions of Bach's French Overture, BWV 831," *Essays*, 100.

19. "Rhythm in the Two Versions," 106

20. In every case where he did not, the situation is very simple: a dotted quarter is followed by an eighth, and there are no problems of synchronization with other voices such that only the composer could resolve them with authority (mm. 1, 11, 12, 13, 19, 144, 147, 148, 153, 159, 162). The performer, if so inclined, could readily elongate the quarters in these bars. (As indicated in *NBA* V/2, *KB*, 69, in m. 152 Bach almost certainly forgot to alter the four sixteenths of the second quarter; my account accepts *NBA*'s editorial emendation.)

21. The 1730 "Draft" is found in *The Bach Reader*, 123; for a useful view of Bach's relationship with Dresden, see Robert L. Marshall, "Bach the Progressive: Observations on His Later Works," *Musical Quarterly* 62 (1976): 318–25.

22. For a useful summary and review of the evidence see Joshua Rifkin's review of Johann Sebastian Bach, *Messe in h-moll: Faksimile-Lichtdruck des Autographs*, ed. Alfred Dürr (Kassel: Bärenreiter, 1983), and Johann Sebastian Bach, *Missa h-Moll BWV 232¹: Faksimile nach dem Originalstimmensatz*, ed. Hans-Joachim Schulze (Neuhausen-Stuttgart: Hänssler, 1983), in *Notes* 44 (1988): 791ff.

23. *Critischer Musicus*, new ed. (1745), 62; trans. in *The Bach Reader*, 238.

24. Neumann, "Rhythm in the Two Versions," *Essays*, 106. Emery and Wolff have shown that the Preller manuscript is not derived from Anna Magdelena's copy of the C-minor overture, but probably stems from some earlier source for the piece; in their view, the ornaments (and fingerings) added to the overture in the Preller manuscript are probably Preller's own, since such additions are characteristic of his other Bach manuscripts (*NBA* V/2, *KB*, 15, 48–49, 51).

25. The implications of all this for the performance of other works by J. S. Bach will be briefly addressed in the final chapter of this study.

26. C. P. E. Bach, *Versuch über die wahre Art das Clavier zu Spielen* (Berlin, 1753), III/23–24. See also Neumann, "The Dotted Note," *Essays*, 79–82.

27. Bach's 1787 additions are included in the appendix to the facsimile of the *Versuch*, ed Lothar Hoffmann-Erbrecht (Wiesbaden: Breitkopf & Härtel, 1978), 12–13.

28. I.e., the first (short) note of the Lombard rhythm.

29. Figures VII–IX have been interpolated from C. P. E. Bach's tables; the (unnumbered) musical examples for the 1787 additions are found in the main body of that edition.

30. William S. Newman, "Emanuel Bach's Autobiography," *Musical Quarterly* 51 (1965): 366. Kirnberger and Agricola are two other students of J. S. Bach's who advocate overdotting (see below).

31. *Anleitung zum Clavierspielen* (1755 [and 1765]), 13. According to Neumann ("Facts and Fiction," *Essays*, 128), Johann Samuel Petri's *Anleitung zur praktischen Musik* (Lauban, 1767, 21; 2d ed., Leipzig, 1782, 142) is "in obvious accord with Marpurg" on the issue of notating intended overdotting. But Petri says nothing about overdotting as a performance practice; he merely explains with mathematical precision the value of single- and double-dotted notes, and proceeds no further with the issue.

32. Hays, "F. W. Marpurg's *Anleitung zum Clavierspielen* . . ." chaps. 3–4.

33. Charles Burney, *The Present State of Music in Germany* . . . , 2d ed. (London, 1775), in *Dr. Burney's Musical Tours in Europe*, ed. Percy A. Scholes (London: Oxford University Press, 1959), 2: 160.

34. *Anleitung zur Singkunst* (1757), 133–34.

35. For a useful review of the book's genesis and publication, see Alfred Einstein's preface to the English translation by Editha Knocker, *A Treatise on the Fundamental Principles of Violin Playing*, 2d ed. (London: Oxford University Press, 1951), esp. xx–xxvii.

36. *Versuch einer gründlichen Violinschule* (Augsburg, 1756), I/iii/11, pp. 39–40. This clearly is not "soloistic doubledotting," as Neumann claims in "The Overdotting Syndrome," *Essays*, 157.

37. Mozart concludes VII/ii with the observation (§8) that the foregoing exercises will be "very useful for a beginner [wird einem Anfänger schon sehr nützlich seyn]"; thus, they are not for soloists (and indeed never extend beyond the first position). (Cf. also Mozart's brief comments on dotted notes in IV/11 and 13.) In chap. XII, "Of Reading Music Correctly, and in Particular, of Good Execution," §21, Mozart warns "all ensemble players" to observe each other carefully and especially to watch the leader; in addition, "care must be taken to play . . . the short notes after a dot or rest late and rapidly [*Ubrigens müssen . . . alle die Zusammenspielenden einander wohl beobachten und sonderheitlich auf ihren Anführer sehen. . . . Ferner muß man sich befleissigen die nach einem **Puncte** oder kleinen **Sospir** folgenden kurzen Noten aber spät und geschwind wegzuspielen*]." He then refers the reader to VII/ii/2–3.

38. *Grondig onderwys in het behandelen der viool* (Haarlem, 1766), 43–44, 140–41; *Méthode raisonnée pour apprendre à jouer du violon* . . . , trans. Valentin Roeser (Paris [1770], [ca. 1783], [ca. 1788], [ca. 1800]); ca. 1783 ed., 5, 27–30.

CHAPTER 6.   Later Sources on Overdotting

1. See Otto Rieß, "Johann Abraham Peter Schulz' Leben," *Sammelbände der Internationalen Musik-Gesellschaft* 15 (1913–14): 190ff.
2. *Allgemeine Theorie* . . . (1771–[74]), 2: 873–74. Quantz had also recommended the practice of overtures for good orchestral discipline (XVII/i/11).
3. See Eva Renate Blechschmidt, *Die Amalien-Bibliothek: Musikbibliothek der Prinzessin Anna Amalia von Preußen (1723–1787)*, Berliner Studien zur Musikwissenschaft, vol. 8 (Berlin: Verlag Merseburger, 1965), 25, 67, and passim.
4. It has long been believed that J. S. Bach performed Fasch overtures with the Leipzig Collegium Musicum, but Andreas Glöckner has recently shown that such was probably not the case. Fasch overtures evidently entered the repertoire of the Leipzig Collegium ca. 1747–49, when Gerlach was director; see Glöckner, "Fasch-Ouvertüren aus Johann Sebastian Bachs Notenbibliothek?" *Bach-Jahrbuch* 76 (1990): 65–69.
5. Example cited from Carl Mennicke, *Hasse und die Brüder Graun als Symphoniker* (Leipzig: Breitkopf & Härtel, 1906; reprinted, Hildesheim: Georg Olms, 1977), 113; for additional information on the history of the French overture at the Court of Frederick the Great, see Mennicke, chaps. 3 and 10, and Helm, *Music at the Court of Frederick the Great*, 144–45, 200. (Helm mistakenly provides the date 1768 for the Graun overture cited in Example 6-1.)
6. *Allgemeine Theorie* (1771–[74]), 2: 930: "Doch giebt es auch Fälle, wo der wahre Vortrag dem Punkt eine noch etwas längere Geltung giebt, wie schon im Artikel Ouvertüre errinert worden." Neumann ("Once More: The 'French Overture Style,' " *Essays*, 142) insists that Schulz's "wording merely allows the mild overdotting generated by *notes inégales*," and dismisses the evidence thus: "No matter whether Schultz may have heard in Paris some old-time overture with its *inégalité*, or have relied on hearsay. . . ." ("Facts and Fiction," *Essays*, 132).
7. *Allgemeine Theorie* 2: 722: "**Loure.** / (Musik und Tanzkunst.) / Ein kleines Tonstük zum Tanzen, dessen Ausdruk Ernst und Würde, auch wol Hoheit ist. Der Takt ist $\frac{3}{4}$ und die Bewegung langsam."
8. Loc. cit. Neumann ("The Overdotting Syndrome," *Essays*, 298–99, n. 44) considers this evidence "ambiguous." Moreover, he generally disqualifies the Schulz and Kirnberger articles because of their purported "uniqueness [and] lateness of date." Such an evaluation is ill-founded, as we shall see in the following paragraphs of the present study.
9. See David Beach, Introduction to Kirnberger, *The Art of Strict Musical Composition*, trans. Beach and Jurgen Thym (New Haven: Yale University Press, 1982), xiv–xvi.
10. *Dr. Burney's Musical Tours*, 2: 207; see also Helm, 71–80.
11. Helm, 122–26.
12. *Dr. Burney's Musical Tours*, 2: 182–83.
13. *Ueber die Pflichten des Ripien-Violinisten* (Berlin and Leipzig, 1776), 20–21.
14. Reichardt, 28, 92; see also Reilly's preface to his translation of Quantz, xxxiii.

According to Neumann ("The Overdotting Syndrome," *Essays*, 153–54), in the case of Reichardt's "example" rhythm of dotted sixteenths, "overdotting is technically impossible in the face of an overwhelming tendency to shorten the dot." But this depends to a great extent upon the tempo (which Reichardt does not indicate), and also upon the sort of instrument, bow, and technique utilized; eighteenth-century equipment makes such passages much easier.

Neumann also draws attention to Reichardt's demand that the ripienist "must not deviate a hair's breadth" from executing precisely what is on the page — "not a note, not a [bow] stroke more or different from what is there" (1776, 79–80). But this is nothing more than a paraphrase, in stronger language, of what Quantz had written years earlier (XVII/i/9). Taken in historical context, such remarks rule out willful disruptions of the ensemble — improvised embellishments, non-uniform bowing, and similar antics, which, although condemned by numerous writers, were apparently commonplace in many orchestras (see John Spitzer and Neal Zaslaw, "Improvised Ornamentation in Eighteenth-Century Orchestras," *Journal of the American Musicological Society* 39 [1986]: 524–78). Reichardt's admonition does not, however, preclude overdotting, any more than did Quantz's: any rhythmic alteration would be introduced by the leader, whom the other ripienists were required to follow (Reichardt, 78–81; cf. also Quantz, XVII/i/7, 9, 10, and XVII/vii/15).

15. *C. P. E. Bachs Angangstücke mit einer Anleitung für Clavierspieler . . .* (Berlin, 1790), xii–xiii.

16. *Clavier-Schule . . .* (Leipzig and Züllichau, 1765), 69 (also 1773, 67). The text of the 1791 edition, published after Löhlein's death, is slightly different and includes a general qualification:

> Wenn kurze Noten auf Punktirte folgen, so pflegt man die letztern so zu spielen, als wenn zwey Punkte dabey stünden. Man sehe hierüber die Ausführung des folgenden Beyspiels [examples as in earlier eds.].
>
> Regel ist dieses aber nicht, und es können oft Fälle vorkommen wo diese Ausführung unrecht ist. Daher ist es, zur Vermeidung einer fehlerhaften Ausführung, besser, wenn der Componist dergleichen Stellen genau so schreibt, wie sie gespielt werden sollen. Der Schüler muß sich genau an die Vorschrift der Noten halten.

> When short notes follow dotted notes, one takes care to play the latter as though two dots were present. Concerning this, one should see the performance of the following example [examples as in earlier eds.]
>
> This is not a rule, however, and cases may often arise where this rendering is incorrect. Therefore, to avoid an erroneous performance, it is better if the composer writes such passages exactly as they ought to be played. The student must restrict himself exactly to the recipe of the notes.

17. *Versuch eines Unterrichts zum Klavierspielen* (Leipzig, 1785), 8, and 44 (where the quoted material appears).

18. *Ausführlicher und gründlicher Unterricht die Flöte zu spielen* (Leipzig, 1791), 172. The discussion of the Lombardic rhythm follows on p. 173.

19. Example *l*), p. 171.

20. *Unterricht in der Singekunst* (Halle, 1784), 41.

21. *Kurzer aber deutlicher Unterricht im Klavierspielen,* 2d ed. (Leipzig, 1784), 32–33.

22. *Klavierschule . . .* (Leipzig and Halle, 1789), 361.

23. Ibid., 362.

24. Loc. cit.; "nämlich so" = "namely, thus." Türk's two collections of *Sechzig Handstücke für angehende Klavierspieler* (Leipzig and Halle, 1792, nos. 41 and 53; 1795, no. 56) contain three pieces in which overdotting is indicated by footnote references to the relevant passages of the *Klavierschule* (and also to his later *Kurze Anweisung zum Klavierspielen*, 1792). These are additional instructive cases of where and how Türk would apply overdotting, but they scarcely constitute sufficient basis for broad generalizations about the notation and performance practice of other musicians (cf. Graham Pont, "Rhythmic Alteration and the Majestic," 68–71).

25. *Klavierschule* (1789), 362–63. Türk concludes this section with a small-print comment in which he takes exception to Agricola's consistently short rendition of the Lombardic rhythm, and cites C. P. E. Bach's more flexible approach.

26. Ibid., 392.

27. These examples confute Neumann's claim that seemingly general observations about rhythmic alteration found in eighteenth-century instrumental tutors apply only to solo players of the specific instrument for which a given volume was written: obviously Türk (and Quantz, C. P. E. Bach, and Leopold Mozart) often wrote from the perspective of much broader musical experience. (See also chap. 5, n. 17.)

28. Schlegel, *Gründliche Anleitung, die Flöte zu spielen, nach Quanzens Anweisung* (Graz, 1788), 54–56 plus table IV, figs. 1–9; also 118.

29. Bailleux, *Méthode raisonnée pour apprendre à joüer du violon . . .* (Paris [1798]), 27. We may note in passing that Bailleux makes no mention of French *inégalité*.

30. Watkins Shaw, *A Textual and Historical Companion to Handel's "Messiah"* (London: Novello, 1965), 203–4; Donington, *The Interpretation of Early Music*, 451; Graham Pont, "Rhythmic Alteration and the Majestic," 73–75; idem, "A Revolution in the Science and Practice of Music," *Musicology* 5 (1979): 9–10 and passim; idem, "French Overtures at the Keyboard: 'How Handel Rendered the Playing of Them,' " *Musicology* 6 (1980): 29–50; idem, "Handel's Overtures for Harpsichord or Organ: An Unrecognized Genre," *Early Music* 11 (1983): esp. 317 and n. 54; idem, "A Third Alternative," *Early Music* 14 (1986): 411; Terence Best, ed., *George Frideric Handel: Twenty Overtures in Authentic Keyboard Arrangements*, 3 vols. (London: Novello, 1985).

31. See Neumann, "Once More: The 'French Overture Style' " and "The Overdotting Syndrome," *Essays*, 142–43 and 164–67. On changing traditions in Handel performance see Jens Peter Larsen, *Handel Studies*, special issue of *American Choral Review* 14/1 (1972): esp. 25–27 and 32–41; Burney provides personnel lists for the 1784 festival in *An Account of the Musical Performances in Westminster-Abbey . . . in Commemoration of Handel* (London, 1785), [pt. 2]: 16–24.

32. John Mainwaring, *Memoirs of the Life of the Late George Frederic Handel* (London, 1760), 56–57; the Italian phrase may be translated "But my dear Saxon, this music is in French style, which I do not understand."

33. See Best, preface to *Sechs einzeln überlieferte Instrumentalwerke, Hallische Händel-Ausgabe*, ser. IV, vol. 15 (Kassel: Bärenreiter, 1979), VII. First published by Walsh in 1758 without a specific title, this French overture in B flat survives in manuscript sources dating back to ca. 1720, and is clearly in the style of Handel's early Italian period. The second version ("Sonata del overtura") is found in *G. F. Händels Werke*, vol. 24, ed. Chrysander.

34. It is noteworthy that Corelli's Op. 3 (Modena, 1689) is dedicated to Francesco II of Modena, at whose court French influence had long been strong; thus, the French overture style in Sonata No. 10 may have been intended to please the duke. Donington has already suggested that the 7:1 rhythmic ratios which open the third concerto of Corelli's Op. 6 may well reflect French influence (*The Interpretation of Early Music,* 446); Pont's objection to this, chiefly on the grounds that Corelli does not consistently write such sharp rhythms, misses the stylistic point ("Rhythmic Alteration and the Majestic," 77–79). Corelli may indeed have intended a distinction in performance between the 7:1 and 3:1 rhythms in Op. 6, No. 3 (and elsewhere) – his notation is generally very careful. But this does not diminish the likelihood that the sharper rhythms indicate a somewhat eclectic adaptation of French style. Nor does Pont refer to the trio sonata Op. 3, No. 10, wherein both form and rhythm are obviously related to the French overture.

35. See Best, preface to *Twenty Overtures in Authentic Keyboard Arrangements,* 1: viii–x, and William C. Smith, *Handel: A Descriptive Catalogue of the Early Editions,* 2d ed. (Oxford: Blackwell, 1970), 280–87.

36. The copy believed to be annotated by Battishill, *Handel's Overtures from All His Operas and Oratorios Set for the Harpsichord or Organ . . .* (London: Wright, ca. 1785), is in the Hamburg Staats- und Universitätsbibliothek, MB/1657 (see below, and also Pont, "French Overtures at the Keyboard"); concerning the other editions, see Pont, "Rhythmic Alteration and the Majestic," 72–75.

37. "Once More:" and "The Overdotting Syndrome," *Essays,* 140–43, 165–67.

38. The inconsistency in this and other sources has led Pont to the unlikely hypothesis that the application of rhythmic alteration was generally inconsistent, and that the "paradigm of inconsistency" is going to precipitate a widespread "revolution in the science and practice of music" (1979, 1980, 1983; full citations are found in n. 30). While keyboard players could do much as they wished, unwritten rhythmic alteration must have been applied fairly consistently within a given piece if it were adopted in orchestral performance; see also chapter 7 below.

39. The Hamburg volume contains two annotated copies of the overture to *Faramondo.* One is much worn, trimmed, and has been bound in adjacent to the second copy; it also bears the handwritten indication "this side Copied out." This suggests that the markings in the second copy of *Faramondo,* which is part of the main volume, were transferred from the worn and trimmed exemplar, and comparison of the two supports the hypothesis. All of this led Pont to suppose that the worn, bound-in copy of *Faramondo* was from an older printing, perhaps as early as 1749 ("French Overtures at the Keyboard," 50, n. 48). But the paper on which both copies were printed is actually the same: in both the chain lines run horizontally, 2.8 cm apart, and the (vertical) wire lines are just over 1 mm apart; moreover, the plates have been pressed at virtually the same spot with respect to the chain lines. Thus, the evidence as it stands cannot be dated any earlier than ca. 1785.

40. According to Best's identification of Handel's own overture transcriptions, only four of the eleven arrangements for which Battishill has provided overdotting were made by the composer.

41. In a communication to *Early Music* 7 (1979): 279, David Fuller reported that overdotting was present in a ratio of 4:1, but in "Analyzing the Performance of a Barrel Organ," *Organ Yearbook* 11 (1980): 111–12, he correctly retracted that

assertion; see also Hefling, review of *G. F. Handel, Two Ornamented Organ Concertos*, transcribed with commentary by David Fuller, in *Early Keyboard Journal* (1982–83): 88–89.

42. "Analyzing the Performance of a Barrel Organ," 113.

43. Falkener, *Instructions for Playing the Harpsichord . . .* (London, 1770); 2d ed. (London, 1774), 17, 19.

CHAPTER 7.   Summary Observations

1. Quantz, chap. XVII, sec. 1. See also L. Mozart, XII/21.

2. C. P. E. Bach, letter to Forkel [late 1774], cited in *The Bach Reader*, 277.

3. Choquel, *La musique* (1762), 106 (see also p. 21ff. above).

4. See esp. Ralph Kirkpatrick, "Eighteenth-Century Metronomic Indications," *Papers Read by Members of the American Musicological Society 1938*, 30–50, and Hellmuth Christian Wolff, "Das Metronom des Louis-Léon Pajot 1735," *Festskrift Jens Peter Larsen*, ed. Nils Schiørring, Nils Glahn, and Carsten Hatting (Copenhagen: Wilhelm Hansen, 1972), 205–17; see also (with caution) O'Donnell, "The French Style," pt. 1, and William Malloch, "Bach and the French Overture," *Musical Quarterly* 75 (1991): 174–97.

It should be noted that L'Affilard's tempo indications, expressed in pendulum measurements, have been misinterpreted by Erich Schwandt in his article "L'Affilard on the French Court Dances," *Musical Quarterly* 60 (1974): 389–400 (and also idem, *The New Grove*, s. v. "L'Affilard, Michel"). Schwandt claims, without substantiation, that L'Affilard's "vibration" of the pendulum actually means a full cycle, and that therefore his tempos are only half as fast as Kirkpatrick and others have calculated them. But L'Affilard clearly states that his pendulum and its measurement have been more fully explained by Sauver ("C'est ce que Monsieur Sauver explique plus au long dans ses Principes nouveaux . . ."): this is a reference to Joseph Sauver's article "Système general des intervalles des sons . . . " in *Histoire de l'Académie Royale des Sciences année 1701* (Paris, 1704; the relevant portions are reproduced in Rosamond E. M. Harding, *Origins of Musical Time and Expression* [London: Oxford University Press, 1938], 10–11 and plate 9). Sauver provides detailed scale diagrams for his "Echomètre," and there can be no doubt that it is based on the timing of a single vibration in one direction, lasting one second, and further subdivided. According to Sauver, the vibration of a pendulum that is "3 pieds 8½ lignes de Paris" lasts one second. The *pied de Paris*, equivalent to 1.066 English feet, was divided into 12 *pouces*, and the *pouce* was divided into 12 *lignes*; calculated by formula, $\pi\sqrt{3.26\text{ft.}/(32\text{ft./sec.}^2)} = 1.003$ seconds for a single vibration, which can also be verified experimentally. (Concerning the length of the *pied de Paris*, see John Martin, *Philosophical Transactions (from the Year 1732, to the Year 1744) Abridged, and Disposed under General Heads* [London, 1747], 9: 489–92, and *Webster's New International Dictionary of the English Language*, 2d unabridged ed., s. v. "measure," p. 1523.)

5. We may advert briefly to two: as early as 1668 Bacilly points out that it is appropriate for airs based on dance movements to be sung with greater leisure, freedom, and ornamentation than would be proper for a piece actually to be danced (*Remarques curieuses*, 105–6). And seventy years later Mattheson draws

attention to the stylistic distinctions between dances for playing or singing, and those that are actually danced (*Der volkommene Kapellmeister* [1739], pt. II: chaps. 12–13).

6. See also Fuller, "The Performer as Composer," *Performance Practice: Music after 1600*, ed. Howard Mayer Brown and Stanley Sadie, Norton/Grove Handbooks in Music (New York: W. W. Norton, 1989), 131.

7. Marcou, *Elémens*, 35 (see above, p. 19).

8. The long slurs in mm. 4, 12, 19, and 25 of this piece raise questions about the appropriateness of inequality here; although no French treatise would forbid it, such long slurs are atypical in French dance music. But no autograph sources survive for BWV 1066, and the Leipzig performance parts do not agree on the articulation of the bars in question: the oboe parts generally show groups of four notes slurred (see *NBA* VII/i, *Kritische Bericht*, 20–24, 29).

9. Neumann, "The Overdotting Syndrome," *Essays*, 151–82; Donington, *The Interpretation of Early Music*, 451; Dart, *The Interpretation of Music*, 82 (see above, p. x).

10. It may be the case, however, that the tempo of the French overture became gradually slower during the course of the eighteenth century; this is an important issue that should be carefully investigated.

11. O'Donnell, "The French Style," pt. 2: 344–45; cf. also Neumann, "The Overdotting Syndrome," *Essays*, 160–61.

12. On performance conditions in Leipzig see e.g. Alfred Dürr, "De Vita cum Imperfectis," *Studies in Renaissance and Baroque Music in Honor of Arthur Mendel*, ed. Robert L. Marshall (Kassel: Bärenreiter, 1974), 243–53. Although the piece was probably composed in Cöthen, parts for the C-major suite were copied during 1723/24 in Leipzig, almost certainly for use by the Collegium Musicum (see *NBA* VII/i, preface, [VI]).

13. See chap. 6, nn. 30, 38.

14. See above, pp. 68, 102, 123–24, 94; see also Best, "Interpreting Handel's Rhythmic Notation," 282.

15. For some additional instructive examples, see Neumann, *Essays*, 60–62, 92, 94, and 123–24. As indicated above (chap. 4, n. 9), the issue of synchronizing binary-ternary conflicts leads beyond the scope of this study. But Neumann's claim that synchronization is impractical in the orchestra ("The Overdotting Syndrome," *Essays*, 161–62) is incorrect, and reveals lack of experience with performance based on procedures of the seventeenth and eighteenth centuries.

16. Graham Pont's contention ("Handel's Overtures for Harpsichord or Organ," 317) that these notational inconsistencies embody "conventional yet free use of rubato" makes no sense from the perspective of ensemble performance.

17. See above, p. 113.

18. This is an issue on which Collins ("A Reconsideration of French Overdotting," 112) and Neumann ("Rhythm in the Two Versions," *Essays*, 104–5) have clashed. Although Neumann has refuted Collins's assertion that Handel modernized his notation of upbeats by writing only thirty-second-note flourishes after 1738, he has not challenged Collins's observation that "Lully, Georg Muffat and D'Anglebert never place three or more demisemiquavers after dots or rests in their *ouvertures*. . . ."

19. Mattheson, *Kern melodischer Wissenschaft* . . . (Hamburg, 1737), 64; also *Der volkommene Kapellmeister* (1739), 206.

20. Cf. also Neumann, "The Rhythm in 'Behold the Lamb of God,'" *New Essays on Performance Practice* (Ann Arbor: UMI Research Press, 1989), 85–90.

21. For additional discussion see Sandra P. Rosenblum, *Performance Practices in Classic Piano Music* (Bloomington: Indiana University Press, 1988), 299–304.

22. See William J. Mitchell's introduction to his translation of C. P. E. Bach, *Essay on the True Art of Playing Keyboard Instruments* (New York: W. W. Norton, 1949), 2, 4.

23. Cf. also Neumann, "Facts and Fiction," *Essays,* 129.

BIBLIOGRAPHY

I. Notes Inégales

A. Primary Sources

1535   Ganassi, Silvestro. *Opera intitulata fontegara.* . . . Venice. Facs. ed., Bologna: Forni, 1969.

1550   Bourgeois, Loys. *Le droict chemin de mvsique.* . . . Geneva. Facs. ed., Kassel: Bärenreiter, 1954.

1565   Tomás de Santa Maria. *Libro llamado arte de tañer fantasia.* . . . Valladolid.

1594   Bovicelli, Giovanni Battista. *Regole, passaggi di musica.* . . . Venice. Facs. ed., Kassel: Bärenreiter, 1957.

1602   Caccini, Giulio. *Le nuove musiche.* Florence. Facs. ed., New York: Broude Bros., 1973. Trans. and ed. H. Wiley Hitchcock, Madison, Wis.: A-R Editions, 1970.

1613   Cerone, Pedro. *El melopeo y maestro.* Naples. Facs. ed., Bologna: Forni, 1969.

1615   Frescobaldi, G. "Avvertimenti," *Toccate e partite d'intavolature di cimbalo.* Rome. Reprinted in the facsimile of the 1637 ed., Florence: Studio per edizioni scelte, 1980.

1618   Puliaschi, Domenico. *Musiche varie a una voce.* Rome. Preface reprinted in Gaetano Gaspari, *Catalogo della biblioteca del Liceo musicale de Bologna*, pp. 155–56. Bologna, 1893; reprinted, Bologna: Forni, 1961.

1665   Nivers, Guillaume-Gabriel. *Livre d'orgue contenant cent pieces.* . . . Paris. Facs. ed., Courlay: Éditions J. M. Fuzeau, 1987.

1667   ———. *Livre d'orgue contenant la messe et les hymnes d'eglise.* Paris. Modern ed. by Norbert Dufourcq, Paris: Schola Cantorum, 1956.

1668   Bacilly, Bénigne de. *Remarques curieuses sur l'art de bien chanter et particulierement pour ce qui regarde le chant françois.* . . . Paris. Trans. and ed. Austin B. Caswell as *A Commentary upon the Art of Proper Singing.* Brooklyn, N.Y.: Institute for Mediaeval Music, 1968.

[ca. 1668– 71]   Burwell, Mary. [Lute tutor, English MS]. Facs. ed. by Robert Spencer. Leeds: Boethius Press, 1974. Portions of text, with introduction, in Thurston Dart, "Miss Mary Burwell's Instruction Book for the Lute." *Galpin Society Journal* 11 (1958): 3–62.

1675   Nivers, Guillaume-Gabriel. *Livre d'orgue des huit tones de l'eglise.* Paris.

1678   Printz, Wolfgang Caspar. *Musica Modulatoria Vocalis.* Schwednitz.

[ca.   Perrine. *Pieces de luth en musique.* Paris. Facs. ed., Geneva: Minkoff
1680]   Reprints, 1983.

1685   Gigault. *Livre de musique pour l'orgue.* Modern ed. Alexandre Guilmant
        and André Pirro, Archives des maitres de l'orgue des XVIe, XVIIe, XVIIIe
        siècles . . . , vol. 4. Leipzig: B. Schott's Söhne, 1902.

[ca.   Anon. "Maniere de toucher lorgue dans toute la proprete et la delicatesse
1685]   qui est en usage aujourdhy a Paris." *F-Pa*, MS. 3042, fols. 100–19. Printed
        in William Pruitt, "Un traité d'interprétation du XVIIe siècle." *L'orgue*
        152 (Oct.–Dec. 1974): 99–111. Reprinted with English trans. in idem, "A
        Seventeenth-Century French Manuscript on Organ Performance." *Early
        Music* 14 (1986): 237–51.

1687   Rousseau, Jean. *Traite de la viole.* . . . Paris. Facs. ed., Amsterdam: An-
        tiqua, 1965.

1690   Jullien, Gilles, *Premier livre d'orgue.* . . . Paris. Modern ed. by Norbert
        Dufourcq, Paris: Huegel et Cie., 1952.

1694   L'Affilard, Michel. *Principes tres-faciles pour bien apprendre la
        musique.* . . . Paris. 2d ed., Paris, 1697. 5th ed., Paris, 1705. 7th ed., Am-
        sterdam [1710]. New ed., Paris, 1717.

1695   Muffat, Georg. *Florilegium Primum.* . . . Augsburg. Modern ed. in *Denk-
        mäler der Tonkunst in Österreich* I/2 (1894). English trans. of preface in
        Oliver Strunk, *Source Readings in Music History* (New York: W. W.
        Norton, 1950), 442–45.

1696   Loulié, Étienne. *Elements ou principes de musique, mis dans un nouvel
        ordre.* . . . Paris. Facs. ed., Geneva: Minkoff Reprints, 1971. 2d ed., Am-
        sterdam: Roger, 1698. Trans. and ed. Albert Cohen as *Elements or Prin-
        ciples of Music* . . . , Brooklyn, N.Y.: Institute for Mediaeval Music, 1965
        [including manuscript additions and corrections from *F-Pn*, f. fr. n. a.
        6355, an incomplete revision of the 1st ed.].

1698   Muffat, Georg. *Florilegium Secundum.* . . . Passau. Modern ed. in *Denk-
        mäler der Tonkunst in Österreich* II/2 (1895). English trans. of portions
        of preface in Strunk, *Source Readings,* 445–48; the remainder trans. in
        Kenneth Cooper and Julius Zsako, "Georg Muffat's Observations on the
        Lully Style of Performance," *Musical Quarterly* 53 (1967): 220–45.

1700   Freillon-Poncein, Jean-Pierre. *La veritable maniere d'apprendre a jouer
        en perfection du haut-bois, de la flute et du flageolet.* . . . Paris. Facs. ed.,
        Geneva: Minkoff Reprints, 1974.

[1701] Dieupart, Charles. *Six suittes de clavessin.* . . . Amsterdam. Modern ed.
        by Paul Brunold, Paris: Éditions de l'Oiseau Lyre, 1934.

1701   Marais, Marin. *Pieces de viole* [2d book]. Paris.

1702   MS. 24-Babell. *GB*-Lbm Add. mss. 39569.

1702 Saint-Lambert, Michel de. *Les principes du clavecin.* . . . Paris. Facs. ed., Geneva: Minkoff Reprints, 1982. Reprinted, Amsterdam [ca. 1710].

1705 Brossard, Sebastien de. *Dictionnaire de musique.* . . . 2d ed. Paris. Facs. ed., Hilversum: Frits Knuf, 1965. 3d ed., Amsterdam [ca. 1708].

1707 La Ferté. *Premier livre de sonates pour le violon.* . . . Paris.

1707 Hotteterre-le-Romain, Jacques. *Principes de la flute traversiere, ou flute d'allemagne.* . . . Paris. Reprinted, Amsterdam [1710]; facs. ed., Kassel: Bärenreiter, 1958. New ed., Paris, 1713, reprinted, Paris, 1720; facs. ed., Geneva: Minkoff Reprints, 1973. Trans. Abraham Moubach as *Grondbeginselen over de behandeling van de dwarsfluit . . .*, Amsterdam, 1728. Trans. anon. as *The Rudiments or Principles of the German Flute . . .*, London [1729]. Trans. David Lasocki as *Principles of the Flute, Recorder, and Oboe*, New York: Praeger Publishers, 1968.

1708 Campra, André. *Cantates françoises mélees de symphonies . . . livre premier.* Paris. Facs. ed., New York: Garland, 1990.

1708 de la Guerre, Elizabeth Jacquet. *Cantates françoises.* . . . Paris. Facs. ed., New York: Garland, 1990.

1709 Monteclair, Michel Pignolet de. *Nouvelle methode pour apprendre la musique.* . . . Paris.

1712 Philidor, A. D. *I.ᵉʳ livre de pieces pour la flute traversiere.* . . . Paris.

1712 Piani, Giovanni Antonio. *Sonate a violino solo.* . . . Paris. Modern ed. by Barbara Garvey Jackson, Madison, Wis.: A-R Editions, 1975.

1713 Couperin, François. *Pieces de clavecin . . . premier livre.* Paris. Facs. ed. of second issue (1717 or later), New York: Broude Bros., 1973.

1715 Hotteterre-le-Romain, Jacques. *Premier livre de pieces pour la flûte-traversiere.* . . . Paris. Facs. ed., Florence: Studio per edizioni scelte, 1980.

1717 Couperin, François. *L'art de toucher le clavecin.* . . . Paris. Facs. ed., New York: Broude Bros., 1969.

1717 ———. *Second livre de piéces de clavecin.* . . . Paris. Facs. ed. of reimpression ca. 1745, New York: Broude Bros., 1973.

1718 Dupont. *Principes de musique par demande et par reponce.* . . . Paris.

1719 Hotteterre-le-Romain, Jacques. *L'art de preluder sur la flûte traversiere, sur la flûte-a-bec, sur le haubois, et autres instrumens de dessus.* Paris. Facs. ed., Geneva: Minkoff, 1978.

1722 [Borin.] [Formerly attributed to Didier Saurin] *La musique theorique, et pratique, dans son ordre naturel.* . . . Paris.

1722 Couperin, François. *Troisiéme livre de piéces de clavecin.* Includes *Suplement, Concerts royeaux.* . . . Paris. Facs. of 1724 reimpression, New York: Broude Bros., 1973.

1724 Dandrieu, François. *Livre de pièces de clavecin.* . . . Paris.

1728　　　——. *Second livre de pièces de clavecin.* . . . Paris. Modern ed. by Pauline Aubert and Brigitte François-Sappey, Paris: Éditions de la Schola
Cantorum, 1973.

1728　　　Demotz de la Salle. *Methode de musique selon un nouveau systeme.* . . .
Paris.

1728　　　Monteclair, Michele Pignolet de. *Cantates a une et a due voix* . . . , bk. 3.
Paris. Facs. ed., New York: Garland, 1990. Modern ed. of selected works
in *Cantatas for One and Two Voices,* ed. James R. Anthony and Diran
Akmajian. Recent Researches in the Music of the Baroque Era, vol. 29/
30. Madison, Wis.: A-R Editions, 1978.

[1730]　　Cappus, Jean-Baptiste. *Etrennes de musique.* . . . Paris.

1730　　　Couperin, François. *Quatriéme livre de piéces de clavecin.* Paris.

1731　　　Caix d'Hervelois. *Deuxiéme recueil de pieces pour la flute-
traversiere.* . . . Paris.

[1731]　　Dornel, Antoine. *Pieces de clavecin.* Paris. Modern ed. by Catherine
Caumont, Paris: Éditions musicales transatlantiques, 1982.

1731　　　Prelleur, Peter. *The Modern Musick-Master or the Universal
Musician.* . . . London. Facs. ed., Kassel: Bärenreiter, 1965.

1732　　　Walther, Johann Gottfried. *Musikalisches Lexikon.* . . . Leipzig. Facs. ed.,
Kassel: Bärenreiter, 1953.

1733　　　Vague. *L'art d'apprendre la musique.* . . . Paris.

1733　　　Villeneuve, Alexandre de. *Nouvelle methode tres courte, et tres facile
avec un nombre de lecons.* . . . Paris. Reprinted, Paris, 1756.

[ca.　　　Monteclair, Michel Pignolet de. *Petite methode pour apprendre la
1735]　　 musique.* . . . Paris.

1736　　　Boismortier, Joseph Bodin de. *Quatre suites de pieces de clavecin.* . . .
Op. 59. Paris. Modern ed. by Erwin R. Jacobi, Munich: Leuckart, 1960.

[1736–　　de-La Chapelle, Jacques-Alexandre de. *Les vrais principes de la
52]　　　 musique.* . . . Paris. [Although the *privilège general* is dated 1736, the
volume contains the printed notice "Achevé d'imprimer le quatriéme
janvier 1752."]

1736　　　Monteclair, Michel Pignolet de. *Principes de musique.* . . . Facs. ed.,
Geneva: Minkoff Reprints, 1972.

[1737]　　David, François. *Methode nouvelle ou principes generaux pour apprendre facilement la musique, et l'art de chanter.* Paris and Lyons.

1737　　　Hotteterre-le-Romain, Jacques. *Methode pour la musette.* . . . Paris. Facs.
ed., Geneva: Minkoff Reprints, 1978.

1738　　　Corrette, Michel. *L'ecole d'Orphée: Méthode pour apprendre facilement
a joüer du violon dans le goût françois et italien avec des principes de
musique.* . . . Paris. Facs. ed., Geneva: Minkoff Reprints, 1973.

1738　　　DuTartre. *La volupté, cantate a voix seule.* . . . Paris.

[n.d.] Metoyen, J. B. *Démonstration des principes de musique.* . . . Paris.

[n.d.] Gaumey. *Cantates.* MS, in *Recueil de cantates.* *US*-Wcm, Case M 1613.3 C64 C6.

1740 Dupont [Pierre]. *Principes de violon par demandes et par reponce.* . . . Paris.

1741 Corrette, Michel. *Methode théorique et pratique pour apprendre en peu de tems le violoncelle dans sa perfection.* Paris. Facs. ed., Geneva: Minkoff Reprints, 1972.

[1741] Dupuit, Jean Baptiste. *Principes pour toucher de la viele.* Paris.

[ca. Marpurg, Frederick Wilhelm. *Pieces de clavecin.* Paris. Facs. ed., Paris:
1741– U. C. P. Publications [n.d.].
48]

[ca. Corrette, Michel. *Methode pour apprendre aisèment à joüer de la flute
1742] traversiere.* . . . Paris. Facs. ed., Hildesheim: Georg Olms Verlag, 1975.

1742 Vion, P.F.C.X. *La musique pratique et theorique réduite à ses principes naturels.* . . . Paris.

[1743] Le Menu de Saint Philbert. *Principes de musique courts et faciles.* Paris.

1747 Denis, Pierre. *Nouveau systeme de musique pratique.* . . . Paris. 2d ed.: *Nouvelle méthode pour apprendre en peu de temps la musique et l'art de chanter.* Paris [1757].

[1748] Corrette, Michel. *Methode pour apprendre facilement à jouer du par-dessus de viole.* . . . Paris. Facs. ed., Geneva: Minkoff Reprints, 1983.

1748 de La Feillée, François. *Méthode nouvelle pour apprendre parfaitement les regles du plain-chant et de la psalmodie.* . . . Poitiers. 3d ed., Poitiers, 1777.

[1748] Mondonville, J.-J. Cassanéa de. *Pieces de clavecin avec voix ou violon.* Op. 5. Paris. Facs. ed., London: H. Baron.

[1749] Fouquet, Pierre-Claude. *Les caracteres de la paix.* . . . Paris. Facs. ed., Geneva: Minkoff Reprints, 1982.

[1750– ——. *Second livre de pieces de clavecin.* Paris. Facs. ed., Geneva:
51] Minkoff Reprints, 1982.

[1751] Lagarde. *Aeglé.* Paris.

1752 Buterne, Charles. *Methode pour apprendre la musique vocale et instru-mentale.* Paris, Lyon, and Rouen.

1752 Quantz, Johann Joachim. *Versuch einer Anweisung die Flöte traversiere zu spielen.* . . . Berlin. French trans., *Essai d'une methode pour apprendre à jouer de la flute traversiere.* . . . Berlin, 1752; facs. ed., Paris: Éditions Aug. Zurfluh, 1975. Trans. J. W. Lustig as *Grondig onderwys van den aardt en de regte behandeling der dwarsfluit* . . . , Amsterdam, 1754. 3d [unaltered] German ed., Breslau, 1789; facs. ed., Kassel: Bärenreiter, 1953.

Trans. and ed. Edward R. Reilly as *On Playing the Flute,* New York: Free Press, 1966; 2d ed., New York: Schirmer Books, 1985.

[1753] Dumas, Antoine Joseph. *L'art de la musique.* . . . Paris.

1753 Mondonville. *Titon et l'Aurore.* . . . Paris.

[n.d.] ———. *Isbé.* . . . Paris.

[1755] Bordet, Toussaint. *Méthode raisonnée pour apprendre la musique.* . . . Paris.

1758 Frischmuth, Leonard. *Gedagten over de beginselen en onderwyzingen des clavicimbaals.* Amsterdam. Facs. ed., Amsterdam: A. J. Heuweke-meijer, 1970.

1759 Choquel, Henri-Louis. *La musique rendue sensible par la méchanique.* 2d ed., Paris, 1762; facs. ed., Geneva: Minkoff Reprints, 1972.

[1760] Bordier, Louis-Charles. *Nouvelle methode de musique.* . . . Paris.

[ca. 1760] Anon. *Nouvelle methode pour apprendre à jouer du violon et à lire la musique.* n. p. [F–TLm; photocopies at F–Pn]

[ca. 1760] Morel de Lescer. *Sçience de la musique vocale.* . . . Paris.

[1760] Rollet. *Méthode pour apprendre la musique sans transposition.* . . . Paris.

[ca. 1761] Boüin, Jean-François. *La vielleuse habile.* . . . Paris. Facs. ed., Geneva: Minkoff Reprints, 1982.

[ca. 1761] ———. *Les amusements d'une heure et demie.* . . . Paris.

1763 Brijon, C.-R. *Réflexions sur la musique, et la vraie manière de l'executer sur le violon.* Paris. Facs. ed., Geneva: Minkoff Reprints, 1972.

1764 Duval, L'Abbé. *Principes de la musique pratique, par demandes et par reponses.* Paris.

1766 Lacassagne, L'Abbé Joseph. *Traité général des élémens du chant.* . . . Paris. Facs. ed., New York: Broude Bros., 1967.

1768 Rousseau, Jean-Jacques. *Dictionnaire de musique.* Paris, Amsterdam. Variously reprinted. Trans. William Waring as *A Dictionary of Music.* London [ca. 1775]. 2d ed. London [ca. 1779].

[1769] Dard. *Nouveaux principes de musique.* Paris.

[1770] Bailleux, Antoine. *Méthode pour apprendre facilement la musique vo-cale et instrumentale.* . . . Paris.

[ca. 1770] Quantz, Johann Joachim. *Solfeggi pour la flute traversiere.* . . . MS, *DK-Kk.* Ed. Winfried Michel and Hermien Teske. Wintherthur: Amadeus, 1978.

1771 Bayly, Anselm. *A Practical Treatise on Singing and Playing with Just Expression and Real Elegance.* . . . London.

1771   *Dictionnaire universel françois et latin, vulgairement appelé dictionnaire de Trévoux.* Paris.

[1772]   Cajon, A. F. *Les éléments de musique avec des leçons a une et 2 voix.* Paris.

1772   Raparlier. *Principes de musique, les agréments du chant et un essai sur la prononciation, l'articulation et la prosodie de la langue françoise. . . .* Lille. Facs. ed., Geneva: Minkoff Reprints, 1972.

[ca.   Tarade, Théodore-Jean. *Traité du violon, ou regles de cet instrument. . . .*
1774]   Paris. Facs. ed., Geneva: Minkoff Reprints, 1972.

1775   Anon. *Principes de musique. . . .* Paris. [*US*-NH]

[1775]   Duval, Pierre. *Méthode agréable et utile pour apprendre facilement à chanter juste, avec goût et precision. . . .* Paris. Facs. ed., Geneva: Minkoff Reprints, 1972.

1775   Engramelle, Père Marie-Dominique-Joseph. *La tonotechnie ou l'art de noter les cylindres, et tout ce qui est susceptible de notage dans les instruments de concerts méchaniques.* Paris. Facs. ed., Geneva: Minkoff Reprints, 1971.

[1775]   Pollet, Charles-François-Alexandre. *Méthode pour apprendre a pincer du cistre ou guittare. . . .* Paris.

1775   Roussel, Ferdinand. *Le guide musical ou théorie & pratique abregées de la musique vocale & instrumentale. . . .* Paris.

[ca.   Torlez, C. *Methode de musique. . . .* Paris.
1775]

[1776]   Azaïs, Pierre-Hyacinthe. *Méthode de musique sur un nouveau plan. . . .* Sorèse par Revel.

1777   Mercadier de Belesta, Jean-Baptiste. *Nouveau systeme de musique théoretique et pratique. . . .* Paris.

1778   Bedos de Celles, Dom François. *L'art du facteur d'orgues.* Paris. Facs. ed., Kassel: Bärenreiter, 1966. [Section on cylinder organs written by Engramelle, in collaboration with Bedos de Celles and Balbastre.]

[1779]   Mussard. *Nouveaux principes pour apprendre à jouer de la flûte traversiere. . . .* Paris.

1779   Lorenzoni, Antonio. *Saggio per ben sonare il flautotraverso. . . .* Venice. Facs. ed., Bologna: Forni, 1969.

1782   Marcou, Pierre. *Elemens théoriques et pratiques de musique.* London and Paris.

[1782]   Corrette, Michel. *L'art de se perfectionner dans le violon. . . . Cet ouvrage fait la suite de l'ecole d'Orphée methode pour le violon.* Paris. Facs. ed., Geneva: Minkoff Reprints, 1973.

[1783]   Corrette, Michel. *La belle vielleuse. . . .* Paris. Facs. ed., Geneva: Minkoff Reprints, 1984.

1786   Cleret fils. "Principes de musique vocale ou l'art du musicien mis en pratique." MS. *F-Pn* Rés 2327.

1787   Meude-Monpas, J. J. O. *Dictionnaire de musique.* . . . Paris. Facs. ed., Geneva: Minkoff Reprints, 1981.

B. Selected Secondary Sources

Babitz, Sol. "Concerning the Length of Time That Every Note Must Be Held." *Music Review* 27 (1967): 21–37.

———. "A Problem of Rhythm in Baroque Music." *Musical Quarterly* 38 (1952): 533–65.

———, John Byrt, and Michael Collins. "Three Further Views on Notes Inégales." *Journal of the American Musicological Society* 20 (1967): 473–85.

Best, Terence. "Interpreting Handel's Rhythmic Notation—Some Reflections on Modern Practice." In *Handel: Tercentenary Collection,* ed. Stanley Sadie and Anthony Hicks, 279–90. Ann Arbor: UMI Research Press, 1987.

Borrel, Eugène. *L'interprétation de la musique françoise de Lully à la revolution.* Paris: Librairie Félix Alcan, 1934; reprinted, Paris: Éditions d'aujourd'hui, 1976.

Brown, Howard. *Embellishing Sixteenth-Century Music.* London: Oxford University Press, 1976.

Caswell, Judith Carls. "Rhythmic Inequality and Tempo in French Music Between 1650 and 1740." Ph.D. diss., University of Minnesota, 1973.

Collins, Michael. (See above under Babitz.)

Cossart-Cotte, Françoise. " 'Documents sonores' de la fin du XVIIIe siècle: Leurs enseignements pour l'interprétation." In *L'interprétation de la musique française aux XVIIe et XVIIIe siècles,* ed. Edith Weber, 139–52. Paris: Éditions du Centre National de la Recherche Scientifique, 1974.

Dart, Thurston. *The Interpretation of Music.* London: Hutchison and Co., 1954; reprinted, New York: Harper Colophon Books, 1963.

Dolmetsch, Arnold. *The Interpretation of the Music of the Seventeenth and Eighteenth Centuries Revealed by Contemporary Evidence.* London: Novello, 1915; new ed., London: Novello, 1946.

Donington, Robert. Communication to *Journal of the American Musicological Society* 19 (1966): 112–14.

———. *The Interpretation of Early Music.* New York: St. Martin's Press, 1963; new version, New York: St. Martin's Press, 1974.

———. "A Problem of Inequality." *Musical Quarterly* 53 (1967): 503–17.

Fuller, David. "Dotting, the 'French Style,' and Frederick Neumann's Counter-Reformation." *Early Music* 5 (1977): 517–43.

———. "Mechanical Musical Instruments as a Source for the Study of *Notes inégales*." *Musical Box Society International* 20/5 (Summer 1974): 281–93. Reprinted, Cleveland: Divisions, 1979 (with sound recording).

———. "More on Triplets and Inequality." *Early Music* 15 (1987): 384–85. [re: Cappus, *Etrennes de musique,* ca. 1730]

———. "Notes and *inégales* Unjoined: Defending a Definition." *Journal of Musicology* 7 (1989): 21–28.

———. "Notes Inégales." *The New Grove Dictionary of Music and Musicians.* 6th ed. London: Macmillan, 1980.

———. "Notes Inégales." *The New Grove Dictionary of Musical Instruments.* London: Macmillan, 1984.

———. "Notes inégales." *The New Harvard Dictionary of Music.* Cambridge: The Belknap Press of Harvard University Press, 1986.

———. "The Performer as Composer." In *Performance Practice: Music after 1600,* ed. Howard Mayer Brown and Stanley Sadie, 117–46. Norton/Grove Handbooks in Music. New York: W. W. Norton, 1989.

———. "Rhythmic Alteration—If Any—in Bach's Organ Music." *American Organist* 21/6 (1987): 40–48.

———. "You Can't Prove It by Notation: Thoughts on Rhythmic Alteration." *Diapason* 72 (March 1981): 3.

Herz, Gerhard. "Lombard Rhythm in the *Domine Deus* of Bach's B Minor Mass: An Old Controversy Resolved." In idem, *Essays on J. S. Bach,* 221–29. Ann Arbor: UMI Research Press, 1985.

Houle, George. *Meter in Music, 1600–1800.* Bloomington: Indiana University Press, 1987 (with sound recording).

Italienische Diminutionen: die zwischen 1553 und 1638 mehrmals bearbeiteten Sätze. Ed. Richard Erig and Veronika Gutmann. Prattica Musicale, vol. 1. Zürich: Amadeus Verlag/Bernhard Päuler, 1979.

Johnson, Jane Troy. "How to 'Humour' John Jenkins' Three-Part Dances: Performance Directions in a Newberry Library MS." *Journal of the American Musicological Society* 20 (1967): 197–208.

Lully, Jean-Baptiste. *Ballet royal d'Alcidiane* (1658). Modern ed. in *Oeuvres complètes de J.-B. Lully, Les ballets,* vol. 2. Ed. Henry Prunières and Andre Tessier. Paris: Éditions de *La revue musicale,* 1936.

Mather, Betty Bang. *Interpretation of French Music from 1675 to 1775. . . .* New York: McGinnis & Marx, 1973.

Neumann, Frederick. Communication to *Journal of the American Musicological Society* 19 (1966): 435–37. Reprinted in idem, *Essays in Performance Practice* (Ann Arbor: UMI Research Press, 1982), 55–58.

———. *Essays in Performance Practice.* Ann Arbor: UMI Research Press, 1982.

———. "External Evidence and Uneven Notes." *Musical Quarterly* 52 (1966): 448–64. Reprinted in idem, *Essays in Performance Practice* (Ann Arbor: UMI Research Press, 1982), 59–72.

———. "Facts and Fiction about Overdotting." *Musical Quarterly* 63 (1977): 155–85 (esp. 165–68). Reprinted in idem, *Essays in Performance Practice* (Ann Arbor: UMI Research Press, 1982), 111–35 (esp. 118–21).

———. "The French *Inégales,* Quantz, and Bach." *Journal of the American Musicological Society* 18 (1965): 315–58. Reprinted in idem, *Essays in Performance Practice* (Ann Arbor: UMI Research Press, 1982), 17–54.

———. *New Essays on Performance Practice.* Ann Arbor: UMI Research Press, 1989.

———. "The *Notes inégales* Revisited." *Journal of Musicology* 6 (1988): 137–49. Reprinted in idem, *New Essays on Performance Practice,* 65–76.

O'Donnell, John. "The French Style and the Overtures of Bach," pt. 1. *Early Music* 7/2 (April 1979): 190–96; pt. 2, *EM* 8/3 (July 1979): 336–45.

Pont, Graham. Communication to *Journal of the American Musicological Society* 19 (1966): 437–39.

Powell, Newman W. "Rhythmic Freedom in the Performance of French Music from 1650 to 1735." Ph.D. diss., Stanford University, 1959.

Pruitt, William. "Un traité d'interprétation du XVIIe siècle." *L'orgue* 152 (Oct.–Dec., 1974): 99–111. English version: "A Seventeenth-Century French Manuscript on Organ Performance." *Early Music* 14 (1986): 237–51.

Ranum, Patricia M. "*Piquer ou Pointer:* A Word Changes Meaning, 1690–1770." Unpublished paper [1980].

Reilly, Edward R. *Quantz and His* Versuch: *Three Studies.* American Musicological Society, Studies and Documents, no. 5. New York: Galaxy Music Corp., 1971.

Saint-Arroman, Jean. "Les inégalités." In *L'interprétation de la musique française aux XVIIe et XVIIIe siècles,* ed. Edith Weber, 67–85. Paris: Éditions du Centre National de la Recherche Scientifique, 1974.

———. *L'interprétation de la musique française 1661–1789.* Vol. 1, *Dictionnaire d'interprétation.* Paris: Librarie Honoré Champion, 1983.

Wilson, John, ed. *Roger North on Music.* London: Novello, 1959.

II. Overdotting, and Variable Value of the Dot

A. Primary Sources

1623   Titelouze, Jean. *Hymnes de l'eglise pour toucher sur l'orgue.* . . . Paris. Modern ed. Alexandre Guilmant, in *Oeuvres completes d'orgue de Jean Titelouze,* Archives des maîtres de l'orgue des XVIe, XVIIe, XVIIIe siècles . . . , vol. 1. Leipzig: B. Schott's Söhne, 1903.

[ca. 1650–61]   MS. 32-Oldham [L. Couperin autograph]. London, private collection. [Concerning this and other manuscripts of French harpsichord music, see Bruce Lester Gustafson, *French Harpsichord Music of the Seventeenth Century.* Ann Arbor: UMI Research Press, 1979.]

[post? 1658]   MS. 38-Gen-2348/53. *F*-Psg.

1670   Chambonnières, Jacques Champion. *Les pieces de clavessin.* . . . 2 vols. Paris. Facs. ed., New York: Broude Bros., 1967.

[post-1676]   MS. 35-Bauyn. *F*-Pn, Rés. Vm7 674–675. Facs. ed., Geneva: Minkoff Reprints, 1977.

[ca. 1677–80]   MS. 33-Rés-89ter. *F*-Pn. [D'Anglebert autograph]

[post-1687]   MS. 44-LaPierre. *F*-Pn, Rés, Vmd. ms. 18. Facs. ed., Geneva: Minkoff Reprints, 1983.

1688   Raison, André. *Livre d'orgue.* Paris. Modern ed. Alexandre Guilmant. Archives des maîtres de l'orgue des XVIe, XVIIe, XVIIIe siècles . . . , vol. 2. Leipzig: B. Schott's Söhne, 1897.

[post-1689]   MS. 46-Menetou. *US*-BE, MS. 777.

[ca. 1690]   MS. 36-Parville. *US*-BE, MS. 778.

[ca. 1690?]   MS. 47-Gen-2356. *F*-Psg.

1690   Muffat, Georg. *Apparatus Musico-Organisticus.* . . . Salzburg.

1696   Loulié, Étienne. *Elements ou principes de musique.* . . .

[post-1697]   MS. 48-LaBarre-6. *US*-BE, MS. 775.

1702   MS. 24-Babell. *GB*-Lbm Add. mss. 39569.

1705   L'Affilard, Michel. *Principes tres-faciles pour bien apprendre la musique.* . . . 5th ed.

1705   Sperling, Johann Peter. *Principia Musicae.* . . . Budissin.

1713   Clérambault, Louis-Nicolas. *Cantates françoises mellées de simpho-nies. . . . Livre II.ᵉ* Paris.

1714   Raison, André. *Second livre d'orgue. . . .* Paris.

1719   Hotteterre-le-Romain, Jacques. *L'art de preluder. . . .*

[post-   MS. 51-LaBarre-11. *US-BE,* MS. 775.
1724]

1735   Bach, J. S. *Zweyter Theil der Clavier Ubung. . . .* Leipzig. Facs. ed. by Christoph Wolff. Leipzig and Dresden: Edition Peters, 1984. Facs. ed. of Bach's *Handexemplar* by David Kinsela. Godstone, England: Gregg International, 1985. Modern ed. in *Johann Sebastian Bach: Neue Ausgabe sämtlicher Werke,* ser. V, vol. 2. Ed. Walter Emery and Christoph Wolff. Kassel: Bärenreiter, 1977.

1737   Hotteterre-le-Romain, Jacques. *Methode pour la musette. . . .*

1737   Mattheson, Johann. *Kern melodischer Wissenschaft.* Hamburg.

[n.d.]   Metoyen, B. *Démonstration des principes de musique. . . .*

1752   Quantz, J. J. *Versuch einer Anweisung die Flöte traversiere zu spielen. . . .*

1752   Schmelz, Simpertus. *Fundamenta Musica Cantus Artificialis. . . .* Yresee.

1753   Bach, Carl Philipp Emanuel. *Versuch über die wahre Art das Clavier zu spielen.* Berlin. Facs. ed. by Lothar Hoffmann-Erbrecht. Leipzig: VEB Breitkopf & Härtel, 1978/Wiesbaden: Breitkopf & Härtel, 1978. [Includes appendix of Bach's 1787 additions to the treatise.]

1755   Marpurg, Friedrich Wilhelm. *Anleitung zum Clavierspielen.* Berlin. 2d ed., Berlin, 1765; facs. ed., Hildesheim: Georg Olms, 1970.

1756   Mozart, Leopold. *Versuch einer gründlichen Violinschule.* Augsburg. Facs. ed., Vienna: C. Stephenson, 1922. 2d ed., Augsburg, 1769 and 1770. 3d ed., Augsburg, 1787. 4th ed., Frankfurt and Leipzig, 1791, and Augsburg, 1800. Trans. anon. as *Grondig onderwys in het behandelen der viool . . . ,* Amsterdam, 1766. Trans. and abr. Valentin Roeser as *Méthode raisonnée pour apprendre à jouer du violon . . . ,* Paris, [1770], [ca. 1783], [ca. 1788], [ca. 1800]. Trans. and ed. Editha Knocker as *Treatise on the Fundamental Principles of Violin Playing.* 2d ed. London: Oxford University Press, 1951.

1757   Agricola, J. F. *Anleitung zur Singkunst. . . .* Berlin. Facs. ed., Celle: H. Moeck Verlag, 1966.

1760   Mainwaring, John. *Memoirs of the Life of the Late George Frederic Handel.* London. Facs. ed., Buren: Fritz Knuf, 1975.

[ca.   Morel de Lescer. *Sçience de la musique vocale. . . .*
1760]

1762   Bach, C. P. E. *Versuch. . . .* (pt. 2) [See above, 1753.]

1765   Löhlein, Georg Simon. *Clavier-Schule.* . . . Leipzig and Züllichau. 2d ed., 1773. 5th ed., 1791.

1768   Rousseau, Jean-Jacques. *Dictionnaire de musique.* Paris, Amsterdam.

[ca. 1770]   Quantz, Johann Joachim. *Solfeggi pour la flute traversiere.* . . .

1771–[74]   Kirnberger, J. P., and J. A. P. Schulz. Articles on music in Sulzer, *Allgemeine Theorie der Schönen Künste.* . . . Leipzig.

1772   Raparlier. *Principes de musique.* . . .

1773   Schweitzer, Anton. Overture to *Alceste.* A-Wn, Musiksammlung, Mus. Hs. 16.152. Facs. ed., New York: Garland, 1986.

1774   Falkener, Robert. *Instructions for Playing the Harpsichord.* . . . 2d ed. London.

1774   Hiller, Johann Adam. *Anweisung zum musikalisch-zierlichen Gesange.* Leipzig.

1775   Engramelle, Père Marie-Dominique-Joseph. *La tonotechnie ou l'art de noter les cylindres.* . . .

1776   Reichardt, Johann Friedrich. *Ueber die Pflichten des Ripien-Violinisten.* . . . Berlin and Leipzig.

1779   Rolle, Johann Heinrich. *Lazarus, oder die Feyer der Auferstehung* . . . *Auszug zum Singen beym Klaviere.* . . . Leipzig.

1782   Marcou, Pierre. *Elemens théoriques et pratiques de musique.*

1784   Wolf, Georg Friedrich. *Unterricht in der Singekunst.* Halle.

1784   ———. *Kurzer aber deutlicher Unterricht im Klavierspielen.* 2d ed. Halle.

1785   Petschke, Adolf Friedrich. *Versuch eines Unterrichts zum Klavierspielen.* Leipzig.

1788   Schlegel, Franz Anton. *Gründliche Anleitung, die Flöte zu spielen, nach Quanzens Anweisung.* Graz.

[ca. 1785]   *Handel's Overtures from All His Operas and Oratorios Set for the Harpsichord or Organ.* . . . London: Wright. Copy annotated by Jonathan Battishill, D-Hs, MB/1657.

1789   Türk, Daniel Gottlob. *Klavierschule, oder Anweisung zum Klavierspielen für Lehrer und Lernende, mit kritischen Anmerkungen.* . . . Leipzig and Halle. Facs. ed., Kassel: Bärenreiter, 1962. Trans. Raymond H. Haggh as *School of Clavier Playing or Instructions in Playing the Clavier for Teachers and Students.* Lincoln: University of Nebraska Press, 1982.

1790   Rellstab, Johann Carl Friedrich. *C. P. E. Bachs Angangstücke mit einer Anleitung für Clavierspieler.* . . . Berlin.

1791   Tromlitz, Johann Georg. *Ausführlicher und gründlicher Unterricht die Flöte zu spielen.* Leipzig. Facs. ed., Amsterdam: Frits Knuf, 1973.

1792   Türk, Daniel Gottlob. *Kurze Anweisung zum Klavierspielung: Ein Aus- zug aus der grössern Klavierschule.* . . . Leipzig and Halle.

1792–95 ——. *Sechzig Handstücke für angehende Klavierspieler.* 2 vols. Leipzig and Halle.

1797   Löhlein, Georg Simon. *Anweisung zum Violinspielen . . . zum dritten Mahl mit Verbesserungen . . . von Johann Friedrich Reichardt.* Leipzig and Züllichau.

[1798]   Bailleux, Antoine. *Méthode raisonnée pour apprendre à joüer du violon.* . . . Paris. Facs. ed., Geneva: Minkoff Reprints, 1972.

B. Selected Secondary Sources

Bach, Johann Sebastian. *Neue Ausgabe sämtlicher Werke.* Series V, vol. 2. *Zweiter Teil der Klavierübung, vierter Teil der Klavierübung, Vier- zehn Kanons BWV 1087.* Ed. Walter Emery and Christoph Wolff. Kassel: Bärenreiter, 1977. *Kritischer Bericht* by Walter Emery and Christoph Wolff. Kassel: Bärenreiter, 1981.

Best, Terence. "Interpreting Handel's Rhythmic Notation — Some Reflec- tions on Modern Practice."

——, ed. *George Frideric Handel: Twenty Overtures in Authentic Key- board Arrangements.* 3 vols. London: Novello, 1985.

Bodky, Erwin. *The Interpretation of Bach's Keyboard Works.* Cam- bridge: Harvard University Press, 1960.

Collins, Michael. "A Reconsideration of French Overdotting." *Music and Letters* 50 (1969): 111–23.

Dolmetsch, Arnold. *The Interpretation of the Music of the Seventeenth and Eighteenth Centuries . . .*

Donington, Robert. *The Interpretation of Early Music.*

Dart, Thurston. *The Interpretation of Music.*

Enrico, Eugene Joseph. "Giuseppe Torelli's Music for Instrumental En- semble with Trumpet." Ph.D. diss., University of Michigan, 1970.

Fuller, David. "Analyzing the Performance of a Barrel Organ." *Organ Yearbook* 11 (1980): 104–13.

——. Communication to *Early Music* 7 (1979): 279.

——. "Dotted Notes." *The New Harvard Dictionary of Music.* Cam- bridge: The Belknap Press of Harvard University Press, 1986.

——. "The 'Dotted Style' in Bach, Handel, and Scarlatti." In *Bach, Han- del, Scarlatti: Tercentenary Essays,* ed. Peter Williams, 99–117. Cam- bridge: Cambridge University Press, 1985.

———. "Dotting, the 'French Style,' and Frederick Neumann's Counter-Reformation."

———. "The Performer as Composer."

———. "Rhythmic Alteration – If Any – in Bach's Organ Music."

Graun, Carl Heinrich. *Der Tod Jesu* (1755). Ed. Howard Serwer. Collegium Musicum: Yale University, 2d ser., vol. 5. Madison, Wis.: A-R Editions, 1975.

Gustafson, Bruce Lester. *French Harpsichord Music of the Seventeenth Century.* Ann Arbor: UMI Research Press, 1979.

Hefling, Stephen E. Review of *G. F. Handel, Two Ornamented Organ Concertos,* transcribed with commentary by David Fuller. *Early Keyboard Journal* 1 (1982–83): 83–93.

Harich-Schneider, Eta. "Über die Angleichung nachschlagender Sechzehntel an Triolen." *Musikforschung* 12 (1959): 35–59.

Houle, George. *Meter in Music, 1600–1800.*

Jacobi, Erwin R. "Über die Angleichung nachschlagender Sechzehntel an Triolen." *Musikforschung* 13 (1960): 268–81.

———. "Neues zur Frage 'Punktierte Rhythmen gegen Triolen' und zur Transcriptionstechnik bei J. S. Bach." *Bach-Jahrbuch* 49 (1962): 88–96.

Leavis, Ralph. "Double-Dotting and Ultra-Dotting." *Early Music* 6 (1978): 309.

Malloch, William. "Bach and the French Overture." *Musical Quarterly* 75 (1991): 174–97.

Neumann, Frederick. "Conflicting Binary and Ternary Rhythms: From the Theory of Mensural Notation to the Music of J. S. Bach." *Music Forum* 6/1 (1987): 93–127. Reprinted in idem, *New Essays on Performance Practice,* 35–64.

———. "Facts and Fiction about Overdotting." *Musical Quarterly* 63 (1977): 155–85. Reprinted in idem, *Essays in Performance Practice,* 111–35.

———. "Graham Pont's 'Paradigm of Inconsistency.' " *Early Music* 14 (1986): 403–6. Reprinted in idem, *New Essays on Performance Practice,* 77–84.

———. "La note pointée et la soi-disant 'manière française.' " *Revue de musicologie* 51 (1965): 66–92. Trans. R. Harris and E. Shay as "The Dotted Note and the So-Called French Style," *Early Music* 5 (1977): 310–24. Reprinted in Neumann, *Essays in Performance Practice,* 73–98.

————. "Once More: The 'French Overture Style.' " *Early Music* 7 (1979): 39–45. Reprinted in idem, *Essays in Performance Practice*, 137–50, with previously edited passages restored.

————. *Ornamentation in Baroque and Post-Baroque Music*. Princeton: Princeton University Press, 1978.

————. "The Overdotting Syndrome: Anatomy of a Delusion." *Musical Quarterly* 67 (1981): 305–47. Reprinted in idem, *Essays in Performance Practice*, 151–82.

————. "The Question of Rhythm in the Two Versions of Bach's French Overture BWV 831." In *Studies in Renaissance and Baroque Music in Honor of Arthur Mendel*, ed. Robert Marshall, 183–94. Kassel: Bären-reiter, 1974. Reprinted in Neumann, *Essays in Performance Practice*, 99–110.

————. "The Rhythm in 'Behold the Lamb of God.' " *American Choral Review* 28 (October 1986): 18–22. Reprinted in idem, *New Essays on Performance Practice*, 85–90.

O'Donnell, John. "The French Style and the Overtures of Bach," pts. 1 and 2.

Oldham, Guy. "Two Pieces for Five-Part Shawm Band by Louis Cou-perin." *Music, Libraries and Instruments*. Hinrichsen's Eleventh Music Book. London: Hinrichsen, 1961.

Pont, Graham. "French Overtures at the Keyboard: 'How Handel Ren-dered the Playing of Them.' " *Musicology* 6 (1980): 29–50.

————. "Handel and Regularization: A Third Alternative." *Early Music* 13 (1985): 500–5.

————. "Handel's Overtures for Harpsichord or Organ: An Unrecognized Genre." *Early Music* 11 (1983): 309–22.

————. "A Revolution in the Science and Practice of Music." *Musicology* 5 (1979): 1–66.

————. "Rhythmic Alteration and the Majestic." *Studies in Music* (Aus-tralia), no. 12 (1978): 68–100.

————. "A Third Alternative." *Early Music* 14 (1986): 409–11.

Rosenblum, Sandra P. *Performance Practices in Classic Piano Music: Their Principles and Applications*. Bloomington: Indiana University Press, 1988.

Saint-Arroman, Jean. *Dictionnaire d'interprétation*.

Scheibert, Beverly. "French Overdotting." *Early Music* 15 (1987): 443–44.

Shaw, Watkins. *A Textual and Historical Companion to Handel's "Messiah."* London: Novello, 1965.

Wulstan, David. "Glorious Uncertainty." *Early Music* 14 (1986): 406–9.

———. Communication to *Early Music* 15 (1987): 141.

III. Related Issues

A. Primary Sources

1558   Zarlino, Gioseffo. *Le istitutioni harmoniche.* . . . Venice. Pt. 3 trans. Guy A. Marco and Claude V. Palisca as *The Art of Counterpoint.* Music Theory Translation Series, vol. 2. New Haven: Yale University Press, 1968. Reprinted, New York: W. W. Norton, 1976.

1625   Diruta, Girolamo. *Il transylvano.* . . . [5th ed.] Venice. Facs. ed., Bologna: Forni, 1969.

[ca.   Bernhard, Christoph. *Tractatus Compositionis Augmentatus.* MS;
1657]   printed with idem, *Ausführlicher Bericht vom Gebrauche der Con- und Dissonantien* and *Von der Singe-Kunst oder Manier,* in *Die Kompositionslehre Heinrich Schützens in der Fassung seines Schülers Christoph Bernhard,* ed. Joseph Müller-Blattau. Kassel: Bärenreiter, 1963. All three treatises trans. and ed. Walter Hilse as "The Treatises of Christoph Bernhard," *Music Forum* 3 (1973): 1–196.

1687   Kusser, Johann Sigismond. *Composition de musique suivant la methode françoise.* . . . Stuttgart.

1694   *Le dictionnaire de l'Académie françoise.* Paris.

[ca.   North, Roger. *Cursory Notes of Musicke.* Ed. Mary Chan and Jamie C.
1698–   Kassler. Kensington, Australia: Unisearch/University of New South
1703]   Wales, 1986.

1702   Raguenet, François. *Paralèle des italiens et des françois, on ce qui regarde la musique et les opéra.* Paris. Trans. [J. E. Galliard] as *A Comparison between the French and Italian Musick and Opera's.* London, 1709; partially reprinted in Oliver Strunk, *Source Readings in Music History* (New York: W. W. Norton, 1950), 473–88.

1704   Sauver, Joseph. "Système general des intervals des sons. . . ." In *Histoire de l'Académie royale des sciences année 1701.* Paris. Portions concerning the *echomètre* reproduced in Rosamond E. M. Harding, *Origins of Musical Time and Expression* (London: Oxford University Press, 1938), 10–11 and plate 9.

1705   Le Cerf de La Viéville de Fresneuse, Jean-Laurent. *Comparaison de la
[–06]   musique italienne et de la musique française.* . . . 2d ed. Brussels. Reprinted in Jacques Bonnet, *Histoire de la musique et de ses effets . . .* (Amsterdam, 1725); portions trans. in Oliver Strunk, *Source Readings in Music History* (New York: W. W. Norton, 1950), 489–507.

1717   Taubert, Gottfried. *Rechtschaffener Tanzmeister oder gründliche Erklärung der Französischen Tanz-Kunst.* . . . Leipzig.

[1718]   Philidor, Pierre Danican. *Trio premier oeuvre contenant six suites.* . . . Paris. Facs. ed., Florence: Studio per edizioni scelte, 1980.

1718   Telemann, Georg Philipp. "Lebens-Lauff . . . 1718." In Johann Mattheson, *Grosse General-Baß-Schule.* . . . 2d ed. Hamburg, 1731. Facs. ed., Hildesheim: Georg Olms, 1968.

1723   Tosi, Pier Francesco. *Opinioni de' cantari antichi e moderni, o sieno osservazioni sopra il canto figurato.* Facs. ed. included as supplement to J. F. Agricola, *Anleitung zur Singkunst* . . . (Berlin, 1757; facs. ed., Celle: H. Moeck Verlag, 1966). Trans. J. E. Galliard as *Observations on the Florid Song; or, Sentiments on the Ancient and Modern Singers,* London, 1742. 2d ed., 1743; facs. ed., New York: Johnson Reprint Corp., 1968.

1726   Couperin, François. *Les nations: Sonades; et suites de simphonies en trio.* . . . Paris.

1732   Walther, Johann Gottfried. *Musikalisches Lexikon.* . . .

1739   Mattheson, Johann. *Der volkommene Kapellmeister.* . . . Hamburg. Facs. ed., Kassel: Bärenreiter, 1954.

1745   Scheibe, Johann Adolf. *Critischer Musikus, neue, vermehrte und verbesserte Auflage.* Leipzig. Facs. ed., Hildesheim: Georg Olms, 1970.

[1747]   Forqueray, Antoine. *Pieces de viole . . . Livre Ier.* Paris.

[1747]   Greene, Maurice. *Six Solo Anthems Perform'd before His Majesty at the Chapel Royal.* . . . London: Walsh.

1747   Martyn, John. *Philosophical Transactions (from the Year 1732, to the Year 1744) Abridged, and Disposed under General Heads.* . . . Vol. 9, *The Anatomical and Medical Papers . . . and the Historical and Miscellaneous Papers.* London.

1749   Marpurg, Friedrich Wilhelm. *Der critische Musicus an der Spree,* no. 27 (2 Sept. 1749). Reprinted, Berlin, 1750; facs. ed., Hildesheim: Georg Olms Verlag, 1970.

1756   Pauli, Carl. *Elémens de la danse.* Leipzig.

1758   Adlung, Jakob. *Anleitung zu der musikalischen Gelartheit.* . . . Erfurt.

1760   Mainwaring, John. *Memoirs of the Life of the Late George Frederic Handel.* London.

1763   Marpurg, Friedrich Wilhelm. *Anleitung zur Musik überhaupt, und zur Singkunst besonders.* Berlin.

[1764]   Roeser, Valentin. *L'art de toucher le clavecin . . . par M. Marpourg . . . mis au jour par M. Valentin Roeser.* . . . Paris.

1767   Petri, Johann Samuel. *Anleitung zur praktischen Musik.* Lauban. 2d ed., Leipzig, 1782.

1769   Roussier, Jacob. *Méthode de musique sur un nouveau plan.* Paris.

1771–   Kirnberger, Johann Philipp. *Die Kunst des reinen Satzes in der*
79   *Musik.* . . . Berlin. Facs. ed., Hildesheim: Georg Olms, 1968. Partially
          trans. David Beach and Jurgen Thym as *The Art of Strict Musical Com-*
          position. Music Theory Translation Series, vol. 4. New Haven: Yale Uni-
          versity Press, 1982.

1775   Burney, Charles. *The Present State of Music in Germany.* . . . 2d ed.
          London. Reprinted in *Dr. Burney's Musical Tours in Europe.* Ed. Percy A.
          Scholes. 2 vols. London: Oxford University Press, 1959.

1785   ———. *An Account of the Musical Performances in Westminster-Abbey*
          . . . *in Commemoration of Handel.* London.

B. Secondary Sources

Augsbach, Horst. *Johann Joachim Quantz: Thematisches Verzeichnis der musikalischen Werke, Werkgruppen QV 2 and QV 3.* Studien und Materialien zur Musikgeschichte Dresdens, vol. 5. Dresden: Sächsische Landesbibliothek, 1984.

Bach, Carl Philipp Emanuel. *Sinfonia in G,* Wq. 182/1. Ed. Traugott Fedtke. Frankfurt: Henry Litolff's Verlag, 1975.

Bach-Dokumente. Supplement zu Johann Sebastian Bach: Neue Ausgabe sämtlicher Werke. Vol. 3: *Dokumente zum Nachwirken Johann Sebastian Bachs 1750–1800.* Ed. Hans-Joachim Schulze. Kassel: Bärenreiter, 1972/Leipzig: VEB Deutscher Verlag für Musik, 1972.

Bach, Johann Sebastian. *Neue Ausgabe sämtlicher Werke.* Ed. Johann-Sebastian-Bach Institut, Göttingen, and Bach-Archiv, Leipzig. Kassel: Bärenreiter, 1954–. [*NBA*]

———. *Werke.* Leipzig: Bach-Gesellschaft, 1851–99. [*BG*]

The Bach Reader. Ed. Hans T. David and Arthur Mendel. New York: W. W. Norton, 1966.

Blechschmidt, Eva Renate. *Die Amalien-Bibliothek: Musikbibliothek der Prinzessin Anna Amalia von Preußen* (1723–1787). Berliner Studien zur Musikwissenschaft, vol. 8. Berlin: Verlag Merseburger, 1965.

Boyden, David. *The History of Violin Playing from Its Origins to 1761.* London: Oxford University Press, 1965.

Collingwood, R. G. *The Idea of History.* Ed. T. M. Knox. Oxford: Oxford University Press, 1946; reprint ed., New York: Oxford University Press, 1956.

Corelli, Arcangelo. *Les oeuvres.* Ed. Joseph Joachim and Friedrich Chrysander. London: Augener, 1888–91.

Curtis, Alan. "Musique classique française à Berkeley." *Revue de musicologie* 56 (1970): 123–64.

Dürr, Alfred. "De Vita cum Imperfectis." In *Studies in Renaissance and Baroque Music in Honor of Arthur Mendel*, ed. Robert L. Marshall, 243–54. Kassel: Bärenreiter, 1974.

Dreyfus, Laurence. "Early Music Defended against Its Devotees: A Theory of Historical Performance in the Twentieth Century." *Musical Quarterly* 69 (1983): 297–322.

Fleischhauer, Günter. "G. Ph. Telemann als Wegbreiter des 'vermischten Geschmacks' im Musikleben seiner Zeit." In *Die Einflüsse einzelner Inter-preten und Komponisten des 18. Jahrhunderts auf das Musikleben ihrer Zeit*, 35–48. Studien zur Aufführungspraxis und Interpretation von Instrumentalmusik des 18. Jahrhunderts, vol. 13. Konferenzbericht der IX. Wissenschaftlichen Arbeitstagung, Blankenburg/Harz, 27 bis 29 Juni 1980 [n.p, n.d.].

Fock, Gustav. *Der junge Bach in Lüneburg, 1700 bis 1702*. Hamburg: Merseburger, 1950.

Fürstenau, Moritz. *Zur Geschichte der Musik und des Theaters am Hofe zu Dresden*. 2 vols. Dresden: Verlagsbuchhandlung von Rudolf Kunze, 1861–62.

Glöckner, Andreas. "Fasch-Ouvertüren aus Johann Sebastian Bachs Notenbibliothek?" *Bach-Jahrbuch* 76 (1990): 65–69.

Goldstein, Leon J. "Collingwood's Theory of Historical Knowing." *History and Theory* 9 (1970): 3–36.

Gustafson, Bruce Lester. *French Harpsichord Music.* . . .

Handel, George Frederic. *Sechs einzeln überlieferte Instrumentalwerke. Hallische Händel-Ausgabe*, ser. IV, vol. 15. Ed. Terence Best. Kassel: Bärenreiter, 1979.

———. *Werke*. Ed. Deutschen Händelgesellschaft. Leipzig: Breitkopf & Härtel, 1859–95.

Harding, Rosamond E. M. *Origins of Musical Time and Expression*. London: Oxford University Press, 1938.

Hays, Elizabeth Loretta. "F. W. Marpurg's *Anleitung zum Clavierspielen* (Berlin, 1755) and *Principes du clavecin* (Berlin, 1756): Translation and Commentary." Ph.D. diss., Stanford University, 1976.

Helm, Ernest Eugene. *Music at the Court of Frederick the Great*. Norman: University of Oklahoma Press, 1960.

Kirkpatrick, Ralph. "Eighteenth-Century Metronomic Indications." In *Papers Read by Members of the American Musicological Society 1938*, 30–50.

Klenz, William. *Giovanni Maria Bononcini of Modena*. Durham: Duke University Press, 1962.

Landmann, Ortrun. "The Dresden Hofkapelle during the Lifetime of Johann Sebastian Bach." *Early Music* 17 (1989): 17–30.

———. "Französische Elemente in der Musikpraxis des 18. Jahrhunderts am Dresdener Hof." In *Der Einfluß der französischen Musik auf die Komponisten der ersten Hälfte des 18. Jahrhunderts*, 48–56. Studien zur Aufführungspraxis und Interpretation von Instrumentalmusik des 18. Jahrhunderts, vol. 16. Konferenzbericht der IX. Wissenschaftlichen Arbeitstagung, Blankenburg/Harz, 26. Juni bis 28. Juni 1981. [n. p., 1982]

Larsen, Jens Peter. *Handel Studies*. Special issue of *American Choral Review* 14/1 (1972).

Linnemann, Georg. *Celler Musikgeschichte bis zum Beginn des 19. Jahrhunderts*. Celle: Schweiger & Pick (Ernst Pfingsten), 1935.

Little, Meredith. "French Court Dance in Germany at the Time of Johann Sebastian Bach: *La Bourgogne* in Paris and Leipzig." In International Musicological Society, *Report of the Twelfth Congress Berkeley 1977*, ed. Daniel Heartz and Bonnie Wade, 730–34. Kassel: Bärenreiter/The American Musicological Society, 1981.

———, and Natalie Jenne. *Dance and the Music of J. S. Bach*. Bloomington: Indiana University Press, 1991.

Lonati, Carl'Ambrogio. *Die Violinsonaten: Mailand 1701*. Ed. Franz Giegling. Winterthur: Amadeus, 1981.

Lonergan, Bernard. *Method in Theology*. 2d ed. New York: Seabury Press, 1973. [Esp. chap. 9, "History and Historians."]

Malloch, William. "Bach and the French Overture."

Marshall, Robert L. "Bach the Progressive: Observations on His Later Works," *Musical Quarterly* 62 (1976): 313–57.

Mennicke, Carl. *Hasse und die Brüder Graun als Symphoniker. Nebst Biographien und thematischen Katalogen*. Leipzig: Breitkopf & Härtel, 1906; reprinted, Hildesheim: Georg Olms, 1977.

Mink, Louis O. "Collingwood's Dialectic of History." *History and Theory* 7 (1968): 3–37.

Monson, Craig A. "Eine neuentdeckte Fassung einer Toccata von Muffat." *Musikforschung* 25 (1972): 465–71.

Die Musik in Geschichte und Gegenwart [*MGG*]. Ed. Friedrich Blume. Kassel: Bärenreiter, 1949–79.

The New Grove Dictionary of Music and Musicians. Ed. Stanley Sadie. London: Macmillan, 1980.

Newman, William S. "Emanuel Bach's Autobiography." *Musical Quarterly* 51 (1965): 363–72.

Page, Janet K. "The Hautboy in London's Musical Life, 1730–1770." *Early Music* 16 (1988): 359–71.

Purcell, Henry. "O Give Thanks unto the Lord" (1693). Modern ed. in *The Works of Henry Purcell*, vol. 29, Sacred Music, pt. 5, Anthems. Rev. ed. by Anthony Lewis and Nigel Fortune. London: Novello, 1967.

Reilly, Edward R. *Quantz and His* Versuch. . . .

Répertoire international des sources musicales. Ser. BVI$^{1–2}$: Écrits imprimés concernant la musique. Munich: Henle, 1971. [*RISM*]

Rieß, Otto. "Johann Abraham Peter Schulz' Leben." *Sammelbände der Internationalen Musik-Gesellschaft* 15 (1913–14): 169–270.

Rifkin, Joshua. Review of Johann Sebastian Bach, *Messe in h-moll: Faksimile-Lichtdruck des Autographs*, ed. Alfred Dürr (Kassel: Bärenreiter, 1983), and Johann Sebastian Bach, *Missa h-moll BWV 232^I: Faksimile nach dem Originalstimmensatz*, ed. Hans-Joachim Schulze (Neuhausen-Stuttgart: Hänssler, 1983). *Notes* 44 (1988): 787–98.

Saint-Arroman, Jean. *L'interprétation de la musique française 1661–1789*. Vol. 1, *Dictionnaire d'interprétation*. Paris: Librarie Honoré Champion, 1983.

Salmen, Walter. "Der akademische Tanzmeister." In International Musicological Society, *Atti del XIV congresso della Società Internazionale di Musicologia*, 1: 83–88. Torino: Edizioni di Torino, 1990.

Schulze, Hans-Joachim. "Wie enstand die Bach-Sammlung Mempell-Preller?" *Bach-Jahrbuch* 60 (1974): 104–22.

Schwandt, Erich. "L'Affilard on the French Court Dances." *Musical Quarterly* 60 (1974): 389–400.

Smith, William C. *Handel: A Descriptive Catalogue of the Early Editions*. 2d ed. Oxford: Blackwell, 1970.

Spitzer, John, and Neal Zaslaw. "Improvised Ornamentation in Eighteenth-Century Orchestras." *Journal of the American Musicological Society* 39 (1986): 524–78.

Taruskin, Richard. "The Pastness of the Present and the Presence of the Past." In *Authenticity and Early Music*, ed. Nicholas Kenyon, 137–207. New York: Oxford University Press, 1988.

Terry, Charles Sanford. *Bach's Orchestra*. London: Oxford University Press, 1932.

Treitler, Leo. "History, Criticism, and Beethoven's Ninth Symphony." *19th Century Music* 3 (1980): 193–210.

Wolff, Christoph. "Johann Sebastian Bach." *The New Grove Bach Family*. New York: W. W. Norton, 1983.

Wolff, Helmuth Christian. "Das Metronom des Louis-Léon Pajot 1735." In *Festskrift Jens Peter Larsen*, ed. Nils Schiørring, Nils Glahn, and Carsten Hatting, 205–17. Copenhagen: Wilhelm Hansen, 1972.

INDEX

A

Adlung, Jakob, 48, 49
Agricola, Johann Friedrich, 48, 50,
    56, 116, 183 n. 63
    on binary *vs.* ternary rhythms, 185
    n. 9
    on overdotting, 86, 97, 107–108,
    109, 111, 140, 157, 158, 190 n.
    9, 191 n. 16, 196 n. 25
Airs de mouvement, 165 n. 20
Alfonso IV d'Este, 59
Allemande, 25–26, 50
Amalia, Princess of Prussia, 114, 115
Anon.
    "Manière de toucher l'orgue" (ca.
    1685), 6–7
    Nouvelle methode . . . du violon
    (ca. 1760), 14, 23–24, 33, 176 n.
    71
appuyer, 13, 14
Augsbach, Horst, 179 n. 27
August I, 99
Azaïs, Pierre-Hyacinthe, 27, 28, 29,
    40

B

Babell, Charles, 53, 74
Bach, Carl Philipp Emanuel, x, 42,
    48, 50, 100, 107, 112, 115, 117,
    124, 127, 159, 196 n. 27
    on binary *vs.* ternary rhythms, 185
    n. 9
    on overdotting, 85, 86, 101–5, 106,
    107, 108, 110, 111, 118, 138,
    139, 140, 148, 149–50, 158, 159,
    196 n. 25
    on synchronization, 151
    slur-and-dot notation, 167 n. 40

Bach, Johann Christian, 59
Bach, Johann Ernst, 48
Bach, Johann Sebastian, x, xi, 42, 48,
    49, 94, 107, 111, 112, 113, 114,
    116, 139, 141, 144, 145, 146,
    148, 149, 150, 151, 185 n. 9, 194
    n. 4
    Domine Deus, B-minor Mass,
    BWV 232, 180–81 n. 43
    orchestral suites, BWV 1066–69,
    x, 114, 149, 150, 151, 153, 199
    nn. 8, 12
    Ouverture, BWV 831/831a, x, 98–
    99, 100, 101, 111, 113, 115, 116,
    132, 140, 147, 148, 149, 191 n.
    12, 192 nn. 18, 20, 24
Bach, Wilhelm Friedemann, 99
Bacilly, Bénigne de, 5–6, 14, 16, 18,
    32, 37, 198 n. 5
Bailleux, Antoine, 129
Banister, John (i), 51
Battishill, Jonathan, 131, 135–36,
    148, 197 nn. 36, 39, 40
Bayly, Anselm, 53–54, 56, 183 n. 60
Bedos de Celles, Dom François, 19
Beethoven, Ludwig van, x, 145, 158
Benda, Franz, 48, 127
Berlin, 48, 49, 50, 61, 83, 97, 98,
    107, 111, 116, 117, 139, 140, 148
Bernhard, Christoph, 181 n. 45
Bernier, Nicolas, 21
Best, Terence, 53, 130, 131, 135, 196
    n. 33, 197 n. 40
bien pointer, 6
Binary *vs.* ternary rhythms, xii, 185
    n. 9, 199 n. 15
Bologna, 58, 81, 82
Bononcini, Giovanni Maria (i), 59
Bononcini, Giovanni, 40
Bordet, Toussaint, 23, 30
Borin, 27

Borrel, Eugène, 37
Bourgeois, Loys, 3, 5, 6, 7, 49
Bovicelli, Giovanni Battista, 4
Brossard, Sebastien de, 21, 22, 37, 49, 50, 54, 81
Buffardin, Pierre Gabriel, 43, 83, 181 n. 43
Burney, Charles, 83, 107, 116, 196 n. 31
Burwell lute tutor, 51–52
Byrd, William, 70

C

Caccini, Giulio, 4
Caix d'Hervelois, 21
Cambert, Robert, 51
Campra, André, 22
Cappus, 31
Celle, 42–43, 53, 111
Cerone, Pedro, 4
Chambonnières, Jacques Champion, 41, 70, 71, 72, 74, 78
Charles II, 51, 80
Choquel, Henri-Louis, 21, 142
Clay, Charles, 53
Cleret fils, 17
Clérambault, Louis-Nicolas, 21, 70
Cöthen, 49, 199 n. 12
Collasse, Pascal, 148–49
Collingwood, R. G., xi
Collins, Michael, xi, 163 n. 14, 167 n. 40, 178 n. 17, 181 n. 45, 183 n. 69, 188 n. 34, 199 n. 18
Colombi, Giuseppe, 59
Contraction, of upbeats or tirades, 93, 100, 111, 151, 152, 153, 190–91 n. 12, 199 n. 18
Corelli, Arcangelo, 38, 40, 59, 82, 133, 197 n. 34
  and Handel's overtures, 130, 131, 148
Corrette, Michele, 13, 26, 38, 40, 54
Couperin, François, 12, 13, 14, 15, 18, 21, 22, 25, 26, 32, 33, 37, 38, 39, 49, 54, 61, 67, 143, 144, 146, 147, 166 nn. 37, 39
Couperin, Louis, 41, 70, 71, 73, 74, 78

Courante, 50, 144, 145
croches égales, 21
croches inégales, ix
Croft, William, 53, 54
Crotch, William, 132
Curtis, Alan, 76

D

d'Anglebert, Jean-Henri, 70, 199 n. 18
Dandrieu, François, 21, 24, 25, 49
Dard, 14, 23
Dart, Thurston, x, xi, 145, 173 nn. 30, 35
David, François, 17, 38
de Grigny, Nicolas, 49
de-La Chapelle, Alexandre, 16, 32, 149
de La Feillée, François, 15
de la Selle, Thomas, 42
Demotz de la Salle, 22, 28, 31, 36, 49
Denis, Pierre, 18
Dieupart, Charles, 30, 31, 53
Diruta, Girolamo, 35
Dolmetsch, Arnold, x, 173 n. 35
Donington, Robert, x, xi, 60, 130, 145, 183 n. 68, 188 n. 34, 197 n. 34
Dornel, Antoine, 18, 21
Dortmund, 148
Dots and strokes, 21, 22
Dotted notation. See also Double dotting (notated)
  and ornaments, 68
  and synchronization, 68, 185 n. 9
  standard meaning of, 65, 78, 80, 82, 188 n. 32, 193 n. 31
  substitute for tie, 66, 67–68
  substitute for triplets, 68
  variable duration of, 66
Double dotting (notated), 70, 79–80, 158, 159, 160, 186 nn. 20, 22, 189 n. 2, 193 n. 31
  in French keyboard MSS, 70, 71, 72, 73, 74, 76, 78, 187 nn. 23, 24, 29
  in Italian sources, 188 n. 29

Dresden, 47–48, 49, 50, 61, 83, 97, 98, 99, 110, 114, 115, 116, 121, 130, 140, 147, 148, 150, 179 n. 25, 180 n. 43, 192 n. 21
Dreyfus, Laurence, 162 n. 18
Dumas, Antoine, 28, 29
Dumont, 70
Dupont, 14, 65, 184
Dupuit, Jean Baptiste, 17, 166–67 n. 40
Duval, L'Abbé, 17
Duval, Pierre, 18, 21, 23

E

Emery, Walter, 192 n. 24
Engramelle, Père Marie-Dominique-Joseph, 14, 15, 19–20, 36, 69–70, 82, 96, 98, 116, 142
Entrée, 79, 80, 81, 97, 98, 148
 tempo of, 149
Erlebach, Philipp Heinrich, 43

F

Falkener, Robert
 on overdotting, 86, 138
Fasch, C. F. C., 117
Fasch, Johann Friedrich, 113, 114, 148, 194 n. 4
Fischer, Johann, 42, 50
Forkel, Johann Nicolaus, 48
Fouquet, Pierre-Claude, 14
Francesco II (Duke of Modena), 197 n. 34
Frederick the Great, 48, 50, 83, 97, 98, 105, 107, 114, 115, 116, 120, 127, 144, 158, 179 n. 27
French bowing style, 92–96, 189–90 n. 9, 190 n. 11, 191 n. 16
French dance music, 93–98, 115, 151, 158, 189 n. 9, 190 n. 11. See also Allemande; Entrée; Gigue; Loure; Sarabande
 tempo of, 142, 198 n. 4, 198–99 n. 5
French dancing, 46, 48–49, 143
French keyboard MSS
 23-Tenbury, 53

24-Babell, 30, 31, 53, 74, 175 n. 56, 187 n. 23, 188 n. 29
32-Oldham, 70, 74, 187
33-Rés-89ter, 70, 74
35-Bauyn, 70, 74, 187
36-Parville, 74, 78, 187
38-Gen-2348/53, 74
46-Menetou, 74, 76, 80, 81, 98, 147, 187
47-Gen-2356, 74
51-Labarre-11, 74
French overture, 74, 81, 97, 98, 112, 113, 114, 115, 116, 130, 131, 135, 139, 148, 149, 150, 158, 191 n. 16, 194 nn. 4, 5, 6, 197 n. 34, 199 nn. 10, 18
 tempo of, 142, 148, 199 n. 10
"French Overture style," x, 145
Frescobaldi, Girolamo, 4, 14
Friedrich August II, 99
Frischmuth, Leonard, 50
Froberger, Johann Jakob, 41
Fuller, David, xi, 60, 70, 169 n. 68, 171 n. 6, 172–73 n. 26, 174 n. 41, 176 n. 71, 183 n. 60, 186 n. 22

G

Galliard, J. E., 53, 56, 57
Gaultier, Jacques, 51
Geneva, 3, 4
Gerber, Ernst Ludwig, 48
Gerlach, Carl Gotthelf, 194 n. 4
Giegling, Franz, 188 n. 29
Gigault, 6, 29, 32, 67, 68, 151
Gigue, 6, 50, 163 n. 14, 172 n. 21, 190 n. 11
 tempo of, 142
Glöckner, Andreas, 194 n. 4
'Good' and 'bad' notes, 35–36, 44–47, 56, 58, 143, 176 n. 71
Grabu, Louis, 51
Graun, Carl Heinrich, 48, 113, 114, 116, 127, 148, 158
 Der Tod Jesu, 123–25
Graun, Johann Gottlieb, 48, 113, 114, 127, 148, 158
Graz, 128

Greene, Maurice, 56, 58, 183 n. 60
Gustafson, Bruce L., 76, 175, 187 nn.
    23, 24

H

Halle, 83, 97, 120, 121, 130, 140
Hamburg, 135
Handel, George Frideric, x, 40, 53,
    82, 94, 113, 114, 134, 139, 148,
    157, 199 n. 18
  French overtures, 152–55
  keyboard arrangements of over-
    tures, 131–32, 135–37, 148, 197
    nn. 39, 40, 199 n. 16
  organ concertos, 136–38
  the 'Handel Tradition,' 130–38
Hasse, Johann Adolf, 48
Haydn, Franz Joseph, x, 158
Hays, Elizabeth Loretta, 107, 167 n.
    40
Hebenstreit, Pantlon, 42, 178–79 n.
    21
Herz, Gerhard, 181 n. 43
Hiller, Johann Adam, 119, 140
Holland (organ builder), 53, 136,
    137–38, 148
Homilius, Gottfried August, 116,
    118, 121, 140
Horn, Johann Caspar, 43
Hotteterre-le-Romain, Jacques, 23,
    37–38, 49, 50, 53, 69, 70, 82, 96,
    146, 182 n. 57, 185 n. 12, 186 n.
    17
Houle, George, 19, 169 n. 69, 177 n.
    72, 181 n. 45
Humfrey, Pelham, 51

I

inégaliser, ix, 18
inégalité, 18

J

Jommelli, Niccolò, 70
Jullien, Gilles, 6, 29

K

Kirnberger, Johann Philipp, 97, 112,
    114, 115–16, 140, 147
  Die Kunst des reinen Satzes, 115
Kirnberger/Schulz, 131, 139
  on contraction of upbeats, 113,
    191 n. 12
  on French overture, 112–16, 126
  on overdotting, 87, 113, 115, 118,
    140, 147, 148, 194 nn. 6, 8
  on the loure, 115
Kusser, Johann Sigismund, 42, 50,
    53, 178 n. 20

L

L'Affilard, Michel, 49, 50, 68, 78–79,
    142, 188 nn. 33, 34
  tempo indications, 198 n. 4
La Barre, 70
La Ferté, 21, 25
Lacassagne, L'Abbé Joseph, 17, 22,
    26
Lanier, Nicholas (ii), 51
Larsen, Jens Peter, 196 n. 31
Le Cerf de La Viéville de Fresneuse,
    Jean-Laurent, 59
Le Roux, Gaspard, 49
Leipzig, 49, 83, 99, 114, 118, 119,
    130, 140, 148, 150, 194 n. 4, 199
    nn. 8, 12
Löhlein, Georg Simon
  on overdotting, 118–19, 195 n. 16
Lombardic rhythm, 14, 90, 92, 102,
    109, 110, 119, 124, 129, 180–81
    n. 43, 195 n. 18, 196 n. 25
Lonati, Carl' Ambrogio, 188 n. 29
London, 51
Lorenzoni, Antonio, 54, 56, 58, 183
    n. 69, 184 n. 70
Louis XIV, 51, 76
Louis XV, 65, 184 n. 1
Loulié, Étienne, 13–14, 16, 17, 18,
    22, 23, 24, 37, 50, 54, 58, 66, 78,
    79, 187 n. 24, 188 n. 34
Loure, 115, 116, 139, 149, 190 n. 11
lourer, 16, 22, 167–68 n. 43, 170 n.
    6, 179 n. 24

Lully, Jean-Baptiste, 30, 37, 41, 42, 43, 51, 53, 70, 74, 76, 77, 81, 98, 112, 116, 135, 139, 146, 150, 178 n. 20, 189 n. 37, 199 n. 18
Lüneburg, 99

M

Magdeburg, 127
Mainwaring, John, 130, 131
Marais, Marin, 14, 25, 26
Marchand, Louis, 47, 49
Marcou, Pierre, 18, 32
Marpurg, Friedrich Wilhelm, 14, 48, 49, 50, 61, 107, 109, 140
  on overdotting, 97, 106, 110, 111, 191 n. 16
  slur-and-dot notation, 167 n. 40
marqué, 21–22
Marshall, Robert L., 99, 192 n. 21
Martini, Padre Giovanni Battista, 58
Martinozzi, Laura, 59
Mather, Betty Bang, 173 n. 30
Mattheson, Johann, 48, 49, 61, 198–99 n. 5
  on dotted style in vocal music, 155, 157
Mayr, Rupert Ignaz, 42, 50
Mazarin, J. Cardinal, 59
Mazzinghi, Joseph, 132
Moneton, Françoise-Charlotte de Senneterre de, 76
Mercadier de Belesta, Jean-Baptiste, 31, 176 n. 71
mesuré, 21, 25
Metoyen, J. B., 67, 69, 79, 82, 96, 187 n. 24
Meude-Monpas, J. J. O., 22
Michel, Winfried, 179
Modena, 59, 61, 82, 197 n. 34
Mondonville, J.-J. Cassanéa de, 24, 25, 26, 38
Montéclair, Michele Pignolet de, 12, 13, 14, 18, 28, 33, 34, 36, 38, 49, 79, 80, 81, 98, 143, 147, 166 n. 37
Monteverdi, Claudio, x, 145
Morel de Lescer, 22, 29, 69, 70, 76, 82, 96, 98, 146

Mozart, Leopold, x, 117, 129, 181, 196 n. 27
  on ensemble leadership, 193 n. 37
  on overdotting, 86, 109–10, 111, 138, 140, 148, 158, 193 n. 37
Mozart, Wolfgang Amadeus, x, 158, 160
Muffat, Georg, 12, 32, 33, 37, 41, 49, 50, 70, 142, 150, 186 n. 20, 199 n. 18
  on *tirades*, 190 n. 12
Mussard, 40

N

Naples, 59
Neuff, Augustin, 179 n. 27
Neumann, Frederick, xi, xiii, 7, 18, 60, 99, 101, 102, 135, 145, 163 n. 14, 165 n. 23, 166 n. 39, 168 nn. 50, 53, 170 n. 71, 173 n. 35, 175 n. 56, 180–81 n. 43, 181 n. 45, 185 n. 10, 186 nn. 17, 22, 187–88 n. 29, 189 nn. 38, 9, 190 nn. 9, 12, 191–92 n. 16, 192 nn. 17, 24, 193 nn. 31, 36, 194 nn. 6, 8, 14, 195 n. 14, 196 n. 27, 199 nn. 15, 18
Nivers, Guillaume-Gabriel, 5, 14, 16, 18, 29, 32, 37
North, Roger, 51, 52–53, 56, 57, 80–81, 98, 147, 148, 189 n. 37
notes inégales, ix, 3 ff., 70, 78, 79, 82, 83, 97, 98, 107, 116, 129, 141–42, 157, 194 n. 6
  and MS variants, 60
  and overdotting, ix, 68–70, 74, 76, 79–81, 82, 96–98, 115–16, 131, 143, 145–46, 148, 149, 151, 191–92 n. 16
  and slurs, 21, 44, 45, 47, 78, 170–71 n. 6, 180 n. 30, 199 n. 8
  and tempo, 17, 44, 45, 47, 142–43
  cancellation of, 21–22, 25, 44, 58, 81, 142
  cumulative, 27
  defined, ix

notes inégales (Cont'd.)
  descending, 26–28
  'first' and 'second' 8ths, 69–70, 78,
    82, 186 n. 16
  French tutors not discussing, 49,
    181 n. 46
  in allemandes, 18, 25–26, 50, 71
  in meter $\frac{3}{4}$, 27–28, 174 nn. 42, 44
  in meter C, 28–30, 31
  in orchestral music, 165 n. 23
  in stepwise motion, 12–13
  meter-inequality relationship, 3–4,
    6–12, 50, 54, 58, 71, 96, 142
  mixed with syncopations, 26
  notes detachées vs. notes articu-
    lées, 23, 176 n. 21
  outside France, 37 ff., 143–45
  ratio between, 5–7, 13–20, 43, 70,
    98, 142, 146, 149, 186 n. 17,
    191–92, n. 16
  terms for, ix
  trochaic *vs.* iambic, 13–15, 142
  vs. "dragging" (Tosi), 54, 56, 57
  vs. 'good' and 'bad' notes, 35–36,
    44–47, 58, 176 n. 71
  vs. dotted notation, 18–19, 24,
    32–33, 60, 143, 169 n. 66. *See*
    also tables 1-1 and 1-2, pp. 8–11

O

O'Donnell, John, 149, 163 n. 14, 168
  n. 43, 169 n. 66, 173 n. 29, 185
  nn. 10, 12, 186–87 n. 22, 188
  nn. 34, 35
Ornaments
  with dotted rhythms, 68
Overdotting, ix, x, 65 ff., 83 ff.,
  84–88 (table 5-1), 140 (table 6-1),
  185 ff. *See also under individual*
  authors (listed in table 5-1, pp.
  84–88)
  and vocal music, 107–8, 120–21,
    123–25 (ex. 6-2), 155, 157
  concomitant with *notes inégales,*
    ix, 68–70, 74, 76, 79–81, 82,
    96–98, 115–16, 145–46, 148,
    149, 151, 191–92 n. 16
  defined, ix

P

Page, Janet K., 188 n. 29
Paisible, James, 53
Pajot, Louis-Léon (Count D'Onzem-
  bray), 142
Paris, 4, 48, 50, 51, 59, 61, 76, 110,
  116, 150, 194 n. 6
Pasquini, Bernardo, 59
passaggi, 5, 41
passer les croches, ix, 145
Pepusch, John Christopher, 40
Perrine, 6, 7, 29
Petri, Johann Samuel, 193 n. 31
Petschke, Adolf Friedrich, 118
  on overdotting, 119, 140, 158
Pezold, Christian, 47
Piani, Giovanni Antonio, 38, 39
piquer (piqué), 16, 22–25, 171 nn.
  14, 16, 172–73 nn. 17, 26, 29
Pisendel, Johann Georg, 43, 47, 48,
  114
plain-chant musical, 15
poincts alternatifs, ix, 6
pointement, 6
pointer (pointé, pointez), ix, 16, 18,
  22, 32, 50, 59, 79, 169 n. 66, 185
  n. 12
Pollet, Charles-François-Alexandre,
  31
Pont, Graham, xi, 70, 130, 132, 135,
  151, 183 n. 60, 196 n. 24, 197
  nn. 34, 38, 39
pontato, 59
Porpora, Nicola, 40
Preller, J. G., 99, 100, 101, 148, 192
  nn. 18, 24
Prelleur, Peter, 53, 182 n. 57
Printz, Wolfgang Caspar, 41, 49
Prussia, 97, 107, 115, 120
Puliaschi, Domenico, 5
Purcell, Henry, x, 51, 53, 54, 55

Q

Quantz, Johann Joachim, x, xiii, 14,
  37, 48, 50, 58, 61, 65, 83, 116,
  117, 128, 142, 147, 195 n. 14,
  196 n. 27

Quantz, Johann Joachim *(Cont'd.)*
  on 'good' and 'bad' notes, 44–47
  on binary *vs.* ternary rhythms, 185
    n. 9
  on contraction of upbeats, 93, 113,
    147, 152, 190 n. 12
  on ensemble leadership, 141
  on French dance music, 94–95, 96,
    98, 99, 115, 189 n. 9, 190 n. 11,
    191 n. 16
  on French overtures, 95, 96–97,
    98, 115, 126, 191 n. 16, 194 n. 2
  on majesty, 91–92, 93, 95–96, 97,
    190 n. 9, 191 n. 16
  on *notes inégales*, 43–45, 47, 49,
    98, 144, 184 n. 70
  on overdotting, 83–85, 89–98, 99,
    101, 102, 105, 106, 107, 108,
    110, 118, 120, 127, 129, 131,
    138, 139, 140, 147, 148, 158,
    189–90 n. 9, 191–92 n. 16
  on pickups in dotted contexts, 94,
    151
  on slurs cancelling inequality, 44,
    171 n. 6
  on universal rules of good execu-
    tion, 91
  Solfeggi, 43, 44, 90–91, 179 n. 27
Querelle des Buffons, 61

R

Raguenet, François, 59
Raison, André, 70, 71, 74, 186 n. 22
Rameau, Jean-Phillipe, xi, 33, 49,
  115
Ranum, Patricia, 173 n. 29
Raparlier, 31
Reichardt, Johann Friedrich
  on overdotting, 116–17, 140,
    194–95 n. 14
Reilly, Edward R., xiii, 47, 58, 189 n.
  4, 190 n. 10
Rellstab, J. C. F., 116, 132
  on French overtures, 117, 118, 126
  on overdotting, 117, 118, 139, 140,
    148, 158, 159, 189 n. 9
reposer/passer plus viste, 18
Ricci, Francesco Pasquale, 59

Richard, 70, 78
Richter, Johann Christian, 47
Rifkin, Joshua, 192 n. 22
Roeser, Valentin, 167 n. 40
Roger, Estienne, 50
Rogers, John, 51
Rolle, Johann Heinrich, 126, 127,
  128, 139, 148, 151
Rollet, 16
Rome, 59
Rousseau, Jean, 7, 16, 22, 32, 49, 50
Rousseau, Jean-Jacques, ix, 18, 22,
  25, 38, 50, 53, 54, 58, 61, 68
Roussier, Jacob, 14, 35, 159

S

Saint-Arroman, Jean, 5, 173 n. 29
Saint-Lambert, Michele de, 17, 26,
  32, 36, 49, 50, 186 n. 16
Salzburg, 140
Sammartini, Giuseppe, 188 n. 29
Santa Maria, Tomás de, 4, 14
Sarabande, 149
Sauver, Joseph, 198 n. 4
Scarlatti, Alessandro, 40, 60
Scheibe, Johann Adolf, 97, 100, 126,
  131
Scheidt, Samuel, 49
Schein, Johann Hermann, 49
Schlegel, Franz Anton
  on overdotting, 128–29
Schmelz, Simpertus, 67, 68
Schmidt, Johann Christoph, 47
Schmierer, Johann Abraham, 43
Schulz, J. A. P., 97, 112, 116, 140,
  147
  on overdotting, 115
Schütz, Heinrich, 49
Schwandt, Erich, 198 n. 4
Schweitzer, Anton, 126, 127, 139,
  148, 151
Shaw, Watkins, 130
Slur-and-dot notation, 14–15,
  166–67 nn. 39, 40
Smith, John Christopher, 130, 135
Sperling, Johann Peter, 67, 68
Steffani, Agostino, 42, 60
Sulzer, Johann Georg, 48, 112

Sweelinck, Jan Pieterszoon, 51
Synchronization
    of pickups in dotted contexts, 94,
        151, 158

T

Tarade, Théodore-Jean, 17, 30, 98
Tartini, Giuseppe, 40
Taruskin, Richard, 162 n. 18
Taubert, Gottfried, 46
Telemann, Georg Michael, 48
Telemann, Georg Philipp, 42, 48, 49,
        61, 113, 114, 130, 139, 144, 148,
        178–79 n. 21, 179 n. 25
tenir/passer, 18
Teske, Hermien, 179 n. 27
Thysius, Johan, 51
Titelouze, Jean, 66
Torlée, J. C., 49
Tosi, Pier Francesco, 50, 54, 56, 57,
        183 n. 60
Triplets, rhythmic alteration of, 30–
        31, 185 n. 9
Tromlitz, Johann Georg, 48, 118
    on overdotting, 119–20, 140
Türk, Daniel Gottlob, 97, 132, 181
        n. 45, 196 n. 27
    on French overtures, 122–23,
        126–27
    on overdotting, 121–22, 123, 127,
        139, 140, 148, 151, 158, 159, 189
        n. 9, 196 n. 24
    on pickups, 124–26
    on synchronization, 123–24,
        127–28

U

Uccellini, Marco, 59

V

Vague, 12, 16, 18, 32
Valentine, Roberto, 40, 178 n. 13
Vincent, 70
Vion, P. F. C. X., 40, 188 n. 32
Vitali, Giovanni Battista, 59
Vivaldi, Antonio, 40
Volumier, Jean Baptiste, 43, 47
Vulpio, 60

W

Walsh, John, 132, 135
Walther, Johann Gottfried, 43, 49
Watts, John, 132
Weimar, 127
Wolf, Georg Friedrich
    on overdotting, 120–21, 140, 158
Wolff, Christoph, 180 n. 37, 192 n.
        24
Wright, H. (publisher), 135, 136
Wulstan, David, 188 n. 34

Z

Zarlino, Gioseffo, 35
Zerbst, 114

.